About the Author

Nigel Gann BEd, MPhil, FRSA taught in UK secondary education to headship level and in adult and teacher education. He is now a consultant and has worked with schools throughout England, Wales and abroad. Nigel has made programmes for BBC TV & Radio and published widely. He has been a governor in nine schools. He currently coaches headteachers and governors. In 2007, Nigel was presented with a National Teaching Award.

This book is dedicated to all those parents, governors, school staff and others who have fought – and are still fighting – successfully or otherwise – to keep their school ownership in the communities they serve. And of course, to the children who, like Finley, Jack and Jesse, Summer and Callum, attend schools in England.

It was written in admiration of the dedication of the teachers, support staff and governors who kept schools open and safe during the unprecedented events of 2020, and in shame at those politicians and school sponsors whose first concern was with their own careers and interests.

Nigel Gann

THE GREAT EDUCATION ROBBERY

How the Government Took our Schools and Gave Them to Big Business

AUSTIN MACAULEY PUBLISHERS™
LONDON • CAMBRIDGE • NEW YORK • SHARJAH

A CIP catalogue record for this title is available from the British Library.

ISBN 9781398432710 (Paperback)
ISBN 9781398432727 (ePub e-book)

www.austinmacauley.com

First Published (2021)
Austin Macauley Publishers Ltd
25 Canada Square
Canary Wharf
London
E14 5LQ

Table of Contents

Endorsements

Warwick Mansell, writer/editor of the website Education Uncovered.
"Nigel Gann's carefully researched analysis should be read by anyone who is interested in the reality of how control of our schools has become much less democratic. Putting his experience of the dubious shenanigans around the change of control of a small primary school into a national context, the account of this experienced school governor and teacher makes compulsive reading."

Chris James, Emeritus Professor of Educational Leadership and Management, Department of Education, University of Bath
"Nigel Gann has created a quite remarkable text and I recommend it wholeheartedly to all those who have a serious interest in the school system in England. Drawing on a significant moment for him and his local community – the forced academization of the village school – he provides a well-researched, thorough and securely-grounded account of the way the school system in England is changing. Nigel highlights not only the flaws in this trajectory but also the defects in the way the policies underpinning the pathway were created.

The picture he paints is of schools being 'taken away' from their local communities by a system that is increasingly centralized and corporate in nature, as schools fall under a direct management hierarchy from the Secretary of State, to schools' commissioners and multi-academy trusts to schools. Nigel points to the dangers of schools losing touch with the local communities they serve and the harm that will do. However, he doesn't just paint a negative picture, he sets out alternative approaches in a constructive way.

Very importantly, Nigel has written a very engaging book that is based on very sound educational and moral principles. The book is an excellent read and Nigel's standpoint as a committed educator shines through the text. I recommend it to all those involved in the school system in England – you will gain new and important insights."

Dr Andrew Wilkins, Goldsmiths, University of London

"Weaving together novel insights and empirical evidence from case study material, policy commentary and education research, Nigel Gann offers an impassioned rebuke and rejection of the celebrated gains of 'academisation' in the English education system. Tracing the history of these reforms and their present-day effects, from diminishing community consultation and bargaining to intensive and costly legal and political wrangling, Nigel Gann carefully details the technocratic exceptionalism upon which the fate of schools is now decided. Responding to these crises in public sector organisation and the growing public demand for democratic accountability, Nigel Gann avoids any excessive fatalism by communicating a new vision of education, with public trust, transparency and localism at its core."

Raj Unsworth, parent, chair of governors, trustee, special advisor to Headteachers Roundtable.

"I thoroughly recommend this book to anyone working in or with an interest in the education sector in England, including parents, governors and trustees. The book makes for uncomfortable reading at times and will, I suspect, resonate with those who have perhaps been through similar experiences. It is especially timely as we are still in the throes of a pandemic which has served to highlight exactly why every school, irrespective of structure, should be part of its local community. As Nigel Gann points out, the corporatisation of schools in the public sector has resulted in less democratic institutions. The loss, in particular of accountability to parents and communities is not acceptable.

A well researched, well written, warts and all account of the current state of play in 2020."

About This Book

The Meaning of Corporatisation

This book is about the widespread corporatisation of state-funded schools in England.

Corporatisation is the removal of state schools from the overall responsibility of their local authority and the transfer of their leadership and governance to independent trusts accountable directly to the government department overseeing English education. That existing schools should become corporate academies, either voluntarily or compulsorily, and that all new schools would be 'free schools' with similar independent status, became the policy of the new Conservative-led coalition government in 2010, and continued throughout the following decade. It was a distinctive twenty-first century Conservative policy, although the seeds had been sown in the early 1990s and watered and fertilised by the Labour government from 1997 to 2010. By 2020, the large majority of secondary schools and a substantial minority of primary schools in England had become academies. Initially, some of these were free-standing independent schools, but in the latter half of the decade, schools were encouraged or required to join existing 'multi academy trusts'. Academies are literally 'independent schools' funded by the state, so academisation is often referred to as 'privatisation'. However, I prefer the word 'corporatisation' because the schools become the property of corporate bodies rather than private individuals – although in some cases it is difficult to see the difference.

Since education is a devolved responsibility, Wales, Scotland and Northern Ireland were not required to implement this policy and chose not to follow a similar path.

Why this matters will become clear throughout the book. For now, we just need to recognise that state-funded schools have been publicly owned since 1870 and managed by elected local authorities since the turn of the twentieth century. They have been part of the public domain, accountable to a combination of national and local government, for all that time. Although there has always been an important partnership with the churches' diocesan boards of education, significant decisions about them and the responsibility for their performance have belonged to elected representatives and were always ultimately subject to democratic accountability.

Academies and free schools are different. They are literally independent from government, other than having to comply with certain performance requirements laid down by the Department for Education. Members and trust boards are self-appointed. There are few meaningful obligations to parents or pupils in terms of accountability for their conduct. Individual schools within trusts have no independent legal status.

That is an outline of the national picture, as will become clear throughout the book. Academisation has national consequences and raises the question: Since schools are run with publicly-raised money, who should own them and govern them? Once they were identifiable as 'belonging' to their communities – neighbourhoods would talk about 'our school'. But a minority government enacted a policy to end that relationship throughout the country, and to 'give' those schools to independent trusts. Many of those trusts, as we shall see, as well as a new establishment of educational leaders, are populated by people with a background not in education, but in business and finance.

The Consequences of Corporatisation for Schools

Academisation also has a powerful bearing on local communities and raises the question "Whose school is it, anyway?"

So we start by looking at how the policy of 'forced academisation' was applied in a single small school in a 'typically English' rural village community – a community which had always had a meaningful relationship with its school. Local people formed the majority of its governing board. Many staff lived locally. Most parents walked their children to school and were on familiar terms with its leaders – the headteacher and the governors. The legal structures underlying the school's status had changed little over the years, becoming only more democratically accountable to the community and more open to local participation in its governance. Its stability and long standing meant that its presence and its status were largely taken for granted by the community. If things did ever go wrong, however, and the headteacher and governors couldn't sort it out, a county councillor would be living in or very near the village, and the local education authority (LEA) was just a few miles away. The LEA, as the responsible authority, would have both the power and the disinterested capacity to put things right.

This history starts as a little local wrinkle. A few lies here, a deception, a bit of cronyism, then an escalation into something that, six years on, holds up a mirror to the way this country is being governed in every aspect of its national politics.

How the Book Was Born

The story begins when I was working in my office at the bottom of our Somerset garden in the summer of 2014. The phone rang. A friend wanted to call round and ask my advice about what was happening in their nearby local school.

Those events, which we will look at later, turned out to have ramifications with which we are still living. This started out as a story about a few local government officers deciding that they had no obligation to safeguard the interests of the people living in a small Somerset village, but instead felt duty-bound to follow the dictation of a government department. That department, it turned out, had been entirely reconstructed over the course of four years into a laboratory for what we could call 'neoliberal disruptive politics'. The core belief of this was that, in every branch of government provision, the concept of any provision as a 'public good' was inefficient and outdated – a relic of an age when it was taken for granted that certain public services and safety nets underpinned the workings of any nation state, for the benefit of its people and, ultimately, for its own effective working even in a pragmatic capitalist society.

For if 'the market' is to predominate, only a fanatic would deny that the nation still needs a firm, well-maintained and constantly improving infrastructure in, for example, transport, planning, health provision, welfare and education to provide the means by which capitalism can operate. If you neglect these basics, the outcomes are dire but foreseeable. If you set out purposefully to disrupt them, the outcomes become entirely unpredictable. When that happens, those who pay the highest price are ordinary people living lives that they probably thought could never seriously be affected by 'politicians' and 'their' politics.

So the forced academisation of their village school, insignificant as it may have seemed for many of the Somerset villagers, was the harbinger of a series of events that have come to haunt us all. It was dramatic enough to impact everyone involved in education in England, and it shifted the ethical basis of school provision which had been largely taken for granted since the introduction of compulsory free education one hundred and fifty years before. Not content with that, the new thinking overturned a consensus on international cooperation and trade which had dominated political thinking for more than sixty years.

Disastrously, it then became the prevailing model for the way the United Kingdom would handle a global crisis which, at the time of writing, is on track to disrupt the livelihoods of, infect and actually kill more of the population of these islands than any other event since … who can say?

From Decree to Dispute

So the tale starts here in the quiet southwest of England – a sequence of historical events that is generally accepted as true – though there are very different views on what the story is about, and who played what part in it. The outcome is generally agreed, although a bewildering number of people involved in the story did not want to talk about how it came about, or their role in it. Why did they not want to? How did it come about that the leadership and governance of a school of fewer than two hundred five to eleven-year-olds could become an issue? Since the late 1980s, the school had been overseen by Somerset Education Department, and locally governed by a combination of staff and community governors, including a proportion of parents. This structure of limited local responsibility and accountability – a partnership between professionals and lay people – was probably not much understood by parents and children, but it was accepted and possibly, like much about local affairs, largely taken for granted. Whether it would be missed if it disappeared is a moot point. But having become the subject of a briefly intense controversy – the subject of public meetings, petitions, applications to the MP, even having its own Facebook page – why did it fade away so quickly?

In other parts of England, other similar disputes were arising, and getting publicity through educational and local press, Facebook and Twitter. Many of these were still running, months, even years later, and similar disputes continue to appear regularly, more than five years on.

Sometimes, evidence condemning a system or a strategy can pile up, and up, until one small event turns the tide. A homeless man dies on the street, a child refugee is photographed dead on a beach, and a migrant health worker makes a tweeted plea for support in bereavement. This wasn't one of those, though soon enough other school protests would hit the national press and turn up again and again on front pages. Here, after two or three months of protest and agitation, the local opposition to the plans that the Somerset Local Authority and the Department for Education had for the school seemed to melt away as quickly as it had arisen[1].

In the time we are studying here, the policy of forced academisation of schools deemed to be 'inadequate' or 'failing', was causing enormous disruption in some areas of the country, perhaps particularly urban areas, while going almost unremarked in others. In south Somerset, the reaction of the community of the first school to be subjected to this was very combative for about two months. All the surrounding primary schools were relatively successful – 'good' or 'outstanding' according to Ofsted's inspection reports – and the County's policy of requiring some schools to become academies, come what may, was consequently not making much headway. And then the opposition disappeared, and parents, staff and governors submitted in the handover of their school to a trust based on a small-town primary school some 15 miles away.

In this book, we will be looking at some of the tactics used by the officers of the local authority (the LA), the Department for Education (DfE) and the trust concerned to ensure that they got the outcome they wanted, and had agreed among themselves, probably at a very early stage in the process. We will focus on some aspects of the conversion process that may be particularly problematic.

The sources for the story are the minutes of meetings held in the critical period by the school governing board and the directors of the trust[2] – one element of democratic accountability that remains intact is that schools and academy trusts are required to make all but their confidential minutes available to anyone who has an interest. This does not mean, of course, that there were not dozens or hundreds of informal meetings that were not minuted, or that there were not parts of formal meetings designated as confidential without proper cause. I also met

---

[1] I am going to use the term "Department for Education" throughout this book to identify the government department responsible for schools, though at various times throughout the period discussed here, it has borne other titles, such as 'Department of Education and Science'; 'Department for Education and Employment'; 'Department for Education and Skills'; and 'Department for Children, Schools and Families'

[2] Currently, the body responsible for governing a maintained school is called a 'governing board', although before the period we are writing about here, the preferred term was 'governing body'. Academy trusts have their own terms for any local board, but these have no statutory powers or responsibilities, and can only be advisory

with a number of the parents, staff and governors. Most of them preferred to remain anonymous, particularly past and present staff, for obvious professional reasons, and parents. Although perhaps predictable, it is sad that they felt that they or their children might in some way suffer if they were identified as having told their version of events. It is an indicator of the overall atmosphere engendered by the process, and fostered by the key players, often in the cause of not damaging the school or, in consequence, the children. The parents' action group started a Facebook page on which were posted opinions, news of meetings and so on. This was available to me, though lying sadly neglected like an abandoned brownfield site.

How The People In Control Behaved

As fascinating as the meetings with participants and observers were, they were somewhat eclipsed by the range of responses I had from those people who were not prepared to participate in a discussion about the key issues we identified. The CEO and the Chair of Redstart Trust received from me a request as follows:

"To ensure that we fairly represent the Redstart Trust, the governing board of the school, the local community of Stoke sub Hamdon, and other participants in the process, we would welcome the opportunity to have a face-to-face conversation with you. While we would want to source you on substantive issues, we will, of course, observe confidentiality 'off the record' on any matters on which you would not want to be quoted." The reply, on behalf of both of them, was: "The Redstart Learning Partnership is committed to the principles of school to school support and is dedicated to effectively meeting the needs of all pupils within its schools."

The LA officer who saw the process through the autumn term to conversion received a similar request and replied: "Thank you for your query. Somerset County Council has operated a system of 'school to school' support based upon strong partnership working. This concept is based upon the original work by Hargreaves around Creating a Self-Improving School System (2010) and subsequent updates. For some time many school leaders and LA staff have worked across and beyond any differences between schools and academies to ensure that we respond rapidly and effectively to meet the developing needs of all children and young people in all Somerset settings."

It can be seen that these do not begin to answer the questions we might have asked and appear designed to close down any possibility of dialogue.

The other LA officer, who spoke to the parents in the summer meeting, did not write from the same script, in responding to a more detailed set of questions which arose out of the interviews with parents and staff:

"I have no intention of responding to your questions or of meeting with you. I do not accept the key assumptions contained therein and would strongly advise that you research your facts far more carefully before making public the accusations you have aimed at me and included in your email. 'Subversion', 'neglect' and 'collusion' are verging on slanderous terms and a slight on my professional integrity. However, please note the following:

- My comment to the parents had nothing to do with Redstart. It was a statement of fact. Special Measures means academy conversion. I was there to reassure parents and focus them on supporting the school through a difficult period for the benefit of their children rather than expending time and energy on opposing the process.
- I cannot comment on alleged neglect of the school by the LA before that time as I was not in post until 2014. However, as soon as I was aware of its position, I acted. The school is now providing the quality of education it should have been then. My priority is for the children, not for political point-scoring or having to waste time answering emails such as this.
- I am a school improvement adviser, the only primary adviser at the time of the school's inspection, and I have had no part in the negotiations with the governing body, DfE Academy Broker or Redstart Academy.

I look forward to receiving an apology from you and an undertaking that my name will be removed from any documentation or publication that you are drafting and intend to make public."

This clarification of what was said at the parents' meeting was, in fact, very helpful. It supports what parents said, that they had been told not to oppose the conversion process, as it would be damaging to the school and the children. As will be seen, this was the first occasion on which the statutory process of consultation was perhaps fatally undermined. It repeats the fallacious statement that "Special Measures means academy conversion', which was not legally the case at the time. When this was pointed out, his reply was even more immediate and, perhaps in consequence, even less measured:

"I am certainly not accountable to you, Sir and my conscience is clear. The children of Castle Primary School are in a far better place and it has nothing to do with furthering the LA agenda. Surely, it is not in our best interests to be promoting academies. My priority was to improve leadership at the school which governors had failed to do.

I shall not be entering into any further dialogue with you and politely request that you do not contact me again. Should you do so, I shall refer the matter to our Legal Services Department."

Sadly, the matter was not referred to the County's Legal Services Department, who might have clarified some issues for us all. Nevertheless, it is interesting that this officer seemed to so quickly fly off the handle. These questions were being raised by someone who was the very recent chair of governors of the local secondary school, and a current governor of a federation of two local primaries, which had held recent informal talks with the chair of 'The Castle', and who had himself held senior leadership posts in schools in the past, as well as advising on governance in the formation of a local trust.

When the possible breaches of the statutory process emerged, I wrote to the Secretary of State for Education in June 2015, to receive a misaddressed response from a member of staff, which again avoided the key points I had made. A response to this elicited no reply. Once the evidence cited here had emerged, a further letter was sent in May 2016 to include it in order to support my contention.

Why does this matter? Public officials involved, all receiving salaries or fees from one or other department of 'the state', seemed to be showing in their language and their actions, at best, indifference to the opinion of the public. At worst, contempt for the parents, staff and governors seemed to be a major factor in the attitudes of the DfE, the LA, and the Trust. It stands somewhere on a continuum which leads to a senior civil servant telling a parliamentary select committee that "Human rights are not a priority for this government"[3], or the chair of the parliamentary select committee on education saying in public that he was "less interested in democratic accountability than quality."[4]

---

[3] Ash, Timothy Garton. The Guardian, 13.5.16
[4] Gann, Nigel. 2016. *Improving School Governance: How better governors make better schools.* (2nd edn). London: Routledge: p192

What This Book Is For

The purpose of this book is to explore the impact of radical changes brought about in the English education system from the late 1980s, and in particular since 2010. I explore how these changes have brought in a pattern of schooling that enables, and often seems to encourage, behaviour amongst politicians and school leaders that is ethically indefensible and sometimes criminal. In order to show that decisions made by individuals and political parties have both national and local consequences, I use the experience of this one school to illustrate the impact of politics on a small, lively and engaged community and its local school. We look in some detail at the individuals who, without any knowledge or understanding, and very little practical experience of comprehensive state education, have led these changes, and we see how they are now influencing UK politics across the board, through the application of the Brexit referendum to the deeply flawed management of the 2020 pandemic.

I invite you, in this journey, to do what all sensible investigators do when exploring wrongdoing – follow the money.

Finally, I suggest a way out of the present chaotic state of English schooling based on an ethical approach to policy making and implementation.

Section I Schooling in England (chapters 1-4) explains the background to the current state of education in England and presents the stories of some of the key people responsible for bringing it about.

Section II Capturing the Castle (chapters 5-8) introduces the school and community that generated this book and recounts the key moments in the process of the school's forced conversion into an academy. The school's results started to deteriorate after the retirement of the headteacher in 2009 and culminated in an Ofsted inspection in the spring of 2014. The conversion process was completed in March 2015. We look at a few schools with similar stories and explore the links between people involved in them.

Section III Foul Play (Chapters 9-12) looks in turn at three elements which were manipulated by the authorities to drive through the conversion. These are: what we mean by – and whatever happened to – the legal procedure of public consultation; how the perversion of language serves the purposes of politicians and officials; and the application of democratic accountability. While focusing on the story of the school, I draw parallels with changes and developments on a national scale across the political spectrum. Each one demonstrates the capacity for some politicians and public officials to get their way despite the building up over years of safeguards to public engagement. The wider background to this dilution of democratic influence is drawn in chapter 12, with some thoughts about power and powerlessness in communities.

Section IV Corporatising our schools (Chapters 13-21) looks at the processes and outcomes of the academisation of schools in England. It draws largely on mainstream media accounts of events in the field of education at all levels. Many illustrations are given, in order to pre-empt any suggestion that these are isolated examples. On the contrary. The key argument of the book is that the many weaknesses and faults in the current structure of schooling in England are endemic in a dysfunctional system that carries the seeds of its own destruction. I identify the seven deadly sins which beset schools in the middle of the decade. But by 2015, state-funded education was by no means the only arena where this was happening. Across national politics, as the neoliberal contingent became stronger and more practised in their dark arts, its impact spread. There had probably been some sort of dry run in the use of misinformation and a highly targeted use of the new social media in the run-up to the 2004 referendum on a northeast regional council. The skill set was now being sharpened for the EU referendum. It worked, probably beyond anyone's imagination. So comparisons are drawn in this chapter with what was happening alongside the government's management of English schooling – the fact that Welsh and Scottish schools had not fallen for the academisation policy, foreshadowed greater national differences that now threaten the integrity of the United Kingdom. The shenanigans in the build-up to, and the aftershocks of, the referendum results are directly traceable to the personnel and the practices of the Department for Education from 2010 and onwards.

Much of this may have been predictable. But the emergence of Covid-19 seems not to have been foreseen by anyone but a few prescient scientists. Their warnings, like those of many of the unloved 'experts', were ignored by a government fixated by Brexit and austerity. So the most egregious of the tactics honed in the once innocent world of education – and the seven deadly sins – were now firmly embedded in government and brought into play in the early months of 2020. This gives us an opportunity to ask some important questions which expose behaviour that is now commonplace throughout government. Those questions include: "Who is asking about how school leaders are behaving? Who is auditing what's going wrong with the systems we have in place? Who's counting the costs – financial and moral? Who knows and cares? And who knows and doesn't care?"

And from those questions we can start to voice some more basic concerns. What happened to this country's natural, though not unquestioning, respect for experts? How did money come to elbow aside the mission in the minds of so many educational leaders? Why did all this come about? How have our precious schools become the victims of the half-formed ramblings of a rather undistinguished journalist from the court of a manipulative Australian press baron, and his close friend, a failed airline magnate with skills in thuggishness and mendacity, having mysterious links with Russian financiers and extremist politicians?

The final chapter, What might be considers how education – and in particular the nation's schooling – might be used as a platform for a return, not to an outdated model, but to the values which once underpinned a national system. So, based on my own work and the work of many others, I propose a radical restructuring to restore the ethics of public service in the English schooling system.

A Declaration of Interest

I was a governor in four Somerset schools at various times between 2000 and 2015. The book centres around the practice of forced academisation of schools, using as a case-study the deceptions practised by the DfE, the LA and a multi-academy trust to transfer control of a small village primary school in Somerset. A contract was agreed with a specialist education publisher in 2017 and the book was due to be published in 2018. By July, it had been read, approved, legally cleared and the launch date agreed. However, the publisher, out of the blue, emailed the author to say that he no longer wanted to publish it. The reason for this change of mind only became clear six months later, when I learnt that the managing director of the publishers was also one of the three responsible members of a multi academy trust that had been awarded the sponsorship of a Hertfordshire primary school (see Chapter 8). This school was the victim of very similar tactics to those described in the book, and the subject of a prolonged but ultimately unsuccessful struggle against the combined forces of the DfE, the LA and Ofsted.

Thanks

I am grateful to my publishing team for taking on this poor homeless orphan of a book after it had been so unexpectedly rejected.

Although I take full responsibility for the contents and views expressed here, it could not have been written without the work of academics, journalists and commentators on English education. The research and reporting of Warwick Mansell and his enormously influential blog, Education Uncovered, journalists of the Guardian newspaper such as Aditya Chakrabortty, and Laura McInerney and her colleagues of Schools Week, as well as the staff of BBC Education, the Times Educational Supplement and other mainstream media have been critical in gathering examples of behaviour and throwing light on dark corners. Education experts on social media, many of whom are friends as much as colleagues, have also added much, particularly Raj Unsworth, John Eccleston and Shena Lewington. The Anti-Academies Alliance under the leadership of Alisdair Smith has continued to collect and broadcast some of the most powerful education stories of the last decade.

This is not an 'academic' work. Despite the references to evidence and research, it is a personal response to the state of schooling in England. Nevertheless, I am also fortunate to be stimulated and sustained by colleagues from the academic world who study the phenomenon of school leadership and governance, in particular, Professor Chris James, Emeritus Professor of Educational Leadership and Management at the University of Bath, Dr Ron Hill of the University of Stirling, Dr Andrew Wilkins of Goldsmiths, University of London, and Dr Andrew Allen. Other members and occasional visitors to the Research Interest Group of the British Educational Leadership, Management and Administration Society have offered valuable insights.

Some of the embryonic ideas and experiences recounted here have been published previously in different forms in issues of the education journal Forum[55]. I am grateful to the editors, especially Clyde Chitty, Howard Stevenson and Patrick Yarker, and the editorial board for providing an occasional platform for me in the years between 2011 and 2020.

I first walked into a classroom to stand at the front more than 50 years ago and have engaged in and studied that world ever since. For forty years, I have endeavoured to support those who work in schools, and to help people participate

---

[5] Forum, for promoting 3-19 comprehensive education, Symposium Books Ltd, PO Box 204, Didcot, Oxford OX11 9ZQ ISSN 0963-8253 www.wwwords.co.uk/FORUM

in the leadership of schools and other organisations that affect their lives. My work in teaching, leadership, research, consultancy, coaching and writing has been sustained over the last 38 years by Cathy Wood, without whom none of it would have been possible.

My fervent thanks to those named here, and all the schools, teachers, governors and others I have been honoured to meet and with whom I continue to be privileged to work.

Nigel Gann
Lichfield, September 2020

Section I
Schooling in England: How It Was, How It Is And the Men Who Changed It

Chapter 1
Who Owns Our Schools?

Which recaps the basic principles on which schools in England have operated since 1870, and what has happened to them since 1986. And lays down the key issues of academisation that the book will address.

How Schools Worked, 1870-1988

For people not in daily touch with education, the structure of state schooling in England is remarkably opaque. While we talk about the system of English schooling, some eminent authorities declare that there is no system at all[1].

While Scotland and Northern Ireland have largely trodden their own paths in the provision of statutory schooling, England and Wales have generally walked in step. Indeed, as Lloyd George is reputed to have said, the Welsh take it a lot more seriously: "The Welsh have a passion for education. The English have no real objection to it." If there is any truth in this, it could explain why, while sharing the English model in almost every respect since 1870, the charms of the academy model have never appealed to the devolved government of Wales.

In both countries, until lately, there has been a partnership of convenience between government, local authorities and the churches. It is often overlooked that the churches still provide a substantial proportion of both primary and secondary state schools: of some 23,000 state funded schools in England, a quarter of primary schools and over 200 secondary schools are Church of England; there are more than 2200 Catholic schools, academies and colleges in England and Wales educating over 850,000 pupils. The Catholic Church and the

---

[1] Glatter, Ron. 2018 The 'independent state school' and its aftermath: Which way now?, Keynote paper for British Educational Leadership, Management and Administration Society (BELMAS) UK Review conference on England, Birmingham, 25-26 September 2018. London: BELMAS

Church of England together provide one-third of all the state-funded schools in the country.

The history of state schooling in England since 1870 can be summed up in a series of phases:

- From 1870, the provision of primary schools for all.
- From the early 1900s, the provision of all-through elementary schools taking children up to 14.
- From the 1920s, the provision of separate secondary schools.
- From 1944, a selective system of secondary education with grammar, technical and secondary modern schools.
- From the 1960s, a shift towards progressive teaching methods in primary schools and the comprehensivisation of most secondary schools.
- From the late 1980s, the imposition of a national curriculum, regular testing of children and rigorous inspection of schools, and moves by the government to remove the local authority tier of responsibility, by enabling and then requiring, state-funded schools to become 'independent', owned and managed by charitable trusts.
  So from 1870, the four key principles of state school provision were:
- The ultimate responsibility for provision and quality of local authorities in partnership with the churches.
- The autonomy of individual schools under the leadership of the headteacher.
- A relatively tokenistic role for school governing bodies, including the engagement of lay members of the community.
- The government's reluctance to interfere with what was taught in schools.

This last feature, until the mid-1970s, was unusual in Europe. Legendarily, you could walk into any classroom in France at any time of the school day and the same subject with the same content would be being taught to the same age group. In England and Wales, the secondary curriculum was dictated largely by the examination system, but allowing for that, schools were entitled to teach pretty well whatever and however they liked – as long as they provided religious education. Of course, there were plenty of academics – "experts" – who joined together with the support of the Department for Education to research and create new approaches and resources. These would be supported by university education departments, professional associations and local authorities. But they were only advisory.

Then, in the last years of the Labour government of 1974-79, two of the four principles came to be questioned.

First, **the role and composition of school governing bodies were under discussion**. School governors were usually chosen from 'the great and the good', from the council chamber, the rotary clubs, the golf clubs and Labour groups. There had been increasing demands throughout the 1970s for more local, and particularly parental, involvement in schools. Very few wanted parents to actually run schools. The Conservatives came a cropper over this when they suggested that the entire governing body should be made up of the parents of the school. But there were two quite different movements going on throughout the country, as most communities became better off, better educated, more questioning of longstanding authority, and more demanding of the quality of goods and services provided to them.

One of these movements was around the role of people as consumers. Throughout all the country, and indeed throughout the western world, ordinary people were getting used to the idea that they should have a bit of spare money left over after buying the necessities. So from daily groceries to life-changing purchases, like houses and cars, consumers were demanding a more reliable quality to what they were being offered. The National Consumer Council, the spread of Citizens Advice Bureaux and the advent of 'Which' magazine, to name but three, showed how people who banded together could get better value for money. And this movement shifted into national services provided through local or national taxation; health, transport, community provision and, of course, education had to recognise that the people to whom they were accountable were no longer the government or shareholders, but were consumers and, yes, customers.

Meanwhile, some people began to recognise that they were not just consumers, but they were also citizens, rather than merely subjects. And citizens, in good Greek manner, could expect to play a part in how the state, and the services provided by the state, were managed. This wasn't a neat provider-customer relationship. To many this was a feeling that local communities had a right to participate in managing the services provided for them, not just to pay for them. The people were beginning to see that a modern democratic state should do more than just hold regular elections to their parliaments and councils. Elected representatives should be clearly transparent, accountable and accessible. In the words of an American journalist observing the engagement of local communities in one of President Roosevelt's most ambitious 'New Deal' projects, the people had begun to catch "the vision of their own powers."[2]

So in widening the scope of school governance, the right-wing thought that they were empowering the voice of consumers – a voice, of course, that would be loudest among the better-off and more confident of the population or, more pertinently, of the electorate. Meanwhile, the left-wing thought that they were empowering ordinary people eager to have a say in services that had historically been determined by the ruling classes. So the voice of the disadvantaged might at last be heard in an education service which, until then, as exemplified by the dominance of grammar and private schools, had belonged largely to the middle-classes.

The Conservative government of the 1980s saw no reason to clarify this confusion. It seems likely that the teaching profession feared that the 'consumer' role would be dominant, but relaxed when they found that actually most people wanted to be participants, not adversaries.

The second educational principle to be challenged in the 1970s was – **who should decide what is taught in schools?**

Turning secondary schools into comprehensives throughout England and Wales was the main political issue of the 1970s, although the project remains incomplete. But in 1976 Prime Minister Jim Callaghan made a speech at Ruskin College that opened a debate on the purpose of education – and therefore its content – which continued throughout the following twelve years under, first, a Labour government and then Margaret Thatcher's Conservative administration. In fact, by the end of the 1980s, Thatcher was regarding education as the last big issue she wanted to address. The debate in the '80s had been largely around the nature of provision. This included both how parents should access state schooling for their children – much of this revolving around a plan to distribute vouchers to them to provide a platform for choice – and the content of the

---

[2] Daily, Decatur, Alabama: *Editorial, 18 May 1943*, quoted in Lilienthal, David. 1944 *TVA Tennessee Valley Authority: Democracy on the March.* Harmondsworth: Penguin. The quote reads: "We can write of great dams . . . of the building of home-grown industry and of electricity at last coming to the farms of thousands of farm people in the Valley. *Yet the significant advance has been made in the thinking of a people.* They are no longer afraid. *They have caught the vision of their own powers.*" (p44)

curriculum, what children experienced once they got into school – resulting in the national curriculum. Thus, the 1988 Education Act "was ostensibly an attempt to raise educational standards and to extend parental choice"[3]. However, it also contained the seeds of the end of local government being the exclusive provider of state-funded schools.

From 1988-2010

The Education Reform Act of 1988 introduced a national curriculum, local management of schools and the first model of state-funded schools independent of local government. Professor of Education Brian Simon's prescient view was that the aim of the act was "destabilising locally controlled 'systems' and, concomitantly, pushing the whole structure of schooling towards a degree, at least, of privatisation, so establishing a base which could be exploited further."[4]

Was this 'privatisation'? Certainly, there was a significant role developing here for the public in the strategic leadership of schools. The 1986 reform of governing bodies removed the in-built majority of local authority appointees. It was replaced by a stakeholder model with parents as the largest single group, which was designed to weaken the local authority's 'control' of schools. The '88 Act then brought about a radical devolution of responsibility to individual schools, in the local management of school budgets. Now, the major part of the money provided for schools had to be devolved to the governing board with the headteacher. Decisions about staffing and resourcing the schools became a strategic matter for the governors, no longer the sole reserve of the local departments of education. The degree to which schools from then on were 'run' by local departments of education depended upon the determination of local headteachers and governors to exercise their powers and the willingness of the local education authority to enable them to do so. This varied from, often northern, urban authorities who still dictated governing body policies and agendas, to others where schools were assisted in making their own decisions, with not much more than a paternal eye being kept on them. The major constraints from that time on, were coming from central government, via Ofsted's inspections, introduced in 1992, and the government's Department for

---

[3] Chitty, Clyde. 1999 *The Education System Transformed.* Tisbury: Baseline Book Company. p31
[4] Simon, Brian. 1988 *Bending the Rules: The Baker 'Reform' of Education.* London: Lawrence and Wishart p48

Education. Between them – and the relationship between the two was often problematic – they controlled the great part of the formal curriculum, and the 'hidden curriculum'. That is, what was taught in schools, how it was taught, how schools were organised, what their priorities should be, and what standards they should strive to achieve, were actually not in the hands of the governors and staff at all.

The model of governance which took shape in 1988 took time to settle in. New lay governors had to be recruited and trained. Headteachers had to become accustomed to their accountability to these new creatures. Local authorities had to learn to stand back and let heads and governors get used to responsibility for the strategic direction of the school. At the same time, the devolution of large amounts of money to be managed by headteachers and overseen by the governors, was a very new world. Many new governors were nervous of it, and many headteachers resented it. Some were uncertain and deferential; others were defensive and bombastic – on both 'sides'.

Many longstanding headteachers felt themselves considerably deskilled by the coincidence of local management with the new technology then coming into schools. At one school in the East End of London, a primary school head admitted that she had very little input to the staffing arrangements – staffing amounting to around 75%, or more, of a school's budget – because the caretaker was the only person who understood how to use the computer. Sometimes the machismo of a head was judged by the extent to which they could "run rings around the governing body" – one of the characteristics of a good headteacher, according to one director of education in Wales[5].

But the new arrangements did settle down over time. The model of stakeholder governance and local management of schools established a reasonable and workable balance of control and influence over state-funded schools: a reasonable degree of headteacher autonomy, balanced by lay community strategic direction through stakeholder governance, and democratically accountable local government oversight, with overall central government control, supported by professional accountability to Ofsted. This wasn't perfect, but it generally worked, overseeing very significant improvements in school performance while maintaining broad parental confidence. Many headteachers seemed to begin to see parents as allies, often against an overweening or inefficient local authority and central government.

---

[5] Both of these, with varying degrees of horror, were witnessed by the author

Many recognised that parents and other community members brought some of the reality of life from the outside world into the school. They could often help with practical things too, especially overseeing the budget. And if things went slightly wrong, or worse, the governing body could be a useful – and a very common-sense – line of defence against difficult parents or an interfering bureaucracy. There was, in many schools, a recognition of the wider purposes of education, such as personal, social and creative development. A balance between these and the academic progress of the children was something about which most teachers and parents seemed to agree.

However, the seeds of the model's destruction had already been sown. The advent of, first, city technology colleges, then grant-maintained schools, which grew more slowly than the Conservative government might have wished throughout the 1990s, took self-management to a new level, welcomed by some. These schools were rapturously free from the inefficient and tyrannical local authority and received their entire budget from the fantastically well-organised, sympathetic and freedom-loving central government. Nevertheless, no one could escape the fact that, while a large secondary school with a strong, self-directing leadership team and supportive governors could comfortably manage its own affairs, the situation for the majority of primary schools and smaller secondary, middle and special schools was entirely different. Only a half of one percent of primary schools in England have more than 800 pupils. More significantly, more than one third of English primary schools have fewer than 200 pupils, a number often cited as the absolute baseline for financially viable schools under the maintained schools system.

Between 1997 and 2010 the Labour government introduced the notion of requiring 'failing' urban schools to be converted into 'sponsored' academies. So, when the coalition government took office in 2010, the principle of encouraging successful schools by allowing them to become independent of their local authorities was well established.

From 2010 On

So well established it was that it only took, almost literally, the work of a moment for new Secretary of State Michael Gove to use legislative powers which had been established to address terrorism to introduce a bill allowing 'outstanding' schools to apply for stand-alone academy status. Soon they were followed by 'good' and other schools. Working from the further end of the spectrum, this also enabled the DfE to require any 'failing' school to become an academy sponsored by an existing trust or other 'successful' schools.

How big a turnaround was this? Historically, all the policy developments in education from 1870 up to 1988 could be seen as attempts to improve the schooling of the nation's children and young people. They may not always have been popular. They may have been misguided. They may have pandered to one part of the population, and of the electorate, over another. But a rational argument could be put forward to justify the changes based on some belief about how schools might work better for the country and for its young.

But not now. No serious evidence ever suggested that widespread academisation would improve educational standards. The stuttering and staggering from City Technology Colleges through Grant Maintained Schools and Foundation Schools, to the enforced academisation of inner city schools by Labour governments of the 2000s under sponsors expected to contribute significant sums (though many never did) to the Conservative carrot (boosted by large sums of money taken from local authorities' remaining schools) for 'outstanding' schools – alongside the stick of enforced change to 'failing' schools. Where was the logic here? Was academy status a thing to be desired, or feared? Who wanted their local school to dump its historical links with both local government and local people, and instead become an item of property with no individual legal status, of a geographically incoherent and philosophically unaccountable group of self-perpetuating non-educationists?

The acme of academisation was held up to be the 'free school', owned and managed by parents themselves for the benefit of their own children. Of course, these are now only ever opened by existing trusts, because actually and confoundingly, schools turn out to be best managed by people who know something about education. It is as if communities were being encouraged to open 'free' hospitals, funded by the taxpayer, overseen by business people and hedge fund investors, employing the cheapest and lowest-qualified (if qualified at all – unqualified teachers are welcome in academies) doctors, nurses and carers they could find – just like private care homes, indeed. And just like some private care homes, some free schools took years to open, often failed to open, sometimes lasted a couple of years, sometimes wasted millions of pounds of government funding, often closed ignominiously after a couple of years of under-attended and over-financed mismanagement, chucking the clients out to find other proper state-run providers to take them in.

The Roots of Privatisation

This mishmash of deliberately destructive government policy was openly advocated by two disciples of an entirely speculative and wholly unevidenced 1988 right-wing Tory publication designed to reduce the state to the role of backstop insurer. The incoherence of the 'system' shows that 'school improvement' – or at the least 'student enhancement' – was never any part of the ambitions of the policy-makers, any more than the creeping privatisation of the NHS has seen any improvement in either its provision or its capacity to deal with a much predicted pandemic; any more than the privatisation of the cherry-picked parts of the probation service saw any benefits to its users or to the protection of the public, and instead heralded a public emergency rescued, again, by the state; or any more than the most expensive and least efficient railway system in Europe; or than the ludicrous chimera of 'choice' offered by multiple water or energy providers; or any more than the criminally self-protective managers of the post office.

In one possible future, the education service might well be in line for the kind of de-privatisation now happening to the railways and, in its entirety, to the probation service. These, along with other parts of the justice system being remodelled after the disastrous rule of a particular Tory cabinet member, might lead us to hope that the education department itself might one day fall into, and then out of, the hands of former Transport Minister and Justice Minister Chris Grayling. We will look at those possibilities in the final chapters.

As it is, with the experiences of the decade, we might suppose that the only aim of the mass academisation of schools was to put a public good largely into private hands. And, where possible, into the hands of Conservative fellow-travellers.

So how could a policy born out of such an ambition do anything other than serve the desires of the trustees rather than the needs of the pupils? The many good schools and dedicated staff that stand in classrooms directly providing the best and widest education and care for their children are not the products of this system. They are, in fact, the outliers. Because the characteristics of greed and self-aggrandizement seen from the top of the Department for Education running through the system are not bugs in the system. They are the key features of it.

Chapter 2
How Did We Get Here?

Or maybe that should read: Who got us here? This short chapter searches for the origins of the corporatisation of schools, and how it fits into a nationwide narrative.

Neoliberalism For (And By) Dummies

Philosophically – if that's not too grand a word for the incoherent mishmash of change we have been experiencing – the implementations of Michael Gove and his chief adviser, Dominic Cummings, were born of Conservative MP Oliver Letwin's practical translations of neoliberal thinking for Margaret Thatcher in the 1980s. Conviction politicians, like Letwin and John Redwood, saw Thatcher as a suitable vehicle to implement their extreme vision of a small state, low tax, low regulation Britain. Thus were complex and sophisticated global economics reduced to being an issue digestible by the public as 'good housekeeping'.

With what was to have enormous relevance to education, the ideal model for Britain was America. President Reagan (1972-1980) saw government not as the solution but the problem. The United States had no use for a national health service. Instead by 2020 the economic demands of Reaganomics saw it as reasonable and fair that a coronavirus patient in recovery could be presented with a hospital bill of $1m dollars. It was not interested in a comprehensive welfare safety net, or in guaranteed freedoms from Beveridge's five evils of want, disease, ignorance, squalor and idleness. Nor did it want government time to be wasted on addressing such issues as inequality, or in trying to improve the lives and wellbeing of its citizens.

To model the government of the United Kingdom on any other country, of course, was to ignore the fundamental differences between the two. The United States is a young country built on colonisation and all its attendant traits. It did indeed reach out to welcome "your poor, your huddled masses yearning to breathe free". But this welcome, like the country's national anthem, promised freedom to the brave, not support or protection to the needy. The ideal American would be an independent, self-reliant builder of their own wealth. There would be little sympathy for those who didn't make it by themselves. Naturally, the institutions that developed in the States reflected this mind-set. In Britain, such institutions of state and of local government evolved slowly, responsive eventually to need and demand. They weren't always conscious of the needs of the poor. But they were recognised as conveniences for the middle classes. You would expect history scholars at least to recognise this.

The building of a state founded on compromise and convenience, even though the ultimate beneficiary was a society founded on manufacture and trade, meant that the poor and rootless had to be looked after, even if it was primarily to protect the interests and property of the middle classes. Education is one of those arenas.

How ideas and institutions are born, the ground in which they are rooted, is critical to their development and their dominant culture. The stories that form around their foundation, their successes and their heroes, reflect that culture and are difficult, if not impossible to eradicate. A policing model from the States, for example, would be unlikely to survive wholesale replanting in British soil, any more than a French, or a Spanish or a Russian model would. The purchase of ex-military weapons by US police departments is commonplace. When similar attempts have been made in the UK, they are likely, like Boris Johnson's purchase of water cannons from Germany during his mayoralty of London, to end in ridicule.

Nevertheless, the 1980s saw concerted efforts by right-wing politicians to bring American-style approaches to two of our key public services – health and education.

The Privatisation of The World
Oliver Letwin was Margaret Thatcher's key policy adviser whose beliefs underpinned her instincts. While Thatcher did believe in a safety net for the nation's most vulnerable, Letwin wrote a book whose title needs no explanation: "Privatising the World"[1].

---

[1] Letwin, Oliver and Redwood, John. 1980 *Privatising the World: A Study of International Privatization in Theory and Practice*. London: Cengage

The twentieth century had seen a significant focus on the welfare of the population. One motivation for this was to provide a healthy, appropriately educated workforce for an increasingly competitive and global economy. But there was, from Lloyd George's People's Budget of 1909 through Beveridge's post-war reforms and the 1948 creation of the National Health Service and welfare state, a genuine attempt to provide womb-to-tomb support for ordinary people.

By 1980, for some, the state had become too big, too cumbersome, and too messy. The argument that the market was the more natural and the more efficient provider became embedded in what had once been a predominantly paternalistic Conservative party. The winding-down of state provision began in a frenzy of denationalisation, of transport, of the utilities and of the remaining state-run industries. This involved selling off state ownership and reducing state obligations. The entirely indiscriminate dismantling of the way the state had operated since the Second World War was bound, in the end, to address the major provisions of government: health, welfare provision, the justice system, and education.

One of the main problems with reforming state education, unlike almost all other services, is that most of the politicians taking it on have had little or no experience of it. Around seven per cent of children in the UK are privately educated in a self-confident, entitled world, with preferential access to the Holy Grail of Oxbridge. Even those few politicians who have experience of the state sector are most likely to have been to one of the remaining selective schools. Twenty-six ministers were attending cabinet in early 2020. Seventeen of them, that is sixty-five per cent, were privately educated, while two more attended grammar schools. Thirteen – one half of them – attended Oxford or Cambridge. When the bulk of one's first twenty-one years have been spent in a cloistered world of wealth and privilege providing access to a lifetime of the same, it must be difficult to see the value of any other kind of school experience. Certainly they might be attracted to making all state education as much like their own experience as possible. But without the necessary funding, of course.

So how could state education be privatised? Could it be by giving parents a voucher for their children, exchangeable for schooling at an institution of their choice? This idea had been proposed by Letwin and Redwood for health, where the poor would be subsidised to buy health care with vouchers provided through means testing. The health business could then provide generous profits for both insurers and providers. Sir Keith Joseph, in his spell at the DfE from 1981 to 1986, was much enamoured by this. Vouchers for education could be augmented by the better-off to buy places at more desirable schools and would enable those in the know to choose only the best for their own children. Less popular schools would suffer the punishment of the market and close down. Vouchers died the death when it was realised belatedly that opening up unbridled parental choice would make planning of provision impossible. How could an improved school immediately provide buildings, staff and resources for a sudden influx? And how could less successful schools improve if middle class children left in droves to find places elsewhere?

Putting parents onto governing bodies seemed like a good idea but again, making boards exclusively of parents would be dangerous. Safe enough, perhaps, in the leafy suburbs where parents might be aspirational in an acceptable way, but full of unknown and unspeakable perils in the inner cities, let alone in the farthest reaches of the mysterious Labour-dominated north of the country. But the answer could lie in the concept of independent state-funded schooling.

The story in this book of the forced conversion of a single small school to a sponsored academy might strike the reader as relatively insignificant, especially in the context of the wholesale national reorganisation of schooling orchestrated by the Conservative government of 2015. The democratically elected government has a right to determine the structures of state-funded schooling, so that it best meets the nation's needs. The policy of forcing schools deemed by Ofsted to be 'failing' to become sponsored academies, run by a Board of Trustees, was built into the Labour Government's academies programme in 2002. In 2010, in a strange overturning of the rationale, the new coalition government made academy status open to schools deemed 'outstanding' and, later, to all schools. The policy suggested, first, that persistently failing schools required emergency measures of sponsorship by industry, big business or another more successful school. Then it shifted to reframe academisation as something greatly to be desired by headteachers and governors from the grant-maintained/foundation school model of the 1990s, but only available to the 'outstanding' or 'good' schools. Then in 2015, once the back of those pesky Liberal Democrats had been seen, it became a model to be imposed upon all schools, like it or not. The government presented this as a crusade to ensure that all children received the best education the country could offer, and that this was best achieved by the 'autonomy' that academy status appeared to offer headteachers and staff. By contrast, much of the profession, particularly those in primary schools, saw it as a threat to their relative degree of self-management, which had been enshrined in the 1986 and 1988 Education Acts, and provided local authorities with the means to support and maintain schools, not 'run' them, as the government persisted in claiming.

In fact, after an initial period of headteacher suspicion, most schools had learned to like, or even love, the governing boards that the 1986 (No 2) Education Act had established[2], and so had many parents. Local schools had come to be led by an intriguing coalition of school professionals and local people, who often saw themselves as managing a tight ship with the help of, or sometimes in spite of, a local authority sitting somewhere on a spectrum of supportive or controlling, and competent or inept.

Once the Conservative majority government took office in May 2015, the way was clear for the Prime Minister to confirm what had been implied earlier, that the intention was for all schools to become academies. The Education and Adoption Act of 2016[3] removed the need for consultations over conversion for schools required to become sponsored academies by reason of under-performance. It also widened the definition of such under-performance to include 'coasting' schools. So, ironically, the Conservative government came to preside over more failing schools than any government before it. Education was probably the only area of social legislation where the government was changing the definition of failure to include, as opposed to exclude, increasing numbers. Such was its assault on the status quo.

For almost the first year of the government, rumours circulated about its intentions regarding academies, but these were confirmed, strangely, not by the secretary of state, but in the Chancellor of the Exchequer's pre-budget announcement on the 15th March. The subsequent White Paper[4] announced that all remaining maintained schools would be required to have plans in place for academisation, almost without exception in a multi-academy trust, by 2020, and for implementation to be complete by 2022.

The outcry that greeted this, from parents, teachers, governors and others, led to what was publicised as a U-turn (another major U-turn among nine listed

---

[2] HMSO 1986 *Education (No. 2) Act*. London: HMSO

[3] Education and Adoption Act 2016

[4] Department for Education 2016a *Educational Excellence Everywhere* London: The Stationery Office

by The Guardian[5]) but in actuality was not. A subsequent press release[6] confirmed that the government now thought "that it is not necessary to bring legislation to bring about blanket conversion of all schools to achieve this goal." Instead, the government intended to "trigger" conversion where a local authority might not be viable due to the conversion of a "critical mass" of its schools, and "where the local authority consistently fails to meet a minimum performance threshold across its schools, demonstrating an inability to bring about meaningful school improvement."

Once again, the DfE was demonstrating its unerring capacity to know what the best structure for state-funded schools was, while claiming that this would bring about the desired ideal of putting "control of running schools in the hands of teachers and school leaders" (ibid). In fact, of course, this would bring about a situation where, by 2020, the "stand-alone" school with its own governing board would be an endangered species. For the first time since before the 1870 Act requiring the provision of countrywide state-funded schooling, and on its 150th birthday, practically all small schools, as well as most others, were to be managed at a distance from their own sites. The government had, as it later turned out, established its preference for change through stealth and edict rather than transparent legislation, a practice it was already honing in its reform of health provision and in its creation of a hostile environment for immigrants.

Privatising A Small School; Privatising A Country

Castle Primary School in Somerset fell foul of the 2010-15 coalition government's growing plans to impose sponsored academisation on as many schools as it could. Enforcement would take place where Ofsted reported that it could not see capacity for improvement in the school's leadership, and the local authority would be told to find a school or other organisation to take it over. But Ofsted has always been suspected of being unable to deliver reliable judgments about schools[7]. Sometimes, it has been accused of enabling the DfE's policy of enforcing conversion wherever possible. Nevertheless, governors and staff in

---

[5] The Guardian Leader, 9 May 2016, p24

[6] Department for Education 2016b *Next steps to spread educational excellence everywhere announced*, Press release, 6 May 2016

[7] See, for example, *Improving School Accountability: Report of the NAHT Accountability Commission*, National Association of Headteachers, September 2018 and House, Richard. 2020 *Pushing Back to Ofsted*. Stroud: InterActions Publishing

schools in Castle's position were still at that time entitled by law to express disagreement. The school was required to hold a full public consultation on whether the conversion should take place and on the identity of the intended sponsor. Later, these rights were withdrawn by further legislation. But in 2014, the law was clear. As we shall see, the law was ignored by professional educators and politicians, both locally and nationally.

The priority, to take a school away from its community, overrode professional and ethical principles. Why and how did this happen?

This very substantial change in school provision throughout England reflected changes taking place over some forty years in the ownership of Britain's public services.

In the Britain of 1979, this translated as: "A third of all homes were rented from the state. The health service, most schools, the armed forces, prisons, roads, bridges and streets, water, sewers, the National Grid, power stations, the phone and postal system, gas supply, coal mines, the railways, refuse collection, the airports, many of the ports, local and long-distance buses, freight lorries, nuclear fuel reprocessing, air traffic control, much of the car-, ship- and aircraft-building industry, most of the steel factories, British Airways, oil companies, Cable & Wireless, the aircraft engine makers Rolls-Royce, the arms makers Royal Ordnance, the ferry company Sealink, the Trustee Savings Bank, Girobank, technology companies Ferranti and Inmos, medical technology firm Amersham International and many others. In the past thirty-five years, this commonly owned economy, this people's portion of the island, has to a greater or lesser degree become private."[8]

This policy was then extended to state-funded schools. It is not privatisation. It is the transfer of public assets, goods and services, to corporate bodies. It is better described as corporatisation.

In the next chapter, we will explore the roots of this process at the level of national government, for it was there that the policy was forged, and it was there that the behaviour used to intimidate and crush small local institutions was practised by politicians and their advisers. In subsequent chapters, we shall see how this was played out by people who learnt from their masters the tricks which would enable them to suborn the will of the community.

---

[8] Meek, James. 2014 *Private Island: Why Britain Now Belongs to Someone Else*, London: Verso pp8-9

Chapter 3
Who Did This to Our Schools?

Which explains how these things came about, and asks: "Was this down to a clear strategic and philosophical plan – or was it down to a small group of men more interested in a fashionable political theory and their own advancement than in the nation's education of young people?"

Where We Were In 2015

As we have seen, experimentation with the status and funding of schools began in the late 1980s and was handily sustained and developed by a Labour government as disenchanted with local government as its Tory opponents had been. Notoriously, Labour Prime Minister Tony Blair "holding his left arm to signify a mock injury," spoke publicly of "getting change in the public sector and public services – I bear the scars on my back after two years in government. Heaven knows what it will be like if it is a bit longer"[1]. The Labour government tidied up the anomaly of the grant-maintained schools, creating a category of 'foundation schools' which owed limited accountability to their local authority. In response to the increasingly obvious problems of much inner-city secondary education, it then introduced the concept of the sponsored academy in the Education Acts of 2000 and 2002. This was a nod to the American Charter School and could force the closure of a school and its reopening in new premises, with a new name and an 'independent' but state-funded status. Academies would be directly accountable for their performance to the Department for Education. These City Academies grew slowly in response to need and did not seem much of a threat to rural secondaries or suburban and village primaries.

And so to David Cameron's victory in 2010. In order to govern, he had to enlist the collaboration of the Liberal Democrats. Fortunately for him, they were

---

[1] The Guardian, 7th July 1999

led by a small cadre of "Orange Book" liberals apparently even more besotted with the world of private finance than the Tories. Given that, to whom would Cameron entrust the future of the country's education? Who could implement a nationwide 'privatisation' of schooling?

In 2020, journalist Andrew Rawnsley, bemoaning the performance of a government in a pandemic with one of the highest virus death rates in the world, wrote: "The problem with this government is that it is led by journalists"[2]. In fact, the 2019 government was headed up by an Old Etonian comment journalist with a history of being sacked, lying and general thuggery. In 2010, the government had been led by an Old Etonian PR man whose only apparent motivation had been that "I think I would be rather good at it"[3]. Cameron's casual approach to leadership makes it likely that he had no particular thought-out motivation in allowing Michael Gove to transfer directly into the department for education. It was probably just the easiest option. Gove, at least, was an old mate, and he must have had some notion about what state schools were about since he had, almost uniquely in the new Cabinet, attended a state primary. Cameron did put his own personal likes and dislikes above politics in one respect, though. He objected to Gove's adviser, Dominic Cummings. Or at least, his own adviser, Andy Coulson – ironically recruited from the Murdoch paper The News of the World – did. Even so the road was clear for an ideologically driven set of policies. The man entrusted with the education brief also had had a career of sorts as a comment journalist, and was a close associate of a media billionaire with American nationality, eager to get his hands on a potential education market of some £50 billion.

The Brightest And The Best Of 2010?

"They were careless people ...they smashed up things and creatures and then retreated back into their money or their vast carelessness or whatever it was that kept them together, and let other people clean up the mess they had made."

(The Great Gatsby: Scott Fitzgerald, 1925)

---

[2] Rawnsley, Andrew. 2020 *Even Tories increasingly fear they have inflicted the worst of all worlds on Britain*, The Observer, 15th June 2020

[3] Sandbrook, Dominic. 2016 *How Will History Treat David Cameron?* New Statesman, 29 August 2016

The government elected in 2010 after thirteen straight years of Labour rule was a coalition, though dominated by the Conservatives. Its key task was to address recovery from the dramatic world-wide financial crisis of 2008.

The almost unprecedented chaos into which the world had been thrown proved to be a useful cover for the new government to impose some of its most cherished policies, in the guise of 'necessity'. Its superfluous and self-harming commitment to austerity could be laid at the door of Labour 'profligacy', while enabling a series of enormously damaging policy directives. In education, the entire "Every Child Matters" platform, a coherent 'birth to adulthood' multi-agency structure, was dismantled, with the closure of hundreds of children's centres and other multi-agency initiatives. The progressive idea of extended schooling was dumped, along with Building Schools for the Future, a plan to recover school premises from Thatcher's neglect, most of the nation's youth services, community services and careers advice. The new government's 'Search and Destroy' muscles were quickly flexed and brought into play.

Elsewhere, the government took the opportunity to slash and redesign the benefits system for the unemployed, the sick and the disabled, and to introduce the notorious 'hostile environment' for immigration. This, too, was to return years later to haunt them.

Two Must-Haves For A Government: Ideology ... And Competence

Even highly popular and seemingly brilliant political teams have to be competent. As David Halberstam discovered, when he wrote the history of President John Kennedy's 'Camelot' administration of the early 1960s, "The other thing I learned about the Kennedy-Johnson team was that for all their considerable reputations as brilliant, rational managers they were in fact very poor managers"[4]. The Cameron regime had no such reputation when it gained power. When the hostile immigration environment threw up the Windrush scandal in 2018, with Cameron long gone, it became clear that the damage being done to British society was not an unforeseen by-product of benevolent policy, but a critical and intentional feature of government thinking. This managerial carelessness was revealed as the inevitable outcome of barely concealed racism, historical amnesia and blame-laying. It was the Cameron team's seedy and

---

[4] Halberstam, David. 1969 *The Best and the Brightest*, New York: Ballantine Books, p.xvii

casual self-entitlement that lay behind the casual abandonment of British citizens who had arrived here in the 1940s, '50s and '60s, often as children[5]. It was aided and abetted by successive Home Secretaries, including Teresa May's hard-bitten and explicitly racist policy-making, and Amber Rudd's ignorance, laziness and self-protection. Their policies were being implemented by the latest generation of largely white, middle-class civil servants seemingly more concerned with their own smooth ascent of the comfortable ladder of guaranteed salaries and eventual gongs. This was a group of politicians who had never managed anything before in their lives, driven by an ideology, the likely public impact of which they were too stupid, or too slipshod, to foresee. This was not a competent government.

Indeed, the level of incompetence in government over the ten years from 2010 looks so extraordinary that one is tempted to ask if some of it was deliberate. After all, if you want to take a service apart, particularly something as popular as the NHS, you don't want to do it when it's working well. A more sensible strategy is to run it down so far that any reorganisation, even if it breaches the vision of the founders, will be welcomed by an exasperated and under-served public.

While these things were going on at the Home Office and the Department of Health and Social Care then, what was happening at the Department for Education?

Governments, and individual departmental ministers, have to decide two things when they get into office – what they want to do, and whether they have the ability to do it. The Johnson government of 2019-20 was notable for a number of things. The two most evident ones were that, first, it had been elected on its claim to achieve one thing – Brexit. Secondly, it was going to depend on a small rump of believers and an influx of rather surprised new members to achieve it. Certainly, the education department, in the charge of a slightly disreputable former fireplace salesman, did not appear to have any sort of vision for the future.

Back in 2010, there may have been a clear vision of what was wanted, but an absence of any practical experience to achieve it, alongside an inability to envisage the likely side-effects. What lay at the root of this failure was that the policy was about taking something apart – the current system of local authority

[5] See, for example, Gentleman, Amelia. 2019 *The Windrush Betrayal: Exposing the Hostile Environment,* London: Guardian Faber; Goodfellow, Maya. 2019 *Hostile Environment: How Immigrants Became Scapegoats,* London: Verso Books; Yeo, Colin. 2020 *Welcome to Britain: Fixing Our Broken Immigration System,* London: Biteback Publishing

delivery and oversight of schooling – rather than putting something together – in this case, a system ensuring some national coherence and fairness in the provision of a key public good. It was the disruptive, destructive element of the reformation of schooling that was to be the problem. No one had decided even such basic things as the ethical and behavioural standards to be expected of school providers. For such a negative task, you don't need experts – in fact, experts would get in the way, with their carefully-wrought foresight and annoying warnings.

The Man Who Came To Run Education

"Every great institution is the lengthened shadow of one man. His character determines the character of the organization"[6]

All politicians come and go, and most leave little of a mark behind them. At the various departments responsible for education since the second world war, there have been thirty-eight holders of the post, of whom barely a dozen can be said to have been memorable – not all of those in a good way. Some knew little about state education, others seemed to know nothing. But a handful brought real knowledge, understanding and expertise to the post.

Michael Gove, certainly, was no expert, with no identifiable skills in anything to do with administration or governance. As a journalist of considerable Murdoch loyalty – a book Murdoch's publishing arm had commissioned from him with generous advances in 2006 about an obscure eighteenth century Tory politician remains on the backburner – he allowed his personal life to become rather too colourful.

Gove was notorious at Oxford University for 5-in-a-bed romps and public spats over girlfriends. In government, his chief adviser's wife – another comment journalist – wrote an extraordinarily long denial in the right-wing Spectator magazine that the two men were having an affair[7] – a tactic likely to arouse, rather than quell speculation. The adviser in question was Dominic Cummings. Gove and his own wife, Sarah Vine (another comment columnist, this one with the Daily Mail), had not had a trouble-free time since he swapped his journalist's keyboard for a Surrey constituency. First, the Goves found a not insignificant

[6] Emerson, Ralph Waldo. 1841 "Self-Reliance". In Eliot, Charles William (ed.). *Essays and English Traits*. Harvard Classics. Volume 5, with introduction and notes. (56th printing, 1965 ed.). New York: P.F.Collier & Son Corporation. pp. 59–69
[7] Wakefield, Mary 2016 *The Spectator*, 19 November 2016

role in the Daily Telegraph's exposure of MPs' expenses[8], repaying £7K plus for the furnishing of their north Kensington home – much of which had been spent in David Cameron's mother-in-law's 'upmarket interior design company'. This included the cost of a Chinon armchair, a Manchu cabinet, a pair of elephant lamps, a Loire table and a Camargue chair. The incoherence of this personal style comes as no surprise when laid out against Gove's political term of office. Meanwhile, their honeymoon was paid for by Camilla Parker-Bowles' nephew, Ben Elliot's, 'luxury lifestyle firm' – the owner later being given a post by Gove in the government, and appointed by new Prime Minister Johnson as co-chair of the Conservative Party. Elliot was clearly a "good fellow with a very sound head on his shoulders", as Ms Vine wrote beforehand. Ben Elliot is a Non-Executive Director of YouGov Plc, an exclusively Tory-run polling organisation that somehow invariably manages to show a substantial lead for the party. He sits on the board of the Centre for Policy Studies, a right-wing think tank. Of which more later.

More freebies were to follow. Ms Vine's boss, non-domicile (therefore much tax-relieved) Lord Rothermere was able to foot the bill for the Goves' holidays.

On the spending of other people's money:

"I have generally found, in my experience, that it's their own money people are most particular about. I have seen people get rid of a good deal of other people's money, and bear it very well: very well indeed."[9]

Gove In Government

All this would just be laughably vulgar, until Gove's personal profligacy with other people's money began to extend into his governmental roles. At the end of his period of office at education, from 2010 to 2014, the DfE was unable to value the land and buildings over which it had taken control during the academisation process. The National Audit Office reported that the worth of the "incomplete and inaccurate valuation of academies' land and building assets" was around £33 billion:

"Providing Parliament with a clear view of academy trusts' spending is a vital part of the Department for Education's work – yet it is failing to do this. As a result, I have today provided an adverse opinion on the truth and fairness of its financial statements. The Department will have to work hard in the coming

[8] Daily Telegraph, 13 May 2009
[9] Dickens, Charles. *Little Dorrit*

months, if it is to present Parliament with a better picture of academy trusts' spending through the planned new Sector Account in 2017."[10]

Gove seems to have been particularly profligate with property. Shortly before he was removed from the DfE in 2014, he announced that the Department would be moving out of Sanctuary Buildings into the Old Admiralty Buildings. Gove claimed that this would save the rent and free up money to be "reinvested back into the department's budget". By the autumn of 2018, the refurbishment had cost millions, and the scheme was cancelled, with the DfE signing up to another fifteen years in Sanctuary Buildings[11].

Besides that, the half million given to a newly-established charity, run by Rachel Wolf, another erstwhile colleague of, first Johnson and, later, Gove, to provide advice and guidance to the new Free Schools from 2010, was peanuts. Similarly, the DfE advisers engaged to ensure schools did convert, voluntarily or by force, were being paid as off-book advisers up to more than £1,000 a day – a generous daily fee by any standards in the otherwise cash-strapped world of state education.

Picking Winners?

Above many things – though not, perhaps, above everything – Gove seemed to be a sociable chap. Visitors almost invariably reported just how charming and amiable he is. He has indeed collected an impressive band of associates, towards some of whom he displays a remarkable, and sometimes personally costly, loyalty. But perhaps his greatest loyalty has been to his boss of many years – maybe still his true boss – Rupert Murdoch.

Within a week of Gove's appointment in 2010, the first meeting between the new Secretary of State for Education and his (supposedly ex-) employer and billionaire media owner, soon to be humbled by the behaviour of his newspapers, took place. The two men met in Wapping by the river Thames, where Murdoch planned to monetise his former print works by building there – with government money – one of the first academies under Tory rule. He was accompanied by his American Charter School adviser, Joel Klein. Nowhere could it have been clearer that the exploitation of the American Charter Schools for the benefit of private buccaneering was the model for the new British government. The land for the

---

[10] Morse, Amyas. 2016 *Comptroller and Auditor General's Report on the Department for Education's financial statements 2014-15*, London: National Audit Office
[11] Private Eye, 14 December 2018

building was not to be the only source of profit. Klein's work consisted of all sorts of other profiteering from the public money that governments put aside for the education of children: curriculum models to be bought from the owners, expenses to be earned for top employees and consultants, contracts of the Public Finance Initiative type that locked schools into expensive and unbreakable management arrangements.

To be fair, education was not alone here. Gove's seven early meetings with Murdoch almost pale into insignificance against the nearly one hundred meetings that took place between new cabinet ministers and senior News International officials in the first fourteen months of the new Tory administration – a number enviously reported by the Daily Mail.

Murdoch never did set that academy up. Ironically, the reckless hacking by his News of the World newspaper of the phone of a murdered schoolgirl, and his own subsequent 'humble' appearance in person at the public inquiry of the parliamentary select committee, must have proved a bridge too far for Gove's ability to present his boss as the saviour of English secondary education. It did not, however, stand in the way of the secretary of state for education attacking the subsequent Leveson inquiry into the horrific behaviour endemic in Murdoch's business, for none of which the great mogul took responsibility. Rather, Gove "told the Commons press gallery that it was the inquiry that was having a 'chilling effect' on press freedom"[12].

Gove seems always to have been subject to peculiar personal enthusiasms. The demise of the News of the World led to a gap in the Sunday newspaper market quickly filled by News International's Sun on Sunday. A columnist shifting from the Daily Telegraph was equally quickly defending the new cabinet minister against attacks from other journalists, while putting Gove forward as his own personal choice as the next prime minister – a rather gauche thing to do as Cameron had been in post for less than two years himself. Soon Toby Young, for it was he, was opening one of the first new Free Schools in West London. It seems that this particular brand of lazy comment journalism spawns a rapacious appetite for escapades in education. Young's interest in old-fashioned Galtonian eugenics, alongside a historical habit of lascivious tweeting, soon did for his own adventures. Appointed by Jo Johnson, the PM's brother and then minister for higher education, to be a non-executive director on the board of the Office for

[12] Davies, Nick. 2014 *Hack Attack: How the Truth Caught Up with Rupert Murdoch*, London: Chatto & Windus, p.362

Students, Young resigned after just a week of public pressure. Young had been sacked from a News International post earlier in his career for hacking into the computer system; so sacked journalists had become something of a theme in the modern-day Tory party.

Praise the lords And Follow The Money

More useful to Gove than his journalist background has been his fascination with 'business' – although the businessmen he chose were not always productive, but more likely to be people who played with moving money around to their own considerable profit. Like many people who haven't really managed or made anything, Gove appears enthralled by those who can, as well as by those who are able to, make very serious money indeed at the drop of an apparent hat. Theodore Agnew is a great buyer and seller. Now Baron Agnew of Oulton, he was appointed in February 2020 as a Minister of State at the Cabinet Office, serving under Gove as the new Chancellor of the Duchy of Lancaster. In earlier times, he has been a generous donor to the Conservative Party, and then experienced a range of jobs, his qualifications for which are not entirely clear. Agnew was a non-executive board member of the DfE and chair of its Academies Board from 2013 to 2015. He had a brief spell at the Ministry of Justice under Gove again from July 2015. He is also a great trust founder. He founded, and was chair of, the Inspiration Trust which, coincidentally, was Gove's favourite trust (Gove was keen to clone their head for every other school in England) and the home of very traditional, knowledge-based teaching. Agnew's multi-faceted career raised concerns in 2018 when the DfE refused to release documents which cleared him of any conflict of interest between his ministerial role in charge of academies, multi-academy trusts and free schools, and his membership and trusteeship of the Trust[13]. Just a few months later, it was revealed that Agnew had shares in a firm that had recently been added to the DfE's list of suppliers. Again, he was cleared, this time because his shares were in a blind trust[14].

When the pandemic arrived, Lord Agnew "assumed ministerial responsibility for the Government Digital Service, PublicTechnology has learned. In addition to overseeing the work of the digital agency, it is understood that Agnew will also take on responsibility for efficiency, reform and the eight

---

[13] George, Martin. 2018. *Secrecy over Agnew conflicts of interest*, Times Educational Supplement (TES), 30 May 2018

[14] Dorrell, Ed. TES & @Ed_Dorrell, 6 December 2018

cross-government functions that are led from the Cabinet Office, or one of its specialist agencies, such as the Crown Commercial Service, the Infrastructure and Projects Authority, and the Government Property Agency. But, unlike those who have held equivalent posts before him, he will serve as a minister of state for both the Cabinet Office and HM Treasury."[15]

This was very serendipitous for the newly-ermined minister. He had a £90,000 stake in Faculty, a company that was fortunate to have been awarded seven government contracts in the space of 18 months[16]. A star had certainly risen here.

Another mate of Gove's was John Nash. Nash was another businessman who moved money around in a private equity firm, although he had set up and run one of the NHS' biggest contractors. This qualified him to be invited to serve on Chancellor George Osborne's Independent (sic) Challenge Group, advising the government on their spending review and recommending that the NHS find further efficiency savings of £10bn – a policy now looking rather short-sighted. Nash also sat on the board of the Centre for Policy Studies (see above, p.46). Having, with his wife, donated almost £300,000 to the Conservative party, the happy couple must have been surprised and delighted when Gove offered him an important post as schools minister in the DfE and a baronetcy to go with it. This was around the time that Nash's Care UK was awarded a £53m contract to provide health care services to prisons in the north-east. Never knowingly having encountered a state school in his early life, his post in the education department seems to have qualified Nash to set up his own academy trust, where he employed unqualified teachers, and had his own daughter re-writing the history curriculum. The resulting Future Trust (motto: Libertas per cultum – Freedom through education) raises the question as to whose future would benefit most from the work of the Trust. Its (and presumably the Nash's) belief is that the private education provided to the most comfortable seven per cent of children is an appropriate model for 23,000 state schools. In 2020, Future took over a school in Hertfordshire with a chequered history. Its plan for recovery was to appoint a former teacher of classics at Eton and then Cambridge University, and later still,

[15] Trendall, Sam. 2020 *Lord Agnew to take on ministerial responsibility* PublicTechnology.net, 28 February 2020
[16] See, for example, Evans R and Pegg D, The Guardian, 4 May 2020,

head of a girls' day school in Oxford, as the right man to oversee it. One of the first steps in the strategic plan was to make Latin compulsory[17].

Bankers And Other Heroes

Henry de Zoete is another tech entrepreneur who caught Gove's eye. Henry is a member of the de Zoete banking family, which joined together with Barclays Bank to create 'Barclays de Zoete Wedd', Barclays' first foray into investment banking in 1985. Probably his role as Gove's special adviser at the DfE helped him gain the post of digital director of the anti-EU lobbying organisation Vote Leave. He is currently a non-executive director of the Cabinet Office, where Johnson, Gove and Agnew hung out together during the long but lucrative spring and summer of 2020.

"Pity the country that needs heroes"[18]

Despite claims that the heroic age of leadership is now discredited, the word 'hero' appears alarmingly frequently in the circles we are discussing here. Joel Klein, Murdoch's education adviser, described Gove like this: "This country is so lucky to have a man with Michael's vision and commitment ... In my world that makes you a hero, my friend."[19] Quite what constitutes Gove's 'vision' is unclear. But it too comprises heroes.

One of these is the CEO of Agnew's Inspiration Trust: "When secretary of state Michael Gove met Dame Rachel de Souza, he is reported to have said: If anyone asked me what my ideal education policy would be, it would be to clone Rachel 23,000 times"[20]. However, one might not want to be inducted into Gove's hero club. Liam Nolan was also one of Gove's heroes[21]. Nolan was executive head teacher, CEO and accounting officer at Perry Beeches Academy Trust in Birmingham until he resigned in May 2016[22]. Sadly, he was found guilty of professional misconduct, as he interpreted his collection of job titles as a sound enough reason to pay himself more than one salary. Heroically rewarded indeed, he was barred from teaching. But the man most acclaimed by Gove, after

---

[17] Mansell, Warwick. 2020. *Head arrives at under-pressure secondary academy seemingly without experience of working in state education*, Warwick Mansell, Education Uncovered, 27 July 2020

[18] Brecht, Bertolt. 1947. *The Life of Galileo, Bertolt Brecht*

[19] https://politicalscrapbook.net/2011/07/michael-gove-murdoch-links/

[20] The Observer, 17 August 2014
[21] The Guardian 29 June 2014
[22] BBC News, 18 October 2018

Murdoch, is Lord Harris, the carpet salesman turned educational guru. As we will see elsewhere, Harris' academy trust is a family-owned concern that is to be passed down to his children on his death. Successful as a collection of schools may be, this is an odd feature for an educational trust. Perhaps it is the practical application of a major, and rather disturbing, interest of Gove's circle, the pseudo-science of eugenics.

While Gove's enthusiasms abound, Murdoch remains his true hero and, possibly, boss. In 2010, despite his Times column coming to an end in January, his £60,000+ annual salary kept coming, well into his tenure as cabinet minister[23]. Even the revelations of shady and, indeed, criminal behaviour by Murdoch's business did not eclipse Gove's admiration for him. "I think he is a force of nature and a phenomenon. I think he is a great man", he said in October 2011[24]. What does this say about Gove's management of education between his appointment in 2010 and his sacking in 2014?

Preparing For High Office

As has been suggested[25], can there be a less appropriate, less useful preparation for frontline politics than 'comment journalism'? Professions and trades, including local politics, can usually give young people enormously useful disciplines. These include self-discipline: time-keeping, job completion, accuracy and care for detail, and respect for and readiness to learn from people with more experience. There are also practical skills: accurate budgeting, giving reports truthfully and objectively, knowledge and use of data, research, and follow-up. And personal skills that enable you to do your job more effectively – the ability to interpret and meet the demands of customers and clients, to treat them appropriately, to recognise the key elements of competence, consistency and completion. We expect these skills of people in positions of authority, even when we don't readily observe them.

There are thousands of very competent and conscientious comment journalists. But at its worst, comment journalism, of all the trades in the world, is something that, given a facility with language, a superficial gloss of humour and charm, and a fairly simplistic perspective on what your audience wants to

---

[23] https://politicalscrapbook.net/2011/07/michael-gove-murdoch-links/

[24] Watson Tom and Hickman, Martin. 2012 *Dial M for Murdoch: News Corporation and the Corruption of Britain*, London: Allen Lane p277

[25] Wood, Catherine. 2020 in conversation

read, can be hacked for years without displaying any of those characteristics learnt by most people in the later years of their education and their first years of employment. A particular feature of the worst sort of comment journalism is that it provides a platform for the knee-jerk expression of opinions that will make you 'talked about'. And as Boris Johnson notoriously did, it doesn't matter if you propound one point of view one day and the opposite position the next. No one will remember, as yesterday's edition is already in the recycling bin or the cat litter tray. It is as if that old debating exercise where you have to adopt one position and then argue against it has been turned into a life style: It doesn't matter what you say, as long as you can entertain people while you're saying it. Two of the most senior and influential politicians in Johnson's 2019 government have a background in this work. And it shows.

Dealing With People Who Know More Than You

The first major characteristic of Gove's leadership is the dismissal of, and indeed apparent contempt for, experts. Experts, after all, and all people trained for and performing a proper job, are easy meat for a carping onlooker such as an unscrupulous comment journalist. Both Gove and Johnson in their time have behaved like football spectators who hurl mindless abuse at players and referees, without a constructive thought in their heads. This is something that, in the days of Covid-19, infected the entire government. Sometimes this manifests itself in politicians ignoring expert 'scientific' views, opinions, advice. At other times, it is an expectation that advisers go beyond their own professional brief. For example, "Documents published by the UK Government's Scientific Advisory Group for Emergencies (SAGE) throw light on how overarching concerns about the economy derailed efforts to suppress the Coronavirus, resulting in a worst-of-all-worlds scenario: maximum fatality rates combined with the worst economic performance. One of the most consistent themes in the minutes of SAGE meetings is how the Government repeatedly expected its scientists to account for the economic impact of lockdown – even though SAGE was not doing any economic modelling."[26]

By 2020, this appeared to be a government that had no understanding of how to use professional experience and knowledge. It is all very well for politicians to make well-informed choices from a range of advice. But a dangerous point is

---

[26] Ahmed, Nafeez. 2020 *Sagegate: Vote Leave Ideology Trumped Science and Safety*, Byline Times, July 2020

reached when they believe that they don't need any advice, then show little understanding of assessing the varying risks of different choices; and less comprehension of how to put the chosen policy into action, let alone how to measure its outcomes.

The Johnson government, articulating the Govian and Cummings philosophy of 2010-14, embraced 'weirdness': "In a speech, the Cabinet Office Minister Michael Gove backed the chief advisor's agenda ... which will allow scientists unlimited cash to follow their 'crazy' ideas. ... He also attacked the establishment and said that 'the whole culture of Government, and the wider world of political commentary, is hostile to risk, adventure, experimentation and novelty.' "[27] If the very first duty of any government department of education is to protect its children, the first duty of government is to protect its people. To deliberately set out to put that security at risk is a remarkable dereliction.

Re-Enter Rupert

By this time, Murdoch's toxicity had, predictably, faded as far as the Johnson government was concerned. Murdoch was meeting with Boris Johnson within 72 hours of the 2019 general election and met with him twice more in the following six months. There were a further 41 meetings between Murdoch employees and government representatives in that time frame. Meanwhile, editors and executives of Murdoch's UK newspapers met with government ministers or advisers 206 times during 2018 and 2019[28].

The Art Of Managing People

As might perhaps be expected of someone who had never managed people, Gove's handling of his associates and staff was anything but smooth. Early on, he upset his schools minister David Laws, himself only recently returned to grace after his costly brush with the MPs' expenses overseers. Gove's peremptory and probably improper dismissal of the eminently well-qualified Baroness Sally Morgan as chair of Ofsted seems to have been engineered in order to find a spot for the entirely unqualified Theodore Agnew. The brazenness of this attempt seems to have rebounded on Gove, but he was, as we have seen, able to find

---

[27] Hencke, David 2020. *Britain Heads to Elective Dictatorship*, Byline Times, July 2020

[28] Hacked Off 2020. Unelected: The insidious influence of Rupert Murdoch at the heart of the government, July 2020

other equally inappropriate berths for Agnew throughout the 2010s, while Agnew found the time to put together his own academy trust, a train-set that every right-minded plutocrat should own.

Deputy Prime Minister and Liberal Democrat leader in the coalition, Nick Clegg, quickly formed a negative view of Gove's leadership in education, which reminded him of the political TV satire 'The Thick of It'. He thought that Gove "had come to regard the department as his personal fiefdom"[29]. In particular, Gove – whose secondary education was at an independent school – and like so many non-teachers – thought he knew all he needed to know about state education. Margaret Thatcher's consultation papers, apocryphally, were returned to the Department of Education with remnants of her breakfast toast and marmalade on them. Gove was similarly confident about what should be taught – especially in history. Lists of medieval monarchs, and perspectives of the First World War and the glories of the British Empire would imbue young people with the proper "British values". But it would be another seven years before it emerged that his 2013 dismissal of a recommendation to include references to post-Second World War commonwealth immigration in the history curriculum would make the education department's own contribution to the hostile environment and Windrush scandal[30].

At the same time, Gove knew best about testing. He instructed the department to eradicate any trace of continuous assessment from the qualifications regime, and the one-off examination became the preferred method of assessment. This favours the student capable of quick rote-learning rather than considered evaluation, the one with a fast sprint at the end of the race. At the time, this seemed a blow to those who toil hard throughout the length of a course, as well as to those who think carefully and like to produce their best possible work. Who could have foreseen that in 2020 this total reliance on examination outcomes would lead to yet another government-sponsored fiasco, the algorithm dependent on exam performance that favoured students in private schools and small sixth forms, against those in schools serving less advantaged areas?

Tim Loughton, a Tory children's minister, did not think of 'The Thick of It' when he reflected on his own experience at the department (2010-2012), but of

---

[29] Perraudin, Frances. 2015. *Michael Gove ran office 'like something out of The Thick of It'* The Guardian, 7th April 2015

[30] Hazell, Will. 2020. *Michael Gove criticised for dropping the Windrush generation from curriculum*, The i Newsletter, 30th June 2020

'Upstairs Downstairs' in its 'insiders and outsiders' divisiveness. He also compared Gove to the young Mr Grace in the old TV sitcom 'Are You Being Served?' (Not very appropriately as it turned out, as the character's catchphrase was "You're all doing very well" – which certainly was not Gove's opinion of Loughton)[31]. Rather more dramatically, Gove's often-reported superficial charm has been suggested as a cover for an "us-and-them aggressive, intimidating culture" masking "a hard-line ideological revolution."[32] Gove's DfE appears to have accepted bullying as a legitimate practice. Verbal abuse, shouting, demoralisation and fear seem to have been part of the daily routine.

Bullying seemed to have become institutionalised, though Gove characteristically left it to his advisers. Dominic Cummings and James Frayne came into the frame when it was reported that "it took a private settlement of £25,000 ... to stop details of allegations of bullying and intimidation being heard in the London Central Employment Tribunal"[33]. Fortunately, as "a source close to Michael Gove" reported: "No departmental inquiry has found that special advisers did anything wrong". Meanwhile, Cummings and Henry de Zoete were named by The Observer[34] as contributors to an anonymous account, '@toryeducation', listed as an official Conservative account. Tweets were "downright abusive and childish in tone, and often challenged critics of Gove to 'get a real/proper job rather than waste any time subjecting his department to scrutiny ...' The authors were known for cringe-worthy use of a #winning hashtag, repeated characterisation of opponents as 'lefties' and 'comrades', even a comparison of some critics/opponents to Hitler and/or Stalin ... and throughout, nauseatingly effusive praise of Michael Gove."[35]. Even the much-loved author and Children's Laureate Michael Rosen was accused of being a member of the Socialist Workers Party, a claim he furiously dismissed. One of the last messages posted, after Gove had become so toxic in the world of education that Cameron had to move him to the Whips' Office, suggested that

---

[31] Paton, Graeme. 2013. *Gove's department 'run like episode of Upstairs Downstairs'*, Daily Telegraph, 16 January 2013

[32] Cusick, James 2013. *'Dump f***ing everyone': the inside story of how Michael Gove's vicious attack dogs are terrorising the DfE*, The Independent, 15 February 2013

[33] Cusick (ibid)

[34] Helm, Toby. 2013. *Michael Gove's officials act to clean up abusive Twitter feed*, The Observer 16 February 2013

[35] Ireland, Tim. 2015. *Tweet archive of @toryeducation, the abusive sock-puppet of Michael Gove and/or his SPADs*, Bloggerheads https://twitter.com/bloggerheads, 3 March 2015

"It'll take all you Blobbers a lot more than 4 years to glue pieces together & by then computers will have fired you!"[36].

At the time, this was an extraordinary use of taxpayers' money. By 2020, with memories of Theresa May's anti-immigrant 'Go Home' operation, the blatant lies and criminality of the Vote Leave referendum movement, and daily exposure to President Trump's non-stop government by abusive campaign, it seemed almost commonplace. But it set a tone in this country for a dismissive and offensive style of politicking that is now well embedded in Downing Street.

Gove And The Implementation Of The Corporatisation Of Schooling

Why is Gove's history, both before, during and after his spell at Education so significant, in our understanding of the roots of the academisation process? Because, compared to many, if not most, previous secretaries of state for education, Gove had neither experience, nor expertise in educational matters, nor managerial competence, nor the capacity to formulate and implement policy. He was by no means unique in lacking these qualities, but instead of relying on his civil servants, he showed no respect for those whose job it was to help him out. His chosen advisers had no experience or expertise, or even any superficial understanding of educational issues. They were either 'successful' businessmen (in the sense that they had the ability to enable money to make more money) or apparently failed businessmen and lobbyists.

But it is in the field of policy that we most need to understand what Gove was trying to achieve at education, and how he would use the experience to move on to a bigger stage.

In Cameron's first shadow administration, Gove was appointed as shadow minister for housing. But he was shifted to education in a promotion into the shadow cabinet in 2007 and was able to bring Dominic Cummings into his office. But Cummings did not impress Cameron, who may have had him in mind later when he referred to a 'career psychopath' in a speech to Policy Exchange in 2014. Gove's wish to take Cummings with him into the Department for Education in 2010 was vetoed by Andy Coulson, Cameron's Director of Communications. Coulson had probably been foisted on Cameron – he had been Murdoch's editor of the News of the World until he resigned following the first

---

[36] @toryeducation 14 August 2014

criminal conviction of one of his reporters for phone hacking in 2007. Cameron had been warned by the then editor of the Guardian not to take Coulson into Downing Street with him, as he was known to be seriously tainted by the News Corp scandal. He didn't last long. In January 2011 he resigned, and in July he was arrested for involvement in a conspiracy to intercept voice mails. He eventually got a sentence of eighteen months in prison for that. So, criminality and Murdoch were both significant elements in the twenty-first century Conservative party in government from the beginning. As was the party's willingness to live with them and indeed use them as necessary adjuncts to power. Whether the appointment of Gove to education was also a requirement of support laid down by Murdoch is unclear, but it would not be surprising.

Certainly there did not seem to be a coherent overall plan for education in the new administration. What little was said in their manifesto was radical in the field of school structures, and extremely conservative in their approach to the curriculum, both overt and hidden. They claimed to want small autonomous schools along the lines of US charter schools and Swedish 'Free Schools'. But they wanted primary schools to focus on traditional subjects, with tougher SATs tests, and would support uniforms, strict discipline and streaming in secondaries. They seemed paradoxically to favour the forced academisation of 'failing' schools to academy providers, while cutting bureaucracy and inspections. There is no mention of huge multi academy trusts:

"Perhaps the most radical Academy proposals, however, come from the Conservative manifesto. Taken at face value, the Conservative proposals suggest that Academy status is their preferred model for virtually all schools in the English system. Their manifesto states (p53) that 'all existing schools will have the chance to achieve academy status, with "outstanding" schools pre-approved'. Moreover, the manifesto promises to 'extend the Academy programme to primary schools', an area which has hitherto not seen Academy schools set up. In addition, the Conservatives propose (p53) to 'break down barriers to entry so that any good education provider can set up a new Academy school', emulating the Swedish 'Free Schools' system (which allows charities, businesses and parent co-operatives to open new schools). Unlike the Swedish system, however, new Academies will not be permitted to make a profit"[37].

---

[37] Institute for Fiscal Studies, 2010. Education Policy: 2010 Election Briefing

For a party that has been thirteen years in the waiting for power, this is a very thin vision for a reorganisation of education. All three major parties were pledging to extend academies, though the Liberal Democrats wanted to maintain them within local authorities. One strong indicator of Conservative priorities, much reported by individual visitors to Gove's office, was that the most visible item there, was a map of England with the presence of academies marked by coloured pins[38].

---

[38] "Visitors to the Secretary of State's office in the spring of 2011 reported seeing three maps on his wall: one showed the applications for opening free schools, the second showed existing academies, and the third applications for academy status. 'Freeing' schools from their local authorities clearly had a high priority. Immediately after Michael Gove took office in 2010, the legislation enabling every school to convert to academy status was driven through parliament using procedures normally reserved for anti-terrorism laws, receiving royal assent in July." Gann, N (2011): *Academy Conversion: a view from the governing body,* in Forum Vol 53 No 3, Didcot: Symposium Books Ltd p381

Chapter 4
The Coming Of Corporatisation

Which explores how the gang taking over education policy got control and then spread their wings

Who Is Michael Gove?

It is difficult to discern any clear thread to Michael Gove's political career or his thinking. What did he actually believe in when he became the single most powerful figure in English education, other than small states and big business? To which colleagues was he committed? What did he think about the key social issues of the day – of poverty, inequality, of race and of social justice? Even now, after ten years of his high and rising political profile, it is difficult to tell. He is, as we have seen, often described as personally 'charming' (though charm can be something of a backhanded compliment). And since his failed leadership bids, he has more commonly been called 'treacherous'.

Cracked (1)?

Boris Johnson once asked David Cameron if Mr Gove "was 'a bit cracked', after his fellow Leave supporter withdrew his support for Mr Johnson [in 2016] and announced his own leadership bid."[1] Ambitious? In the spring of 2011, certainly: "H [Hugo Swire] stands in for Owen [Patterson, Northern Ireland Secretary] at the National Security Council. Afterwards, he tells me Gove went off on one again, about Libya. I said what the hell was he doing there, he's Education. 'No idea!' replies H. 'And I'm actually starting to think he is ever so slightly bonkers' … I speak to someone who is in the know about MG; he says there is a feeling inside No. 10 that he is exhausted, that he cannot continue at

---

[1] Kentish, Benjamin. 2019. *David Cameron says Boris Johnson asked him if Michael Gove was 'a bit cracked'*, The Independent, 16 September 2019

this pitch. He is also surrounded by young yes-people who are encouraging him to become the voice of neo-conservatism. Later, I talk to H about it … 'he desperately wants one of the top jobs, Chancellor, Foreign or PM.' But there is a view he might well blow himself out before then."[2]

David Cameron's view of Gove reflects this. When it came to the succession after Cameron's resignation in 2016, "he would go for Boris over Michael any day. Michael, he says, is a radical, an iconoclast, that all his ideas are subversive, that he would make a terrible leader, he is too extreme; that Michael, as he once said, 'believes the world makes progress through a process of creative destruction'"[3]

Cracked (2)?

In 2019, a rumour that had been going the rounds for years in political circles was confirmed by Gove himself: "Gove goes on Marr [the BBC Sunday morning news programme] and it's a disaster. He has been all over the papers for admitting taking cocaine. Trouble is, when he was Education Secretary he published a set of regulations on the prohibition of teachers for misconduct. Included in his list of offences that would lead to a lifetime ban from teaching was possession of Class A drugs. An offence which he confesses to have committed several times."[4] So it may be difficult to sort out whether or not the actions he has taken and the words he has spoken are what he genuinely believes when he is sober.

Radicals, Renegades … Or Robbers?

But one constant feature in Gove's life has been the presence, since their first meeting at an anti-Euro breakfast around the turn of the twenty-first century, of Dominic Cummings. Gove was then a leader writer for Murdoch's Times, and Cummings was campaign director for Business for Sterling. Murdoch, of course, had always been anti-Europe. He saw himself as a man of great influence with prime ministers and presidents but knew that he counted for little among the Eurocrats.

Cummings is from the north-east, a scion of an affluent and respected family. From the age of fourteen he was privately educated and studied history at Oxford

---

[2] Swire, S 2020 *Diary of an MP's wife,* London: Little Brown p58

[3] Ibid, p242

[4] Ibid, p450

University under the right-wing Norman Stone. Stone was noted for his role in advising Margaret Thatcher, and his abrasive – not to say, abusive – personality. His mixture of charm and acerbity seem very similar to Gove's. And one would add Cummings, too, were anyone to accuse him of being charming. There is no record I can find of anyone having done so. It is reported that Ted Heath "said of Stone during his time in Oxford: 'Many parents of Oxford students must be both horrified and disgusted that the higher education of our children should rest in the hands of such a man.'"[5]

Cummings' Wikipedia entry records that "One of his professors has described him as 'fizzing with ideas, unconvinced by any received set of views about anything'. He was 'something of a Robespierre – someone determined to bring down things that don't work'"[6]. This suggests a mindset not dissimilar to Gove's – a desire to break the existing order, but with little clear vision as to what might replace it.

After university, Cummings spent a rather mysterious three years in Russia "working on various projects."[7] One of these was an attempt to set up an airline with one plane and, rather crucially, no passengers. His first job back in the UK was at 'Business for Sterling', an anti-Euro pressure group. It was enough to get him noticed by Iain Duncan Smith, the then leader of the Conservative party in opposition, who appointed him as a Director of Strategy for the party. Following that, he joined James Frayne at the New Frontiers Foundation think tank. Once again, the focus was on destruction, this time mainly of the BBC. During this period, he is credited with a key role in the successful campaign against Deputy PM John Prescott's vision of devolution to a north-east England regional assembly. Cummings joined Gove in his shadow education post in 2007 as chief of staff. And so began a long and continuing relationship, through the shadow, then substantive, Department for Education, Vote Leave during the EU referendum, and into PM Johnson's cabinet office after the 2019 general election and the management of the 2020 pandemic. Ironically, Cummings in his post as the PM's chief adviser reached No.10 before his mentor.

In the course of this journey, Cummings was the beneficiary of the absolute loyalty of Gove and Johnson, and the opprobrium of John Major, David Cameron, a significant number of Tory MPs, and journalists of all shades. His

---

[5] Evans, Richard. 2019. *Norman Stone obituary* The Guardian, 25 June 2019
[6] Wikipedia, *Dominic Cummings*, July 2020
[7] Ibid

particular bêtes noires appeared to be members of the education profession, partly because of their perceived 'incompetence', and partly their rejection of his views on the importance of genetics in performance at school. But the science he invoked to support this view is marginal, to say the least. The other thing he seems to hate is the civil service, the current state of which became his target at Number Ten. Again, there is little hard evidence for his claims about civil servants. He is considerably more voluble about what is wrong with the status quo than he is about what should replace it, other than the "weirdos and misfits with odd skills", policy experts and "unusual" mathematicians and computer scientists and "true wild cards" being sought to work in Number.Ten in a recruitment drive in early 2020[8].

Indeed, Cummings' reliance on 'weird and unusual" experts seems odd given his career-long resistance to more mainstream experts, who are generally inclined to back their views up with hard evidence. This was perhaps encapsulated in the Barnard Castle episode, at the height of the Covid-19 lockdown. Bowing at last to the pressure to justify his return to work while carrying Coronavirus symptoms, his journey north with his comment journalist wife, Mary Wakefield of the Spectator, and their child, and their day trip to Barnard Castle "to test his eyesight", he took to the Downing Street gardens to explain himself. In the course of this, he claimed that he had warned on his personal blog in March 2019 "about the possible threat of coronaviruses and the urgent need for planning". This truly breath-taking piece of prophecy suggested that Cummings, as he no doubt would like to be thought, was way ahead of all other scientists and medics throughout the entire world. Although it did rather beg the question as to why this urgent planning hadn't actually happened. Verily, it appeared, Cummings was the Cassandra of British politics.

But it was a lie. It very soon, very quickly and very simply was exposed as an amendment to his original blog, made on the day after he had returned from his Durham trip, on the 14th April 2020, at 8.55 pm. Cummings' accusations that the media ran false stories about him was itself a false story, deliberately fabricated at the moment of his peak vulnerability, to fool people into thinking he had hitherto unsuspected powers of prescience. And, to boot, great worshipper of high tech himself, he didn't know one of the simplest things about online

---

[8] Smith, Beckie. 2020. *Cummings seeks "weirdos and misfits" to work in No.10*, Civil Service World, 3 January 2020

blogging – that any amendments are automatically recorded and publicly accessible.

Even more interest arose in Cummings when it emerged that, just two days after the sighting of him in Barnard Castle, a woman called Alice Cummings became a director of IDOX plc and IDOX Trustees Ltd., which was the company founded by old Thatcher supporter, Peter Lilley. IDOX managed postal votes in the 2019 election and was then awarded a contract by Gove's Cabinet Office, without competitive tender, to manage the electoral register. Despite a burgeoning conspiracy theory, IDOX has assured Reuters that this Alice Cummings is not, however, Cummings' sister[9].

Few people in positions of authority in their profession would survive such exposure. Unaccountably, Cummings did, until November 2020. Perhaps in the offices of Downing Street and amongst members of parliament and the political media, he had become less a figure of fear and more one of ridicule and contempt. At least, behind his back. It has even been suggested in some parts of the media that his survival demonstrated that he must have some sort of hold over Johnson and Gove, in the form of knowledge about their personal lives. But that would be pure speculation. Now at the time of writing, this rather callow middle-aged man is trying to destroy the establishment of Number 10 that he was instrumental in creating. But some of the damage he has done, and continues to do, to the body politic seems irreparable. Abuse, deceit, contempt for learning and experience, are the weapons of ignorance and bad manners. But the evils they can portend are far worse.

Mary Wakefield, Cummings' wife, does have a brother, Jack. He is the former director of the Firtash Foundation. Firtash is a pro-Brexit Ukrainian oligarch who is alleged to have close links with the eastern European mafia. "Firtash is a living example of the kind of wild capitalism favoured by Vote Leave. Britain increasingly resembles the kind of Russian oligarchy he sprouted from, where Bentleys cruise past rough sleepers and politicians prostitute themselves to shady billionaires"[10]. Firtash is currently in Austria fighting extradition to the United States on charges of bribery and racketeering. The pro-Ukrainian mix includes, if it isn't led in Britain, by Pro-Brexit Tory MP John Whittingdale, another member of Gove's gang. He became a junior minister at

---

[9] https://mobile.reuters.com/article/amp/idUSKBN2322VB?__twitter_impression+true
[10] Komarnyckyj, Steve. 2019. *Firtash: How the Trump Impeachment Scandal Leads back to British Brexiters*, Byline Times, 23 October 2019

the Department of Culture, Media and Sport and has long been a leading light of the British Ukrainian Society. Whittingdale is closely linked to Michael Gove and has worked with him on issues concerning the media, as well as at Vote Leave.

The Gove/Cummings Partnership In 2016-2020

After Gove and Cummings' stint at the DfE, they were recruited to head up Vote Leave, the key organisation for delivering Brexit. Vote Leave was powered by the finances provided by a number of hugely wealthy hedge fund managers, some of whom made enormous amounts of money betting against the UK economy. Sir Paul Marshall, the hedge fund financier we shall hear more of later, convinced Gove to head up the campaign and personally donated £100,000. He made £50m from his bets against the UK. Another multimillionaire hedge fund manager, Crispin Odey, a former husband of Rupert Murdoch's daughter, Prudence, made £220m in similar ventures and donated another £100,000. Odey also provided a great deal of support to MP Jacob Rees-Mogg's hedge fund, enabling him to move his operation to Dublin to avoid the impact of Brexit[11]. No wonder these two men, Gove and Cummings, one the adopted child of a Scottish fish merchant, the other from a well-to-do but hardly wealthy north-east England family, were bedazzled by the money, where a few billion quid must have seemed like loose change.

Their usefulness became apparent with the victory of the Leave campaign. The peccadilloes of breaches of the law in overspending money with AggregateIQ, the online comms firm which ran much of the Brexit campaign, could be safely ignored. The problem was that they had passed this money through a patsy who would then forward it to the hi-tech firm. When PM Johnson placed Gove in charge of the Cabinet Office and took Cummings on as his chief adviser, the huge amounts of money and the wizardry of hi-tech must have seduced them, and have dictated the behaviour of the Cabinet Office in the unchecked distribution of contracts during the pandemic. In doing so, they used the emergency powers of the pandemic to bypass proper press and parliamentary

---

[11] PA Media 2020. *Hedge fund boss Crispin Odey in court on indecent assault charge,* The Guardian, 28th September 2020

scrutiny, just as Gove had done in 2010 when he pushed through the Academies' Act using laws introduced to tackle terrorism[12].

It was at this point in the spring of 2020 that, quite transparently, the interests of government and those of big business became indistinguishable.

What Does Michael Gove Believe In?

By this time, we had some indication of Gove's political beliefs. He was not happy with the Northern Ireland Good Friday agreement. He is a dedicated Brexiteer. He would have liked the Queen to have a new royal yacht. He is open-minded about schools being run for profit. And he wants immigration to be confined to those with 'relevant' jobs and the ability to speak good English. But then he also claimed that Brexit would bring "no change to the border between Northern Ireland and the Republic"; and that EU citizens "will automatically be granted indefinite leave to remain in the UK". And he believes in the Single Market[13], but these latter promises look unlikely to be fulfilled.

In a speech on the 27 June 2020, Gove declared that it was part of his job "to help drive change. To help demonstrate the good that Government can do, to reaffirm the nobility of service to the public, and to strive every day to use the money, and the powers, that people have vested in us to improve their lives."[14]

Even so, from his tenure at the Cabinet Office, with responsibility for government contracts, Gove has demonstrated that he is happy to use the opportunities provided by the pandemic to bypass the usual precautionary measures that ensure that the people benefit from the money they contribute. Big Business, embraced by the 2019 government, bears a strong resemblance to the contacts list of Gove and Cummings. As this book goes to print, a complex network of contracts awarded to firms linked to Conservative supporters and donors, and particularly connected to Gove and Cummings, is coming to light.

The awarding of government contracts is overseen by the Cabinet Office, which is headed up by the Minister for the Cabinet Office, the Right Honourable Michael Gove. It is a process normally bound by strict regulations on competitive

[12] Hardy, Lloyd 2020. *Why is Dominic Cummings So Important?*, Open Source Intelligence, lloydhardy.com/news, 31 May 2020

[13] Gove, Michael et al. 2016. *Restoring public trust in immigration policy – a points-based non-discriminatory immigration system*, Statement by Michael Gove, Boris Johnson, Priti Patel, and Gisela Stuart, Vote Leave, 1 June 2016

[14] Gove, Michael 2020 https://www.gov.uk/government/speeches/the-privilege-of-public-service-given-as-the-ditchley-annual-lecture 1 July 2020

tendering and open to public scrutiny. But in March 2020, ministers told Whitehall departments, the NHS, local councils and other agencies that they could award contracts to private firms without competition or tendering if they needed to, in order to deal with the emergency[15]. During the pandemic, the Cabinet Office itself has been awarding contracts for medical supplies, including personal protective equipment (PPE), for the collection of data, and for specialist communications projects. In early March 2020, the Cabinet Office agreed a contract with a firm to test the effectiveness of the government's 'messaging' about coronavirus. "There was no advertisement for the work, and no competition. No official notice of the award has yet been published"[16]. Indeed, there was no written record of the agreement until a letter dated 5th June appeared in the public domain. The contract was with Public First, owned by James Frayne and Rachel Wolf – names that may ring a bell. Actually, although this deal was ostensibly offered under the coronavirus emergency procedures, whereby no competitive tendering was necessary, two of the services being provided by Frayne and Wolf were for EU exit communications. So, emergency procedures were being applied to activities connected, not with the pandemic, but with arrangements for Brexit that the government had been working on since 2016. A sleight of hand here, at best. The 'emergency' coronavirus work didn't appear to start until late in May. In July, this award became the subject of judicial review proceedings against Gove by the Good Law Project[17]. Another partner at Public First is Gabriel Milland, who helpfully wrote an encomium for Rupert Murdoch's Times' newspaper on Simon Case, Johnson's appointment as new Cabinet Secretary in September 2020.[18]

An Artificial Intelligence (AI) firm called Faculty, which had been recruited for the Vote Leave campaign, was awarded seven contracts worth almost £1m over eighteen months up to May 2020 to work on digital technology. The Cabinet Office minister responsible for the use of digital technology in public services was Baron Theodore Agnew. Agnew had at that time a £90,000 shareholding in Faculty, which in May he was still refusing to sell (see Ch3). He was reported to

[15] Evans R, Garside J, Smith J, Duncan P. 2020. *Firms given £1bn of state contracts without tender in Covid-19 crisis* The Guardian, 15 May 2020

[16] Monbiot, George. 2020. *Awarding PPE contracts in secret: that's deadly serious*, The Guardian, 15 July 2020

[17] Good Law Project 2020 *Update: Money for his mates*, https://goodlawproject.org/news/update-money-for-his-mates/, 4 August 2020

[18] Private Eye. 2020. *Best Case Scenario*, Private Eye, 11 September 2020 p7

have 'relinquished' the holding in early September[19]. Faculty's owner is Marc Warner, a data scientist recruited by Dominic Cummings. His brother Ben had also worked for Faculty before he was recruited to Downing Street by Cummings. Both the Warners, with Dominic Cummings, had been attending meetings of SAGE, the scientific advisory group for emergencies providing scientific and technical advice to the government. In July, it was revealed that "a private company owned and controlled by Dominic Cummings paid more than a quarter of a million pounds" to Faculty over two years.[20] In all, Faculty appears to have received government contracts worth about £3m.

Into the autumn of 2020 the awarding of contracts without competition or tendering to members of a small cadre of mates and cronies went wearisomely on. "A lobbying and PR firm co-founded by an ally of Dominic Cummings has been given two government contracts without competitive tenders during the pandemic. The Cabinet Office and Treasury contracts were awarded to Hanbury Strategy, co-founded by Paul Stephenson, who worked alongside Cummings as the director of communications for the Vote Leave campaign. The other Hanbury founder, Ameet Gill, was David Cameron's director of strategy in Downing Street. Hanbury is the fourth Tory-linked firm to have been awarded work since the start of the pandemic ..."[21]

These people who acclaim earned merit and disdain the Establishment's ways of doing things, seem very wedded to their small circle of the deserving rich.

A Nation For Sale

"I sell anything that commands a price. How do your lawyers live, your politicians, your intriguers, your men of the Exchange? How do you live? How do you come here? Have you sold no friend?" (Little Dorrit: Charles Dickens)

Political writers, journalists, educational researchers and academics have spent years analysing the speeches, decisions and actions of the Conservative

[19] Evans, Rob, Shahid, Nimra, Conn, David. 2020. Minister relinquishes control of shares in firm given UK government contract, The Guardian, 3 September 2020

[20] Pegg D, Evans R, Lewis P. 2020. Revealed: Dominic Cummings firm paid Vote Leave's AI firm £260,000, The Guardian, 12 July 2020

[21] Evans R and Pegg D. 2020. Fourth firm with Tory links awarded government work without tendering, The Guardian 5 September 2020

party in government since 2010. 'Neoliberalism' is perhaps the term most frequently applied to its overall direction.

This assumes that the key players, the politicians closest to setting the direction of the party – David Cameron, Teresa May, Boris Johnson, Michael Gove – each have had their own clear philosophy. Perhaps this gives them too much credit. Standing back from the immediate day-to-day mayhem of the Exchequer, the Home Office, the Transport Department, Health and Social Care, Trade and Industry, is it possible to discern any ordered direction of travel other than day-to-day survival?

Those of us who work in education have probably all seen a disordered school. It is rarely led by people with a clear but misguided sense of direction; rather it is run by staff who have lost any sense of purpose they ever had, and who just concentrate on getting through the day. In understanding such disasters, analysing declarations of intent is unlikely to be helpful. It is more useful to look at the characteristics of the organisation's collective behaviours, planned, intentional or not.

What has Michael Gove sought in his fifteen years as a member of parliament, much of it in government? He seeks change, and disruptive change. He is unable to articulate a vision of order and a workable system of schooling. He is unable to say what education is for. He has set about taking apart a coherent pattern of provision and sought to make schools accountable directly to central government, while presenting this as offering schools the opposite, more autonomy. He and Boris Johnson together use and discard 'expert' advice according to whim and are unpredictable in their behaviour. They will say whatever comes into their heads, with little respect or regard for their audience – they will claim, ludicrously and without shame, that they have a hobby of making cardboard models of buses and painting people riding in them (Johnson), or that they too have a habit of going out for a drive with the sole purpose of testing their eyesight (Gove). Through their superficial 'charm', they show their contempt for people who do not serve their purposes.

These are their evident qualities. The political outcome – not a philosophy, by any standards – is that they seek to align government ever closer to business. The effect of their behaviour is to lead us into something resembling a fascist state.

"Mussolini's definition of fascism was that when you can't distinguish corporate power from governmental power, you are on the way to a fascist state", said author John le Carré (David Cornwell) in interview in 2005.[22]

Michael Gove has demonstrated a personal life of variable morality and cupidity, of cronyism, of an interest in profit-making and grasping freebies. He disdains people with expertise and toadies to people in power and with money. He is unable to manage people or to inspire them, while anxious to appear in control. He admires people like Donald Trump, Rupert Murdoch and Dominic Cummings, whose leadership is founded on bullying and abuse. He supports Cummings with his ludicrous eye-testing story, even when evidence shows that the Barnard Castle incident damaged national unity and public trust in politicians.

The 'policies' emerging from this mess can be summarised as the engagement of business in the delivery of a public good, a reduction in direct government involvement in management and delivery and the undermining of politics, the building of the role of the market in all aspects of daily life, the disruption of local government, the civil service, the professions, and any other potential obstacle to government by a small clique focused on the transfer of public assets into private hands.

These are not the characteristics of traditional, paternalistic Conservative governments. The outcome has much more in common with radical neoliberalism and totalitarianism. It includes some of the 'peripheral' behaviours associated with totalitarianism – the cavalier use of language; the disregard of, almost amounting to contempt for, the truth; the inability to work with people who are off-message, leading to small cliques of acceptable people; the odd mixture of superficial charm and abusive bullying; the apparent worship of money, possessions and 'gracious living'; and the need for heroes.

Above all, maybe, there are the absences of qualities one might usually look for in politicians – of empathy, of rationality, of creativity – in particular, the inability to express a clear philosophy about their political beliefs, about the objectives they want to meet – at least, aims beyond the purely utilitarian, such as exam results. Instead, everything is about competition – beating other countries up the PISA tables, comparing unlike schools and universities, being 'world-beating', not 'world-co-operating'. What then has been the purpose of

---

[22] Cornwell, David. 2005. "I do give a damn", Interview with Stuart Jeffries, The Guardian, 6 October 2005

these ten years of government? To protect the people from want, disease, ignorance, squalor and idleness? To benefit the whole people? Like the regime at the education department between 2010 and 2014, and despite what is said in public, the government displays little interest in people.

The day after I had written this passage, I was given a book in which I read: "Symptoms of sociopathy include a lack of empathy, a facility for lying, an indifference to right and wrong, abusive behaviour, and a lack of interest in the rights of others."[23] I am not medically trained, so I am not qualified to hazard a diagnosis, but the similarities between my observations on Gove, Johnson and Cummings and this description were striking. The sentence was written by a clinical psychologist with unique access to and knowledge of another 'populist' politician. Donald Trump also shares another characteristic with Gove, Johnson and Cummings – "his disdain for the expertise of others."[24]

We will see later how the characteristics explored here are reflected in some of the behaviour recorded in the world of education, and in particular, like looking through the wrong end of a telescope, can be viewed in the story of Castle Primary School.

Sitting astride all the themes touched upon here is the ogre of corruption. In the early 2020s, we began to see the exposure of the manifold ways in which the government's behaviour in and outside the pandemic have benefited both the members of government themselves and their close friends, relatives and business acquaintances. From the awarding of contracts, the favouring of building plans, the creation and feeding of new tech businesses, there is a huge area to be mined.

If this book were more about politics and less about education, we might pursue this theme and explore its pernicious dispersal around the world of government. But we are going to look at the impact of these people on our schooling. While we do that, we could keep in the back of our minds the question we have not been able to answer here.

In 2002, shortly after he first met Dominic Cummings, Michael Gove, together with Wykehamist and future Tory MP Nick Boles, then Tory MP and former ASDA chief Archie Norman, and Tory MP and future Lord Francis Maude, founded Policy Exchange (PE). PE has been one of the most influential

---

[23] Trump, Mary. 2020. Too Much and Never Enough: How my family created the world's most dangerous man, London: Simon & Schuster, 2020, p24
[24] Ibid p194

right-wing think tanks, with particular impact on the government's education policy. It is credited with the idea of free schools and advocating the increased frequency of Ofsted inspections, and is now looking at the current issues of 'academic freedom' and the reframing of the nation's history. Not much can be said about its funding, as it is listed as one of the three least transparent think tanks in the UK[25] – defined as "highly opaque"; and graded E, the lowest rating, in the 'Who Funds You' website, the lowest level for transparency.

Adjacent to it in these ratings, is the Institute of Economic Affairs, founded in 1955 to espouse the neoliberal ideas of Friedrich Hayek, inspiration of Margaret Thatcher. The IEA has done much to create the climate in which organisations and institutions founded for the public good can be taken away and handed over to big business.

In 2010 – or rather earlier, in 2007 – was education picked out to be the canary in the mine for the ideas of the new radical right wing of the Conservative party? Or was it mere chance that landed our schools in the laps of Michael Gove and Dominic Cummings?

---

[25] Transparify 2016 How Transparent are Think Tanks about Who Funds Them 2016? www.transparify.org

Section II
Capturing the Castle

Chapter 5
Schooling In A Somerset Village
The Scene Of The Crime

Away from the heady froth of national politics, schools all over England went on doing the job they had always done. But a new shadow was looming over them – a threat of greater changes in their leadership and management than they had seen since the turn of the twentieth century. The threat came, ironically, from a place called Sanctuary Buildings, from a group of people whose knowledge and understanding of state education could have been fitted on a village noticeboard with room to spare.

In 2015, a village school that had belonged to its community for more than 120 years was handed over to an academy trust centred on a school in a town 15 miles away. The governing board comprising staff, parents, local people and representatives of the local authority (LA), Somerset County Council (SCC), was disbanded. In 2021, you will search in vain for any mention of local representation in governance on the school's website.

OK. This sounds like small potatoes. But it isn't small potatoes for the parents, who for years had had easy recourse to a local person, probably a fellow villager, if they had any worries about the school that the headteacher wasn't sorting. If that failed, they could always go to their local county councillor, who happened to live in the next village, or to a district councillor, who lived in their own village. It is of such finely-wrought networks that local – and ultimately national democracy – is made. But who would they go to now? The head of a school in a town they rarely visit? The chair of a trust board they'd never heard of? Even their local MP, who just happened to be a Schools Minister in the Department for Education, was an advocate of academies, and lived in the town where the Trust Board was situated. He had more than once been photographed with that headteacher – now the Chief Executive Officer – scary title – of the

Trust. And of course, that CEO is also a Director of the Trust, which is a doubling-up, frowned upon even by the DfE, as being a potential conflict of interest. After all, how can a director of a charity be her own employee? And if you don't like what this new boss of your school has done, who can you talk to that isn't a mate of hers? Unless, of course, you do what the regulations say, and go straight to the Department of Education. Suddenly your little local school is not so local or so user-friendly after all.

So what's this place like? We're going to have here, a brief account of the village and its context in Somerset, and an overview of local and national politics in the county.

The Village

The parish of Stoke sub Hamdon lies five miles west of Yeovil in South Somerset, between Montacute and the Fosse Way, known more recently but less fondly as the A303. The village measures nearly three miles from east to west, one and a half miles from north to south, and is the largest and most heavily populated of a cluster of pretty hamstone villages just south of the A303. Connections are not bad for somewhere deep in the Somerset countryside; the M5 at Taunton is eighteen miles away and London Waterloo is a two-and-a-half-hour train journey from Yeovil Junction.

It is an area rich in history, dominated to the south by the ramparts of Ham Hill's Iron Age fort – possibly the largest in Europe – and to the north by the Romano-British super-highway. Throughout the Middle Ages, quarrying of the local hamstone, a honey gold Jurassic limestone, and farming provided the villagers' principal occupations. The origins of Stoke sub Hamdon's gloving industry are obscure but by 1844, four gloving factories had been established and continued to contribute to the local economy until the late 1960s.

Ownership of the local estates established in Saxon times passed into the possession of Norman aristocracy during the 11th and 12th centuries. The Mortains and Beauchamps shared the title of local manors with the Abbots of Glastonbury until, during the 15th century, the Dukes of Somerset and Earls of Dorset took turns as local lords of the manor. In 1660, the Duchy of Cornwall assumed direct control of the Manor of Stoke and retains ownership of much local land to the present day.

Stoke sub Hamdon has not always deferred to the Abbots of Glastonbury and the Dukes of Cornwall. The village has a history of non-conformism dating from the late 17th century. Since that time, a succession of Presbyterians, Congregationalists, Quakers and Methodists have challenged the primacy of the Established Church in the village, a tradition still evident in the isolated location of the parish church and the secular status of the village's primary school. This status is now dubious, as the Trust's diocesan representatives now form a majority on the school's Trust Board.

Local tradition tells of Methodist prayer meetings conducted by Charles and John Wesley beneath the branches of the Holy Tree, a giant sequoia, whose descendant still stands at the crossroads of the old toll road on the outskirts of Stoke sub Hamdon. Methodism held a strong appeal for the working poor who, in the mid eighteenth century, felt largely sidelined by the Established Church.

During the second half of the nineteenth century a local man, George Mitchell, continued this tradition of anti-establishment activism when in 1872 he formed and funded the Southwest branch of the National Agricultural Labourers' Union (NALU), whose members and supporters attended huge rallies on Ham Hill to hear speakers demanding better conditions for the labouring poor. Rousing choruses of "To see the thousands on Ham Hill" enlivened NALU rallies and meetings throughout the 1870s and 80s.

No longer a hotbed of radicalism in 2016, Stoke sub Hamdon was represented on South Somerset District Council and Somerset County Council by Liberal Democrat councillors, and in Westminster by Conservative Marcus Fysh, a former financier who overturned the substantial Liberal Democrat majority in May 2015. Yeovil was famous for being one of the largest Liberal Democrat majorities in the country, having been nurtured by their former leader, Paddy Ashdown, who still lived locally. His carefully groomed successor, former banker David Laws, took over the seat in 2001, and famously became a short-lived Chief Secretary to the Treasury in the new coalition government in 2010. An expenses' scandal, in which Laws was discovered to have been charging to parliamentary expenses the rent he paid to his partner, saw him hurried out of office, to return eventually as Schools Minister – a position he held throughout the period discussed here.

Today's village is a culturally homogenous working community with a population of around 2,000. 97.7% of the population is described as being white British, while 96.6% of the population was born in the United Kingdom and 99.2% of households have English as first language.

Despite the recent loss of its Methodist Church, Post Office and a public house, Stoke-sub-Hamdon is served by a small supermarket, a convenience store, several pubs, a Working Men's Club, GP, dental and veterinarian surgeries, a pharmacy and a service station. Local groups provide a range of social, leisure and educational activities, many based at the Memorial and Church Halls located in the centre of the village. It is a community, in a sense that still exists in rural Britain.

While Stoke-sub-Hamdon still has a quarry, a number of light industrial units, and farms and businesses providing employment opportunities for local people, the majority of the village's working-age population travel to Yeovil and beyond in order to access post-16 study and to earn a living. Retail, leisure and service industries, skilled manufacturing and high-tech businesses linked to the local aeronautical industry and a relatively buoyant public sector maintained local unemployment levels at the time at around 3.5% of the economically active population.

Educational provision for the village's pre-school, primary and secondary age children and young people is provided by two pre-schools, a village primary school and a secondary school in East Stoke.

Castle Street Primary School was opened in 1876 for the children of the village who were then said to be "in wretched order ... very ignorant ... very backward". The school was administered by a local committee, elected annually by subscribers, and was supported by school pence and a government grant[1]. The newly-built Stoke Senior School was hurriedly opened and fitted out with desks and chairs by local people at the dead of night in the autumn of 1939 to avoid its being requisitioned as a military hospital.

Both schools have, in the years since 2010, become academies.

The Schools

Castle School was an all-through elementary school in the centre of the village until the building of Stoke Senior School. The son of a local builder told how his father was contacted by the headteacher on the eve of the Second World War, to urgently move furniture into the new building, a mile away, as it would otherwise be commandeered by the War Office. He remembered how he and his father, with the head, drove back and forward between the two schools at night

[1] Baggs, A, Bush, R & Tomlinson, M. 1974 *A History of the County of Somerset, Volume 3*, London: Victoria County History

to enable the new school to open in September 1939. Stoke Senior School, later Stanchester Community School, became a secondary modern after the war, and a comprehensive in 1974. It also served for many years as a genuine community school, part of Somerset County Council's community education network, providing sports, social and adult education facilities. It was in many ways a typical rural comprehensive community school that had grown with the villages around Ham Hill.

Stanchester, again perhaps typically, did not have much of a reputation for academic excellence – which did not mean that it was a bad school at all. On the contrary, it was locally popular, and regularly scored 'satisfactory' in Ofsted inspections. However, when Ofsted's 'satisfactory' became 'requires improvement', this looked less than satisfactory and, in common with other secondary schools in the region, the school came under pressure to improve its examination results. In 2009, the long-serving headteacher retired, and a new head was appointed to bring about the changes needed. In 2010, the head joined together with the three Yeovil secondary heads to talk about academisation, under the new coalition government's scheme offering financial incentives to any but actually failing schools to convert. The governing board approved this in 2011 – not before coming a cropper with the required consultation, when consultees were given little time, inaccurate information and inoperative email connections to respond.

There was, however, no sign of similar movement among local primary schools.

The Primary Schools Of The Hamstone Villages

There are twenty-one small (that is, smaller than one-form entry) primary schools within a five-mile radius of Stoke sub Hamdon. Most of these serve small villages within sight of Ham Hill. Until 2014, all of them were graded by Ofsted as either 'good' or 'outstanding'. Castle Primary School, in the centre of the village, was first graded 'inadequate' in July 2014, placed in special measures, and designated by the local authority for immediate conversion to a sponsored academy. The Redstart Learning Trust, based at Redstart Primary School fifteen miles away in Chard, was selected to be the sponsor by the LA and the DfE broker. Now, fifteen miles may not sound much. But in a rural area like this one, connections are not always simple. Stoke-sub-Hamdon has always looked to Yeovil, just over 6 miles east, and on a direct bus route. It's where people would generally do their shopping, where youngsters go to college, where people go to work. South Petherton is just across the A303, and culturally not dissimilar, also on the bus route. But Chard is a world away. If you're lucky, you might just make the trip by bus in a little under 1½ hours, because you have to go via Yeovil bus station and change. Usually, it will take you more than 2 hours to do the journey one way. Connections are tricky things in the countryside, and the distance that a crow flies is not always the best guide to which communities villagers feel part of.

Despite the grave reservations of its governors and its parents, the Castle Primary School converted to academy status on March 1st 2015. However, Redstart's nominee for the school's headship, the Chard school's then deputy head, had already taken up the post, on 1st January. In April, the CEO of Redstart reported to the Board that Ofsted had revisited and concluded that the school was "not making reasonable progress".

It was initially the approach of a governor of the school in the summer of 2014 that alerted me to the developing situation. I was asked to advise the governors on possible alternative sponsors to those promoted by the LA. They had serious misgivings about the suitability of Redstart. Nevertheless, the LA forced through its choice. Later, the governors expressed concern that the school appeared to be on the path to conversion without any sign of a consultation, as the law required. Even so, the officers of the Redstart Trust signed the declaration required by the DfE, that a proper consultation had been conducted, and conversion went ahead as planned. "The trust has undertaken that they have completed such a consultation when signing the Funding Agreement." wrote the DfE[2], not showing any interest in whether they were telling the truth or not. This expression of concern by the governors led to correspondence with the trust, the former school governors and the DfE, exploring the background to the conversion. In the course of this, other areas of concern arose, suggesting that misleading statements had been made, promises to the governing body broken and essential procedures bypassed in the haste to have the school converted before the deadline imposed by the forthcoming general election and the preceding period of government department 'purdah'.

It is this chain of events that started me on this book. The story took place in the national context we have seen. We will be exploring what happened, why it happened, why the parents, governors and staff of the school were concerned,

---

[2] DfE letter, 8 July 2015

how they expressed that concern, and then how they appeared to drop out of the picture.

In the next section, we will summarise the events and the areas of contention.

Chapter 6
The Curious Conversion
Of Castle School

How the rules were broken, and ordinary people began to see how a corrupt government might impact on their ordinary lives; how bad behaviour by leaders can trickle down through an organisation as all-embracing as the Department of Education; and how the world of schools became a world of money.
   "Move fast and break things" – Mark Zuckerberg

The Nation's Schools

With a growing number of academies and multi academy trusts throughout the country, the DfE recognised the need for some local structure to oversee the new state-funded independent schools, providing a level of management between them and the bureaucrats of Sanctuary Buildings. These Regional Schools Commissioners, appointed directly by the DfE, would work alongside the shrinking LAs. They would be supported by their own chosen Headteacher Boards and exercise a firm grip on statutory education in their districts, while participating in decisions about academising schools that would fulfil a purely party-political agenda. One major performance indicator for an RSC would be the number of LA schools being converted to academies and getting pinned to Michael Gove's office wall.

Regional Schools Commissioners report to ministers but have no obligation to talk to the schools and communities for which they are responsible. Their headteacher boards (HTBs) are elected only from heads of 'outstanding academies' "by existing academy leaders, even though they advise regional school commissioners (RSCs), who now oversee all schools and whose decisions affect everyone in the country."[1] The HTBs are not required to publish minutes

---

[1] McInerney, Laura. 2017. *These Boards are corrupt, self-serving and secretive,* Schools Week 5 May 2017

or discuss their business in any other way. Meanwhile, any vacancies can be filled by the RSC from any constituency whatsoever, with the outcome that in 2020 the HTB for the south east of England comprised three elected headteachers and five co-opted members picked by the RSC. Business leaders and lawyers take up these positions, if the RSC chooses.

In the autumn of 2014, one of the newly-appointed RSCs declared to a conference of school governors and academics that "We don't talk about forced academisation at the DfE any more."[2] Well, they might have stopped talking about it, but they certainly didn't stop doing it. This was a throwaway comment to a roomful of people committed to providing a professional and principled education service across England. It neatly demonstrated the slipperiness of the language now infecting the senior professionals of the DfE regime. Of course, the DfE continued to force schools to convert to academy status, even though they changed the language to cover up what they were about. With a much wider brief to create unaccountable academies than her predecessor could have dreamed about, it now became open season for the new secretary of state, Nicky Morgan, on all remaining maintained schools, initially on those defined as 'coasting'.

It might be thought that the woman who took over at Education in 2014 following the sacking of Michael Gove would display a little more principle than her lupine predecessor. After all, it would be four years before she would attack Boris Johnson in extreme terms, telling the BBC Today programme that all politicians have "a duty to think very carefully about the language we use", adding: "Boris has to make a decision …he's either a journalist or a politician." When asked in September 2018 if she would serve in a Johnson cabinet, were he ever to become PM, she was unequivocal: "I think I'm very unlikely to be asked but the answer is no. I would not serve in a Boris Johnson cabinet." So you'd think there'd been a big change here, someone in charge of education who would never be part of the Johnson-Gove nexus.[3]

Morgan supported Gove in both of his unsuccessful bids to lead the Conservative party. She supported Remain in the 2016 referendum. Boris Johnson became Prime Minister in July 2019 and Nicky Morgan immediately

[2] Quoted in Gann, N. 2016 Improving School Governance: How better governors make better schools, London: Routledge 2nd edition p183

[3] Honeycomb-Foster, Matt. 2018. *Top Tory Nicky Morgan says she would refuse to serve under Boris Johnson*, www.politicshome.com, 10 September, 2018

accepted the offer of a cabinet post as Culture Secretary. She stood down from parliament at the 2019 general election, "stepping back from ministerial life" though staying in the cabinet as the newly elevated Baroness Morgan. Soon, she was a hot tip to be the next chair of the BBC.

Meanwhile, Down In Somerset[4]

The Castle Primary School in Stoke sub Hamdon lost its long-serving headteacher to retirement in 2009. A maintained village community primary school with 150 or so pupils in England or Wales had not attracted large numbers of applicants for a vacant headship for a number of years. The most recent local vacancy of a primary school of that size had drawn 13 applicants – a number that pleasantly shocked local education officers as being twice as many as average. The first round of interviews at Castle did not identify a candidate to satisfy the governors. The deputy head was well thought of, but he was unwilling to move up to headship. Eventually, the governors persuaded him, and in 2011, having served as acting head for nearly two years, and completed the then compulsory National Professional Qualification for Headship (NPQH), he was appointed to the substantive post.

Sadly, during the subsequent two years, the new headteacher suffered several bouts of illness and the school's Key Stage 2 test results, the key measure of a primary school's performance, began to decline. The then deputy head and class teacher similarly had no desire to follow her predecessor into a stressful and increasingly demanding job. Managing a small school can be in many ways more demanding than heading up a large comprehensive. The same legal, financial and personnel responsibilities are still there, albeit on a far smaller scale, but with very little of the infrastructure to support the head.

At this point, a board of governors would expect significant support from its local authority. Most LAs have a pool of serving or otherwise available staff to be able to step in temporarily to support a school in crisis. The governors were disappointed. Somerset could not find anyone to help other than on a very short-term and part-time basis. It is possible to speculate now that this reflected a deliberate policy of the county. The Liberal Democrat regime that had led the county council until 2010 had been sympathetic to small schools and maintained both a supportive funding formula and a substantial staff of advisers. The

---

[4] Much of this section emerged from conversations with staff, parents and other local people, most of whom did not want to be identifiable

Conservative regime that succeeded it, at the same time that the Conservative-dominated coalition took office nationally, was happy to adopt the party's policy of cajoling, bribing and pushing schools away from their LAs towards state-funded independent academy status. While some LAs did their best to hang on to their schools, at least by maintaining support services and working with schools in difficulty, others were happy to see their schools depart the LA fold, and may have used tactics like offering little real help to failing schools, to ensure that they did. Such schools found themselves in a pincer movement. The DfE's hardening strategy, to force schools graded as 'inadequate' to convert to academy status, operated alongside LA unwillingness, sometimes inability, to provide help to them to improve.

Nationally, not all LAs immediately abandoned their schools once they were placed in special measures. Some staved off academisation by putting improvement strategies in place. Others acquiesced in parents' movements to protect the maintained status of their local schools.

A further element, however, was contributed by Ofsted. There appear to have been cases where, despite sympathetic inspections of schools that displayed deteriorating data, suggesting that their leadership did show a capacity to improve, reports were rejected and rewritten in more draconian fashion in order to meet the government's policy.

This may have happened in The Castle's case. The school had for years, like most primary schools in this area, returned 'good' or 'outstanding' Ofsteds. The inspection of the school in early May 2014, conducted by a reportedly sympathetic inspector, awarded 'requires improvement' grades of three to the three key areas of achievement of pupils, quality of teaching and behaviour and safety of pupils, but could fairly only apply an 'inadequate' grade four to leadership & management, on the basis that the lack of stable leadership suggested little capacity to improve.

It is customary for Ofsted reports to be sent to the school and published promptly:

"The final report will be published on the Ofsted website within 19 working days of the end of the inspection. If the school has been judged inadequate, the report is usually published within 28 working days of the end of the inspection."[5]

---

[5] Department for Education. 2015 *Being inspected as a maintained school or academy,* Website last updated: 3rd September, 2015 https://www.gov.uk/guidance/being-inspected-as-a-maintained-school-or-academy

In this case, however, it took a whole fifty working days for Ofsted to, we can only assume, have the report recast in the way it wanted it to appear. In this version, only 'behaviour and safety of pupils' merited a 'requires improvement', all three other areas were graded 'inadequate', and the school was duly placed in special measures.

The idea that the LA would not have been sorry to see this judgment, or even contributed to the circumstances in which it could be made, comes about because of the sudden expedition of its officers after weeks and months of what the governors saw as complete inaction. The report was published on the day before the last day of the summer term, the 17th July, and parents, governors and staff were summoned to a meeting that evening. At the meeting, the adviser speaking for the county did not equivocate. "Special measures means academy conversion", he said, ignoring the matter of the statutory consultation and the governing body's right at that time to make the final decision. He discouraged the parents from any challenge to this outcome, explaining that it would distract from the school improvement agenda and potentially damage the school and the children.

Unsurprisingly, this combative approach fed a conspiracy theory, and a letter to parents from a parent (who also happened to be a local teacher) stated baldly that "There is a clear agenda to push our school towards becoming an academy". There was plenty of evidence for this view. A significant number of parents set up a Facebook group, which quickly acquired sixty-four members. Parents lobbied the MP, by coincidence the Schools Minister David Laws who, if anyone, could have put a stop to the process with a few quiet words back at the DfE. The local newspaper, not renowned at that time for its crusading for local causes, ran photographs and articles featuring 'angry parents' lashing out at the Ofsted report. The governors worked together throughout the summer to establish their rights, but do not seem to have taken formal advice from anyone but the county's own governor services department – a department stripped over recent years of key personnel, and unlikely to offer disinterested counsel.

Each region of the country had a designated academy 'broker', usually self-employed, who was called in by the DfE when a school was designated for forced conversion. By the time the governors met formally in September, with the broker and an LA officer, the die was cast. Brokers, like their bosses, the Regional School Commissioners, of course had targets. Indeed, there was, and probably still is, a league table of RSCs, where they are rated by the number of academy conversions they preside over annually. In order to keep your substantial fees as a broker, and to keep your comfortable job as an RSC, it was very much in your own interest to ensure that conversions went ahead smoothly.

A note here about the role of the Regional Schools Commissioner. Appointed directly by the National Schools Commissioner, who in turn is a choice of the secretary of state, their main responsibilities are to:

- Monitor the performance of the academies in their area.
- Take action when an academy is underperforming.
- Decide on the creation of new academies.
- Make recommendations to ministers about free school applications.
- Encourage organizations to become academy sponsors (ensuring there are enough high-quality sponsors to meet local need, ensuring each region has a strong supply of high quality sponsors).
- Proposing suitable sponsors for poorly performing maintained schools who have been selected by the Department for Education to become sponsored academies.
- Approve changes to open academies, including: changes to age ranges; mergers between academies; and changes to MAT arrangements.[6]

To assist with this work, as we saw above, they have a Headteachers Board. Only academy heads are eligible for this, but that seems to include Trust CEOs.

Despite promises that the governors could seek their own candidate for sponsor, it soon became clear that this, like the consultation, would be a decision taken by the DfE. The Chair of Governors spotted this and expressed the 'grave reservations' of the governors about the ethos of the Redstart Trust, the most likely candidate based on an 'outstanding' primary school some fifteen miles away in the small town of Chard. A local sponsor approached by the governors through an independent contact (the author) was told not to meet with the governors, as the choice had already been made, which came as something of a surprise to the governing board. Clearly, neither DfE regulations nor common courtesies were going to be observed here.

---

[6] Department for Education. 2020. https://www.gov.uk/government/policies/increasing-the-number-of-academies-and-free-schools-to-create-a-better-and-more-diverse-school-system/supporting-pages/regional-schools-commissioners-rscs

On the 14th November 2014, the governors met with the principal of Redstart, their chair and four other staff, a substantial phalanx of staff and trustees. The DfE broker and an LA officer also attended. The minutes show how angry and frustrated the governors were. But there appeared to be some consolatory efforts. In particular, they were reassured when they "were urged to start the process of headteacher appointment with the sponsor whilst in the process of conversion". This, after all, "would be a fair process the most suitable person being appointed"[7](sic). Despite their misgivings, once the visitors had left, and "after some heated debate"[8], the governors passed the broker's resolution to accept Redstart as the sponsor. It is probable that their enthusiasm was dampened after it had been made clear on more than one occasion that, if they demurred, they would be sacked and replaced by an interim executive board to see the process through.

The following day, the broker issued some advice via email to the chair, copying in the LA officer and the Redstart principal:

"Ideally the decision of the governing body would remain confidential until an Academy Order is issued, but I realise that would be very difficult in this instance. Communication to parents and staff needs to say that the governing body has decided to ask that [sic] the Secretary of State to agree to Castle joining the Redstart Learning Partnership. Please don't write anything that suggests that a decision has been made, as Ministers don't like it and both parents and staff would most likely suggest that consultation is therefore invalid. Reassure them that there will be full consultation after the SoS has given agreement in principle, and that you hope this will happen before the end of term, so that there can be consultation in January. It is also important that the message about the benefits of joining the Redstart Learning Partnership are (sic) flagged from the start and that all messages are very positive ones. Personally I would avoid the word 'sponsor' as it can be quite emotive."[9]

The parents' movement had effectively withered away by this point. The supportive local county councillor had arranged to sponsor the presentation of a petition to the council, but no one turned up to deliver it. At a meeting following the governors' decision, the interim headteacher explained that further challenge would, as they had been told four months previously, be useless once the

---

[7] Governing body minutes

[8] Ibid

[9] Email, academy broker to chair of governors

'consultation' got under way. A communication to parents from one of their number explains the process to come, including the reassurance that the popular and well-regarded interim head would stay in post until Easter 2015.

That was not to be either, however. Once the official decision had been ratified, just a week before the end of the autumn term, the interim head was told that she should return to her own school after Christmas. The chair of governors had been summoned to Chard and told to exercise his supposed right to act on behalf of the governors and appoint the Redstart principal's deputy to take on the Castle headship in January.

By that point, the statutory consultation should have taken place. But as parents, governors and staff have all testified, there was no consultation. The 2010 Academies Act, Section 5.2. was then in force, requiring that "The consultation must be on the question of whether the school should be converted into an Academy"[10]. (The requirement for this consultation was removed shortly after these events, when the Liberal Democrats were no longer needed to provide the government with a majority in parliament).

Efforts to retrieve any copies of a letter to parents explaining the options, inviting opinions, and giving opening and closing dates for comments have proved in vain. The school website contained no information about a consultation prior to conversion, merely the DfE document of "Frequently Asked Questions". Governors appear to have been told that one parental meeting constituted the consultation. The invitation letter, dated 16th January, 2015 – more than two months after the consultation supposedly began – invited parents to a meeting to hear "the process of converting to an Academy" and to receive "information on how the Multi Academy Trust will work". The minutes of this meeting, held at 9.00 am on the 30th January 2015, however, contain no reference to any consultation, either before or after the meeting. The conversion to Redstart Trust sponsorship, based fifteen miles away in Chard, is presented to parents as a fait accompli. And the meeting was conducted, not by the governors (who may not even have been present), but by the aspiring executive principal and the 'new' head, already in place. No other interested parties were informed. An 'advertisement in the local community' appeared in a local free magazine in February 2015, suggesting the consultation was only for parents (whose meeting had already taken place) and giving no details, information or closing date.

---

[10] Department for Education (DfE) 2010: *Academies Act 2010,* London: Department for Education

Similarly, no written copy of the required report back on the consultation is available – it has been a statutory requirement that governors show they have taken such a report into consideration.

The School Duly Converted On 1st March 2015

What was going on here? The process for conversion was breached in at least three respects:

- The governors were given, and were therefore able to offer to parents, no choice of sponsor. The DfE and the LA agreed between them who the sponsor would be, and the governors were prevented from exploring alternatives.
- Secondly, a public consultation must meet certain legal requirements – the governing board must agree who it is appropriate to consult; the consultees must be given sufficient and accurate information to make a reasoned judgment; there must be a clear timescale, and the report must be considered by the governors. The consultation must, as the law made clear, address the question "of whether the school should be converted into an Academy"[11]. There is no evidence of any of these fundamental democratic and legal protections being met by the school or by the sponsor.
- Thirdly, the governors were promised a meaningful role in a fair headteacher appointment process, which within days was overruled by the combined forces of the DfE, the LA and the Trust.

Exploration of all the documents that have been made available, and responses from the DfE, the Regional Schools Commissioner, and the Executive Principal, offer clear evidence that the department and the local authority, with the collusion of the trust, breached statutory requirements both in the spirit and the letter of the law.

All this is now in the past. The school converted, and local villagers lost control, on March 1st, 2015 – just in time to avoid 'electoral purdah' leading up to the general election – a major driver, it seems, in this helter-skelter dash to shed local democratic accountability. The fact that the school sat in the

---

[11] Ibid

constituency of the then schools minister, David Laws, did nothing to help its cause. The local newspaper, owned by the Mail group, reported about angry parents in the summer of 2014, but no more was heard from them after that, and efforts to get them to cover the story, or even print letters about it, were in vain. The democratic shutdown was complete; the key players could claim that the parents were in favour, and that the governors could have kicked up a fuss if they had disapproved.

But the authorities are cleverer than that. They said, and governors and villagers in their innocence appear to have believed them, that there was no alternative – here's the sponsor you'll have: "There is a limited choice in a rural community and it is just not possible to put a selection of potential sponsors forward for discussion', said the LA officer from Somerset County Council – even though the DfE had already forbidden one such potential sponsor to meet with the governors. 'Would the headteacher appointment be a fair process?' asked a governor of the academy broker (who, by the by, was paid £2250 for her egregious role in this). Within a few days, the chair had been told to go far beyond his legal powers and appoint a member of staff from the sponsor school as the new head, over the head of his own GB. Even with the process well down the road of completion, one of the governors asked the new executive principal if her trust's ethos statement would incorporate Castle School's emphasis on meeting the needs of the whole child, with a focus that was not just academic. The new principal's reply:

"(She) is not aware of the Castle ethos or what it looks like in practice."

A few months later, the government passed the Education and Adoption Act[12] to unshackle local authorities, regional schools commissioners, DfE brokers and academy trusts, from the very few remaining demands of local democracy and accountability.

---

[12] Department for Education (DfE) 2016: *Education and Adoption Act 2016,* London: Department for Education

Chapter 7
Meanwhile, Elsewhere in England

The Castle Primary School's story is one of the least publicised of its kind. Some governing boards bowed to what they saw as the inevitable and voluntarily 'went academy', so that they could do it 'on their own terms'. But for ten years, instead of being able to concentrate on the progress and performance of children, the leaders of many schools found themselves spending time, energy and public money on the question of their status. Here are some examples.

"The question of the day, at least it seems to me, is: Where ... is the greatest damage to be done, through neglect or mismanagement or malice?"[1]

Meanwhile, Elsewhere In England

The story of the Castle Primary School was not unusual. All around the country, communities were having their schools taken away from them and handed to an unknown quantity. Most growing trusts were either founded on one "successful" school, like Redstart Primary School in Chard, or on a sponsoring body, like Ark Academies, Oasis Community Learning, Harris Carpets and the many diocesan trusts springing up to deal with errant church schools.

For a period, leaders of successful schools (those labelled by Ofsted in their most recent inspection as 'good' or 'outstanding') were told – or rather it was hinted to them by an academy broker or some DfE official in Sanctuary Buildings – that if they wanted to continue to be judged 'outstanding', they must take on an 'inadequate' school nearby. If they did this, they would not be subjected to further inspections. That was quite an incentive. In fact, it became a time-bomb for the DfE:

---

[1] Lewis, Michael. 2019. *The Fifth Risk*, London: Penguin 2019 p94

"One in 20 children in England is in a school that has not been inspected for more than 10 years, the BBC has found. Analysis of official data revealed 24 schools had gone without inspection for more than 13 years. There are 1,010 'outstanding' schools that have not had a visit from Ofsted in a decade – up from 296 in 2017. The Department for Education (DfE) plans to lift an exemption on routine inspections for outstanding schools. It has been in place since 2012 but watchdog Ofsted called for it to end amid concerns about falling standards."[2] The department's desperation to academise everything in sight was now overriding the earlier priority of regular rigorous inspection.

Other schools, with ambitious leaders, eyed local schools rapaciously as their headteachers – usually the driving force in such cases – saw the magic words 'Chief Executive Officer', 'Principal' or 'Executive Headteacher' dangling before them. Not to mention the attendant salary.

Sponsoring bodies arose out of businesses or groups of people, many of whom were already supplying resources or services to schools, or connected with education in some other way, or sometimes with no connection at all.

Church of England and Roman Catholic dioceses saw academisation as a way of holding onto their longstanding church schools. For a period, the churches had reached agreement with the DfE that a 'failing' church school must be offered to its diocese before other sponsors were considered. Of course, there were individual schools who genuinely saw group academisation as an opportunity to form a federation or cluster which could offer better opportunities for local children. But in doing so, unevenness in provision was bound to appear. A secondary school inviting feeder primary schools to join in a trust would usually expect to be the lead school. Some primary schools would be unwilling to accept that, and find themselves excluded from the community, while children within the trust were prioritised for places at the age of eleven. Other secondary schools might cherry-pick the 'best' and most compliant primaries and leave the more challenging school populations to others.

And so arose a new phenomenon, the 'orphan' school that was 'failing' with its local authority, but that no sponsor saw as sufficiently financially viable, let alone profitable, to take on. Despite DfE bribes, such schools were seen as too difficult to turn around. Never before in this country had state schools found themselves with no authority willing to support them. There are three ways in

[2] Wainwright, Daniel. 2019. Ofsted: 1,010 'outstanding' schools not inspected for a decade BBC News, 2 October 2019

which schools become orphans – those that have been designated as needing to be transferred from their LA to a sponsored trust but cannot find a taker; those that have been academised earlier, as stand-alone schools, and find themselves 'failing', so now need a sponsor; and those whose sponsors have withdrawn or collapsed or been forcibly closed down. As well as causing long-term uncertainty and precariousness to children, parents and staff, these schools are also financially costly: "Schools Week has attempted to monitor and calculate the number and costs of re-brokerage: it suggested in 2017 that more than 100 academies are re-brokered each year, and that this has cost up to £30 million in sweeteners, clearing deficit budgets and funding for improvements. In February 2018, The Guardian quoted a DfE spokesperson as unable to say how many 'orphan schools' ... there were."[3] Which meant that even the government department responsible for such schools didn't care much about them. They couldn't even be bothered to count them.

The usual social divisions and inequalities apply. In the narrow quantitative measures applied regardless of circumstance, white middle-class schools in leafy suburbs were always easier to 'succeed in' than others in less advantaged areas. Almost without exception, the orphan schools served less affluent and more challenging areas with high pupil and staff turnover and numbers of children with first languages other than English – the type of school statistically more likely to be failed by Ofsted. So almost as soon as the Academies Act came into force, academisation embedded one more aspect of inequality amongst schools into the system.

Then there were the crooks and the incompetents. Exposés of some of the worst examples became commonplace. That is where websites like Warwick Mansell's Education Uncovered[4] and the (more partisan) Anti-Academies Alliance[5] came in. Mansell describes 2017-18 as the school year "of the collapsing multi-academy trust". Wakefield City Academies, one of the twenty largest MATs in England, dropped its 21 schools early in the new year. Bright Tribe, based in Stockport but making a rare hash of Whitehaven Academy in Cumbria, managed to have a whole edition of BBC Panorama devoted to exposing its 'entrepreneurial' chairman, and in late 2019 became the subject of

[3] Thomson, Pat. 2020. *School Scandals: Blowing the whistle on the corruption of our education system,* Bristol: Policy Press, 2020

[4] Mansell, Warwick, Education Uncovered https://www.educationuncovered.co.uk/

[5] Anti Academies Alliance http://antiacademies.org.uk/

a formal probe by the fraud police. At least one million pounds of money intended for building improvements seemed to have gone missing and only a parent or two seemed to care. The case continues. So many times these collapses and scandals were connected to the loss of huge amounts of money given to trusts by the DfE for the education of children. All these schools and trusts were directly accountable to the department, whose sole responsibility it was to monitor them. Buildings left chronically unsafe, while trust leaders and their families enjoyed generous salaries in comfortable jobs; friends and relatives with lucrative contracts; trustees enjoying weekends in sumptuous hotels or 'research' trips to New York: the opportunities for unlimited junketing by unscrupulous rogues and thieves seemed endless.

Education Fellowship Trust had its 12 schools 'rebrokered', as the jargon has it (passing over the fact that the original brokering process by the DfE must have been desperately faulty). Michael Gove's second favourite trust was the Durand Academy, now closed, with the ambitions of the knighted headteacher's plans matched only by his salary and his £850,000 pay-off. His departure to Dubai to run a college there seems like a journey from knighthood to benighted. But after a year, he was back again, fighting to hold on to his money. Two years after the school reopened under another trust, the original Durand trustees were also fighting for £3m compensation for returning the trust's assets to the public. "Dr Mary Bousted, the joint general secretary of the National Education Union, said there was a lack of due diligence from the government when the school became an academy in 2010. 'This was always going to be the endless result of a hopeless drive to academise without thinking about the assets handed out to sponsors,' she said. 'The loser has been the taxpayer and the public, who have seen their assets sequestered away and now we're seeing the endgame: a charity is demanding money to hand back assets that were given to it for free.'"[6]

Some of these trusts deserve a book of their own. Schools Company and Silver Birch Trusts were casualties of the year of the broken trusts. We will explore more of this behaviour in Chapter 9 – the reader will need a strong stomach.

Three schools that resisted the department's attempts to force them to join this sorry world hit newspaper headlines over a long period.

---

[6] Whittaker, Freddie. 2020 *Durand wants £m to hand back buildings (and they are 'confident' of winning the legal fight,* Schools Week, 28 October, 2020

John Roan Secondary School, Greenwich

When the historic John Roan School in East London was found by Ofsted to be 'inadequate', staff and parents were shocked by how quickly the LA and the DfE reacted. In a scenario reminiscent of the procedure at the Castle Primary, the report was published on the 8th June, 2018 and five days later, The University Schools Trust (UST) , which had been supporting the school's management for over a year, wrote to parents to announce that they had been 'chosen' to take the school over from Greenwich Council. This was quick work by anyone's standards. A disinterested observer might ask a couple of legitimate questions. Why would an organisation that had had all that time to help the school improve, but had clearly not made sufficient progress when Ofsted arrived, be the one chosen to take full control of it? How come the Regional Schools Commissioner had reached this decision in less than five days, and without meeting with his Headteacher Board, the group supposed to advise him? What was it about UST's record, with just two schools, that convinced the RSC and the LA that it was fit for the job? A swift and effective protest resulted in the UST withdrawing after a very disruptive period to the school. As in Stoke sub Hamdon, the school and the children stood at risk of damage, not from the protest, but from the flawed and opaque decision-making by the officers of the trust and the council. The woman who had been chair of governors at the school when the Ofsted report was published was a former director of children's services in Greenwich. After "fourteen years as director of education at Hammersmith and Fulham, (she) was chair of governors at John Roan when she reportedly brought in UST to provide leadership support to the school"[7]. It emerged that she had been a trustee of UST between 2015 and 2016, including a spell as chair. Members of John Roan Resists and NEU staff members were already attending Anti-Academies Alliance meetings by the 16 June.

The school wallowed in uncertainty for months before UST withdrew, and the DfE disbanded the governing board in December, imposing an Interim Executive Board (IEB) in January 2019. The IEB was the vehicle by which a local authority took control of a school when it disbanded a governing board on the way to handing it over to an academy trust. By June – a year since the Ofsted report – Greenwich Council was discussing a takeover by another trust, United Learning. ULT was a very different kettle of fish from UST. With upwards of

---

[7] Mansell, Warwick. 2019. Education Uncovered, 9 May 2019

ninety schools from Carlisle in the north to Poole in the southwest, it was already a slick operation. Agreements were signed and John Roan became an academy within the ULT on the 31st August 2019. The IEB members constituted the new local governing board (LGB), along with the 'executive headteacher' and the clerk. In 2020, the website showed, oddly, that three of the LGB had word-for-word identical profiles[8] (a school's website is a very good indicator of what its leadership cares about – and what it doesn't). The page on the website recounting its 343-year history made no mention of the moment when the school ceased to be a legal entity.

John Roan had a very efficient and committed protest movement, mainly of parents and staff. But it made no difference to the outcome. The majority of staff and parents, it seemed, were strongly opposed to academisation and, the law being what it was by then, had no consultation process to express this. The school is now part of a 'community' of almost 100 schools, with as many miles between the furthest two of its schools as there are days in the year.

Sexey's School, Bruton, Somerset

Another secondary school with a long history and a strongly supportive community is Sexey's School, a Church of England Foundation secondary school with some boarding facilities. However, the community of Bruton is predominantly white and significantly more affluent than much of Greenwich. The attempts of the local Regional Schools Commissioner to change its status were hugely newsworthy, especially as Bruton and the surrounding area had lately become home to a number of members of the London media.

In March 2019, Sexey's was inspected and found to be overall 'inadequate', having previously been found to 'require improvement'. The inspection had found urgent issues with the school's safeguarding procedures.

A short diversion on the subject of Ofsted, safeguarding, compliance, and schools that don't fit the DfE-required mould

Compliance with the increasing safeguarding expectations on schools during the decade was an issue that came to a head with the inspection of several Steiner schools throughout 2019, leading to their transfer to other sponsors. Schools founded on the educational philosophy of Rudolf Steiner have been around for 100 years. In England, they are a well-established part of both the state and the

---

[8] https://www.thejohnroanschool.org.uk/about-us/additional-information/governance

independent school systems. The fact that they have a different approach to, in particular, early years and junior education had not caused problems until compliance became a significant factor in the Ofsted inspection procedure. Some of the Steiner academy schools have been obliged to transfer to other sponsors. One independent school has closed, as its methods were attacked in its Ofsted report, following HMCI Amanda Spielman's request to the DfE in early 2019 that the DfE "carry out a thorough examination of Steiner education."[9] In those examples, Ofsted has been accused of working to an agenda of risk management and compliance essential to the neo-liberalisation of schooling. The capacity of parents to choose any school deviating from the strict performance-centred orthodoxy propounded by the DfE and imposed by Ofsted has become seriously threatened. The DfE is challenging the very 'autonomy' that it lauds, in state-funded and in independent schools.

Battling Bruton

The RSC issued a warning notice to Sexey's in 2019 and the school set about addressing the issues urgently. However, in early October, the parents of the school were informed, quite out of the blue, that "Following detailed consideration, the Regional Schools Commissioner (RSC) for the South West, Hannah Woodhouse, has agreed that Sexey's School Academy should be transferred to another trust... Sherborne Area Schools Trust has been provisionally identified as the most suitable trust to manage the school going forward … Your views are an important part of the process." The letter, dated Monday 7th October, gave warning of a meeting being held by the trust (SAST) on Wednesday the 9th October: "This will be an opportunity to hear more about SAST, the transfer, ask questions and share your views."[10] The tone of the invitation bears a strong resemblance to the so-called 'consultation' held in Stoke sub Hamdon five years earlier. Parents were being given less than 2 days' notice of a meeting about the future of their school. Only current parents and carers were addressed, not the wider community. While some opportunity appears to be given to express their views, the tone of the letter implies that the decision has

---

[9] See, for example: House, Richard. 2020. *Pushing Back to Ofsted: Safeguarding and the Legitimacy of Ofsted's Inspection Judgements – A Critical Case Study*, Stroud: InterActions; and Gann, Nigel. 2020 Book Review: Pushing Back to Ofsted, Schools Week, 26 July 2020

[10] Communication from the RSC's office

been taken. They are then invited to express their views to the RSC by 9am on the following Monday. An entire consultation lasting less than a week is quite ambitious. To call it "an important part of the decision-making process" is, let us say, cheeky. To suggest that there has already been "detailed consideration", to which staff, parents and the community have not been party, is downright dismissive.

The chair of governors gave a detailed rebuttal to the RSC, copying in the National Schools Commissioner, the Secretary of State for Education, the Bishop of Bath and Wells and the Archbishop of Canterbury. The town council also mobilised under the leadership of the mayor of the town, and the local MP was engaged. On the 16th October, SAST issued a statement: "it is evident that there is not an alignment of values or partnership working with Sexeys. Therefore, the Trust will continue to focus on our current schools and others interested in joining in the future, who do share our values."[11]

So community pressure can work – and it may help to have media figures like journalist and BBC presenter Mariella Frostrup on board – and certainly worthwhile to have Warwick Mansell reporting.

Other celebrities adorn the town and its surrounding area. The influx has led the town, which boasts two private secondary schools and a state boarding secondary school, to be labelled the 'next Chipping Norton' and British Vogue called it 'the new Notting Hill'."[12]

Maybe these things make no difference. In other campaigns, as Mansell reported, "the community around Moulsecoomb primary in Brighton forced a second possible sponsor to pull out of a proposed forced academy takeover there. And in West Yorkshire, a trust without primary experience which had been lined up by the RSC to take over Crigglestone Mackie Hill junior and infant school in Wakefield pulled out in July."[13]

So while schools and their communities now have no say – or any statutory role to play – in their forced academisation, according to law, a well-supported and vocal assault on the RSC with significant local figures involved can make a

[11] Statement about Sexey's School, Bruton, Sherborne Area Schools Trust, 16 October 2019

[12] Neate, Rupert. 2020. *'This isn't really Somerset': how the rich took over Bruton*, The Guardian, 10 July 2020

[13] Mansell, Warwick. 2019. Education Uncovered, 17 October 2019

difference. In the pandemic-dominated start to the 2020-21 school year, Sexey's School remained a Church of England Foundation School.

Waltham Holy Cross Primary School

Waltham Holy Cross School in the small town of Waltham Abbey in Essex, not unlike Stoke sub Hamdon's Castle Primary School, is an important focal point in the community, and similarly much valued by parents and children. Despite its name, the school was not a church school but a maintained community primary. Again, like the Castle, the school had been pretty consistently good in inspections in 2010 and 2015. But in December 2017, it was reported to be 'inadequate' in all areas except personal development, where it 'required improvement'. But, again like the Castle, there were inexplicable delays to the publication of the report. The Castle's report took 50 days to emerge. Holy Cross's took 79 days. In that time, as Freedom of Information (FOI) requests revealed, around 60 errors had to be corrected, including the headteacher's name and the number of nursery classes. But it did suggest that a new headteacher was putting things right and indeed an Ofsted monitoring visit in December 2018 said that "Leaders and managers are taking effective action towards the removal of special measures ... the local authority's statement of action was judged fit for purpose."[14] But this cut no ice, because forced conversion was well on its way and would not be diverted. After the delayed publication of the substantially amended report, the Diocese of Chelmsford offered to talk with the governing board about sponsorship, and this was welcomed by the governors. But quickly, the county council declared that "the DfE allocate a sponsor and is discussing this with NETAT". Now, NETAT was the NET Academies Trust, of which the Director of Education for Essex happened to be a trustee. The Holy Cross governors were pretty unhappy about NETAT from the outset. They knew that it was a small and relatively untried sponsor with two inadequate schools already, and they wondered if it would have the capacity to take on a third.

Even so, in May, an announcement appeared on the NETAT website that it was welcoming Waltham Holy Cross to its family of schools. The school was rightly upset about this – and so was the county council, because they complained to the DfE about it. Anyway, by this time the governors had been disbanded and an IEB had been put in place by the LA. Almost their first action was to invite the Chief Executive of NETAT to join them ("but not until after" a meeting with parents because "they need to get the parents on their side", the IEB minutes

---

[14] Ofsted

report). This is already sounding familiar, isn't it? Some of the parents were beginning to cause a bit of a nuisance, checking NETAT's status and record, sending FOI requests to the trust, the county and the DfE. We know that the Regional Schools Commissioner thought this, because her office "mistakenly sent an email to a parent promising to 'close down' her 'line of enquiry' about the long-awaited minutes of a Headteachers' Board meeting which had controversially approved an academy sponsor for her children's school."[15] The meeting had taken place in April and resulted in the premature announcement.

As Guardian journalist Aditya Chakrabortty reported, the Education Policy Institute had suggested that NETAT was the seventh worst primary school group in the country. Chakrabortty goes on to say that "Its board is stuffed with City folk: PFI lawyers, management consultants, accountants – but apparently no working teacher. Even as it drops three of its schools, the trust's aim is to run twenty-five to thirty institutions."[16] By December, the protests were going more strongly than ever, but it didn't seem to be making any difference. NETAT was reported to be ready to take the school over in May 2019. Shortly after a thronged town hall protest meeting, a parent discovered that NETAT had a £4.6m pension deficit.

In January of the new year, 2019, a local newspaper reported that the arrival on NETAT's board of trustees of "an expert financial specialist (with interests in real estate) as a trustee is unconnected to their proposed sponsorship of Waltham Holy Cross Primary School. We have been previously told that there are no plans at present to sell any of the school land. However, once an Academy Trust has been given ownership of the land, we have no guarantees for the future."[17] The takeover date had now slipped to near the end of the summer term.

The closed-door meetings went on and the parents and staff continued to be kept in the dark, although strictly speaking, the minutes of meetings should have been available to them. A march through the town in April "was the latest in a series of unorthodox actions taken by local parents … To uncover details about the fate of their own children's school, they have had to file hundreds of freedom

[15] Mansell, Warwick. 2018 Education Uncovered, 26 June 2018

[16] Chakrabortty, Aditya. 2018 *How parents and teachers are frozen out of our schools*, The Guardian, 30 July 2018

[17] Boyd, Milo. 2019. *NET Academies claims to have no plans to sell Waltham Holy Cross' land when it takes over in July,* East London and West Essex Guardian, 21 January 2019

of information requests and spent many months getting on top of the obscurities of education policy, land agreements and the relationship between different branches of the state."[18]

As in Stoke sub Hamdon, the parents and staff found that the trust's takeover included the arrival of leadership staff in the school, even though no formal agreement had yet been reached. Teachers were now threatening to strike, as NET academies had "been referred to the government's Standards and Testing Agency (STA) over concerns about the administration of the recent SATs testing"[19]. A very temporary reprieve was awarded by the LA while this embarrassing glitch was resolved. The school eventually became an academy in the NET Academies Trust on the 1st November 2019. The headteacher and another senior member of staff 'resigned'.

---

[18] Chakrabortty, Aditya. 2019. *'Accidental Activists': Essex parents fight academy trust's takeover of school*, The Guardian, 28 April 2019

[19] Twitter, @naughtsandcross, 11 June 2019

Chapter 8
Making the Links
Introducing the New Blob

In this chapter, we are going to look behind the shambles that the education 'system' had become in the course of a decade of Michael Gove's destructive drive to total academisation. We have seen how the policy was created and enacted. But who were the people orchestrating its implementation? It takes more than a single politician to win a war. There needs to be plenty of willing – as well as some less willing – foot soldiers.

"There is a passage in The Pool of Vishnu [by L H Myers]: 'If one sees,' he says, 'a man struggling at the bottom of a well, one's natural impulse is to pull him out. If a man is starving, one's natural impulse is to share one's food with him. Surely it is only on second thoughts that we don't do these things? Society seems to me to be like an organized system of rather mean second thoughts.'"[1]

The responsible members[2] of NETAT, designated sponsors of Waltham Holy Cross, during this period were Nick Caulfield, Executive Head of an academy in Slough, Alex Sharratt, managing director and co-owner of John Catt Educational Publishing Company, and Roy Blatchford. The leadership of NETAT has changed, and it is now headed up by four responsible members.

---

[1] Origo, Iris. 1947. *War in Val D'Orcia,* Harmondsworth: Penguin p12

[2] *Guidance Paper: Forming or Joining a Group of Schools: staying in control of your school's destiny,* Association of School and College Leaders; Browne Jacobson education lawyers; National Governors' Association, September 2015: "MATs are . . . required to have a group of members who sit above the board of trustees. The members have a hands-off but significant role. They monitor the performance of the trust and hold the trustees to account. They will intervene if the board is not performing by making changes at board level." p6

Blatchford and Sharratt have stood down, and Caulfield is joined by Andrew Smith, Richard Howard and Richard Carr (gender diversity not being an issue here). The members of a trust must hold the trustees to account for their management of the trust's business, so it is strongly recommended by the DfE that there is a degree of separation between them. In particular, it is not good practice for the chair of the trustees to be a member, because how can the members objectively hold him accountable if he is one of the very small number of them? But at NETAT in 2020, responsible member Richard Carr was also chair of the trustees. He is also an educational publisher. We can assume that this is a pretty tight-knit group of men involved in education and educational publishing, who would stay in touch with each other if the Trust were experiencing difficulties – or damaging publicity.

When the forced conversion of Waltham Holy Cross was being considered by the Regional Schools Commissioner, he consulted his Headteacher Board. Roy Blatchford, serendipitously, responsible member for NETAT, was a member of that HTB. Blatchford later relinquished formal connections with NETAT. But he was also serving on the advisory board of the Education Policy Institute (EPI), the highly prestigious national think tank for education. Fellow advisory board members included Rachel Wolf and Sam Freedman.

EPI trustees included Michael Wilshaw, former Chief Inspector and head of Ofsted (HMCI), Sally Morgan, former chair of Ofsted, sacked by Michael Gove to the disgust of then Schools Minister David Laws, and Lord Nash. The chair of the trustees of EPI was Sir Paul Marshall, the hedge fund financier.

Paul Marshall is a founder and trustee of the educational charity ARK (Absolute Return for Kids), founded in 2001, alongside his business partner, Ian Wace in Marshall Wace Asset Management. Amanda Spielman was an accountant at ARK, and founded the subsidiary ARK Schools, to open and run academies. Spielman became Her Majesty's Chief Inspector of Schools in 2017. In 2016, of the eight trustees of ARK, five were hedge fund managers, and none had a background in education. ARK is closely associated with the knowledge-based curriculum movement expounded by KIPP (the Knowledge Is Power Programme) based in the US and at the centre of the Charter School movement. ARK itself is a prime example of what is now called 'philanthrocapitalism'. Sir Paul Marshall was lead non-executive Board member of the DfE until 2016. That role, from July 2020, was held by John Nash.

Marshall donated £100,000 to the Brexit referendum Leave campaign and £3250 to Michael Gove's campaign for leadership of the Tory Party. He is a trustee of the Sequoia Trust, which receives investment income from hedge funds and donates to various charities (£32 ½ m in 2018-19) including between £700,000 and £750,000 to the Education Policy Institute in that year. The Sequoia Trust, perfectly legally of course, is registered in the British Virgin Islands[3]. It is a strange coincidence that a giant sequoia tree has stood at the crossroads leading to Stoke sub Hamdon since the days of the Wesleys. It symbolises the religious freedom that John Wesley sought, when he faced down the wealthy and powerful church and state establishment.

Marshall was a Lib Dem supporter and co-edited The Orange Book[4], which re-wrote Liberal Democratic doctrine as a right-wing capitalist set of policies. Marshall's co-editor was David Laws. Laws had been a banker at J P Morgan and then at Barclays de Zoete Wedd, a joint venture between Barclays Merchant Bank, a UK stockbroker de Zoete & Bevan and one of the London jobbing firms Wedd Durlacher. This was Barclays' first investment bank. Henry de Zoete, Michael Gove's adviser and Dominic Cummings' colleague at the DfE is a scion of the banking family.

David Laws, during his very brief period of office as Chief Secretary to the Treasury in 2010, was questioned at an event in his constituency about the possibility of the new coalition government tackling the huge issue of tax avoidance, including the use of offshore tax havens. His response was to say that that would do no good, as the bankers were so clever, that the moment one restriction was placed on them, they would find another loophole[5]. Laws, of course, left parliament in 2015 with the expenses scandal hanging over his head and after a disastrous campaign which ended with the loss of one of the Lib Dems' safest seats. However, he quickly found a berth at ARK academies where Marshall was chair of trustees, as an adviser to their international programmes. He advised ARK on the development of global education systems, including quality assurance and value added programmes[6]. He moved onto the Education Policy Institute as Executive Chairman, where Marshall, again, was a trustee and

---

[3] Offshore Leaks https://offshoreleaks.icij.org/nodes/161856

[4] Laws, David and Marshall, Paul. 2004. *The Orange Book: Reclaiming Liberalism,* London: Profile Books

[5] Personal recollection, Catherine Wood

[6] https://arkonline.org/

major donor. But in 2014, Laws had been MP for the constituency in which the Castle Primary School stood. He was also Schools Minister in the DfE. But he did not engage with the school. Instead, he happened to live just outside Chard, where Redstart Primary School was his nearest school, and where he was photographed with the headteacher by local press more than once[7]. Although little more than a nudge would have been needed from him to sort out the Castle School's issues, he appeared not to engage. Oddly, one parent who did get to meet with him in the early summer of 2014, very soon after the publication of the Ofsted report, came away with the strong impression that he knew exactly who the new headteacher would be – six months before anyone in the village – and that he was a bit surprised that she herself didn't know.

This is the new Blob. This is the new educational establishment. The main difference between this blob and the old one that was Gove's sworn enemy – the "enemies of promise" as he dubbed them – was that these people, almost exclusively white middle-class men, had little or no experience of state education. They did not know anything about schooling. They had never stood in front of a raucous crowd of five-year-olds, or a sulky bunch of year elevens on a Friday afternoon. And they never would. They come from, and mainly live in, a world of money. There is no room for parents and children here, and precious little space to hear the views of teachers and classroom assistants. In fact, there seems to be little room for people, except for people like themselves.

Some will feel grateful that they spend so much of their costly time on education. Others may think that our schooling should be the business of the state.

The Business Of Education

Taking over the direct management of maintained schools in a way that had rarely happened in the days of local authority oversight (a proviso had been written into the 1988 Act that enabled LAs to suspend local management from a school in extreme circumstances) means that the school loses its legal status as an independent organisation and becomes entirely subsumed into the trust. That process is not reversible. So any local authority (that is, public) assets transferred to the school following the 1988 Act establishing the local management of schools – buildings, grounds, equipment – become the property of the trust and

---

[7] See, for example, The Western Gazette: https://www.somersetlive.co.uk/

are disposable by them. But this wasn't the only way that control could be monetised after Gove's reforms.

While individual schools fell victim to Gove and Cummings' dreams of state-funded independent schooling, global businesses saw the pound signs of services to the new, less regulated and less monitored world of statutory education. Vosper Thornycroft, later Babcock, for example, is better known for its supplies to the defence industry. Nuclear submarines and school improvement apparently make comfy bedfellows, with Babcock providing school management for Worcestershire LA. Capita supplies a lot of healthcare services including recruitment, legal, financial and construction services. Capita has worked for the Home Office, telling migrants they had to 'go home' when they didn't, and for the Department for Work and Pensions, taking so long for terminally ill people to get the benefits due to them, that they often died before they got them, and inaccurately assessing so many disabled people for benefits that more than sixty per cent of appeals against their decisions were granted. Even so, renamed 'Crapita' by Private Eye magazine, they work with Staffordshire County Council in supplying educational services in the form of a joint venture called Entrust.

Serco runs the notorious Yarl's Wood Immigration Removal Centre, where it was accused of covering up systemic sexual abuse of women migrants and asylum seekers. Asylum seekers in Glasgow found themselves being housed and then dehoused by Serco employees, who tended to be premature in evicting them before their appeals had been completed. Serco's management of the electronic tagging service for the Ministry of Justice was so criminally fraudulent that they ended up paying more than £20m in fines, with two employees awaiting their court hearing[8]. It has become familiar to us all through its contract to run the less than world-beating Test and Trace service on behalf of the NHS during the pandemic for an alleged £12bn. Its management of that has not been without criticism. Serco has run the education service in Bradford, in Walsall and in Stoke-on-Trent.

As assessed by Gove and Murdoch in 2010, education is a multi-billion-pound industry, with the capacity for stupendous profit-making from money

---

[8] Yeo, Colin. 2020. *Welcome to Britain: Fixing our Broken Immigration System,* London: Biteback Publishing: "These are not isolated examples of an otherwise humane system now and then malfunctioning. At the time of writing, the charity Inquest had recorded thirty-seven deaths in immigration detention centres since 2000 and a further fourteen deaths of immigration detainees held in prisons under immigration laws." p228

supposedly dedicated to the education of England's children and young people. There was a time when all these services would have been provided by local education authorities on a non-profit-making basis.

This, then, is the face of corporatisation. The interests of the government are no longer distinguishable from the interests of big business.

The Possibilities Of Change

Shortly before the arrival of the 2020 pandemic, Ofsted's visits to schools followed a new inspection framework. One early effect was that schools became "less likely to move out of 'requires improvement' rating"[9]. During the pandemic, forced conversions continued and the new arrangements made them more likely and easier to impose.

Between 2016 and 2019, more than 300 primary schools were forced to become academies against mounting opposition from parents[10]. Schools were also transferring between trusts at an increasing rate. Not because they chose to – these schools have no independent existence any more. That was lost when they were converted and subsumed into a trust. They are transferred when their trust fails, so more disruption, more blocking out parents and children and staff.

But people are resisting. They see the examples used here and, successful or not, they begin to see what is possible. Some of them have "caught the vision of their own powers"[11]. Protests across Essex, Kent, London, West Yorkshire, East Sussex, Dorset, and Hertfordshire are cited, including some victories in Newham, Lewes and Redbridge[12].

Perhaps the ground is shifting.

For the parents of the Castle Primary School, the die is, for the moment at least, cast. We have seen why and how academy status was forced on it, and how those methods were replicated widely elsewhere. And we have seen who was involved in some of those conversions.

---

[9] Speck, Dave. 2020. *Fewer schools 'outstanding' under new Ofsted framework,* Times Educational Supplement, 26 March 2020

[10] See, for example, McIntyre, N and Weale, S. 2019. *More than 300 English primary schools forced to become academies*, The Guardian, 11 July 2019.

[11] Lilienthal, David. 1944. TVA Tennessee Valley Authority: Democracy on the March. Harmondsworth: Penguin p44

[12] Weale, Sally 2019. *Academisation rebellion: parents resist school takeovers*, The Guardian, 5 May 2019

In the following three chapters, we are going to look at three key elements in ensuring that the views of parents, staff and governors could be discounted throughout a conversion process managed by the combination of a DfE academy broker, a Regional Schools Commissioner, LA officers, and the trustees of the designated sponsor. These three elements are the attitude towards public consultation and information, the manipulation of language, and changes in the democratic accountability of state funded schools.

Section III
Professional Fouls

Chapter 9
How To Consult ... And How To Avoid It

People used to be protected by the process of statutory consultation. What happened? Increasingly, democratic safeguards against the actions of the unaccountable have been lost. It stands as a warning that we are losing long-standing protections against summary government actions.

Listening To The Public

A major part of the Conservative Party's enthusiasm for academies is that local and elected elements can be removed from their governance. While contractually bound to have at least some parent views represented in their structures, they can easily shovel these away into the backwaters of their procedures. It is likely that the proponents of the 1986 Act[1] thought that the reconstruction of the governing bodies of maintained schools to include elected parents and staff and co-opted members of the community would be a stick with which to beat the senior professionals in schools. Headteachers would be further disempowered, then, by the contents of the 1988 Act, the National Curriculum and standardised testing, and the 1992 Act creating Ofsted with its rigorous, performance-centred inspections.

No doubt to their disappointment, it rarely turned out that way. The interests of parents and teachers, it transpired, were not generally opposed. On the contrary, there was widespread consensus around a liberal and humane regime in schools with a balanced curriculum meeting a wide range of individual needs. Academies would stunt the growth of a public expectation for transparency, accountability, accessibility and a degree of democratic participation in their

---

[1] Department of Education and Science1986. Education (No 2) Act 1986, London: HMSO

schools. Add to this the far greater opportunities to make an honest profit from a £50 billion business, what was there not to like about academies?

But there was still a problem. Over decades since the Second World War, in response to a growing demand for accountability, a complex system of public scrutiny had developed. It had even invaded parliament itself, with its twice-weekly Prime Minister's Question Time and the comprehensive select committee system. The public now assumed that local and national plans for developments in land use, transport services, industry, hospital provision and schools would be subject to, first, publicity and, second, consultation. As far as schools were concerned, you had to hold a consultation if you wanted to open one, and you had to hold a consultation to close one. If you wanted to change the nature of a school, if you wanted to alter the times of opening and closing the school day, or to change the holiday dates, you had to hold a consultation. The purpose of all this was to ensure both that local people knew what was happening to the organisations that served them, and that they had a chance to express a view about it which had, by law, to be taken into consideration.

This seemed such a confounded nuisance to people who wanted to change the whole school system, especially when most people seemed content with what they had. Other regulations similarly were there to protect the public. Nationally, planning laws and by-laws slowed down business development, acting as a brake on housing and industrial money-making. When the regulations required that you spend money on such socialist flummery as cheap housing for essential workers, or play spaces for children, or community centres for local people to enjoy, clearly the law itself had become far too responsive to the needs of the public. The decimation of legal aid, so that justice would be beyond the reach of the average person, the limitations on freedom of information, even the diminution of the centuries-old jury system would ensure that the money-makers were put back where they belong, at the front of the queue for human rights.

In 2010, the Liberal Democrats, whose support was essential to David Cameron's first period of office, had had no qualms whatsoever about ditching their unreserved manifesto commitment to the abolition of higher education tuition fees, in order to gain a sniff of power. But even they jibbed at supporting an unrestrained government capacity to remove schools from local authority oversight at will. So Michael Gove's 2010 Academies Act[2] included a procedure

---

[2]Department for Education (DfE) 2010: Academies Act 2010, London: Department for Education

whereby any school wishing, or even being forced by the DfE, to become an academy was required to conduct a public consultation.

What Is Expected Of A Consultation

The concept of consultation before significant decision-making is well-embedded in English law. In the past, it has perhaps been best known nationally in the form of government green papers, designed to promote discussions which will pave the way for legislation, and subsequent white papers, which are policy documents produced by the Government that set out their proposals for future legislation. Consultation procedures appear most frequently in the process of relevant authorities making planning decisions, on any matter from the building of a conservatory on the back of a house in a conservation area, to the decision on a third runway at London Heathrow Airport.

In education, local authorities have for many years been required to consult with the public over the proposed closure of, or significant changes in the provision of, maintained schools.

There are some general legal requirements for authorities to follow when undertaking a public consultation, *even where to do so is itself not legally required*. The following key issues are taken from the blog of David Wolfe of Matrix Chambers[3]:

"In short, anyone who undertakes consultation must let people know what they are proposing and why, give them a chance to comment, and conscientiously take into account their responses with an open mind before deciding whether or not to do what was proposed." Wolfe goes on to state unequivocally that a public body, having once decided to consult (even if not required to) "must comply with the following overarching obligations (unless detailed statutory rules supplant these):

- Consultation must be at a time when proposals are at a formative stage.
- The proposer must give sufficient reasons for its proposals to allow consultees to understand them and respond to them properly.
- Consulters must give sufficient time for responses to be made and considered.

---

[3] Wolfe, David. 2016. http://davidwolfe.org.uk/wordpress/archives/268

- Responses must be conscientiously taken into account in finalising the decision.

All of those are aspects of an overriding requirement for 'fairness'. The process must be substantively *fair* and have the *appearance of fairness*." (Original emphasis).

The Castle School's 'Consultation'

Castle Primary School governors met for the last time on the 26th February 2015. At this meeting, they went through the statutory requirements for conversion to academy status, including receiving a report on the school's consultation.

Following lobbying from the then National Governors' Association (NGA), the 2010 Act added at the last minute the requirement that a school hold a consultation before the signing of the funding agreement that sealed the deal and turned a school into an academy. The consultation had to be 'appropriate' – as any public consultation must be. That means that, once the governing body has agreed who it is appropriate to consult, it must genuinely seek to establish the views of the consultees; the consultees must be given sufficient and accurate information on the subject; and consultees who are chosen because they are representative of certain organisations or bodies must be told why they have been consulted, given time to respond, and given accurate addresses to which to respond. It must, in other words, meet the requirements of the general law on public consultations and must not be able to be perceived in any way as a merely token operation.

Advice from the NGA was that governing bodies should keep all those involved with the school (parents, pupils, staff, local authority, local community, neighbouring & feeder schools and diocese, if appropriate) informed of their plans throughout the process and that consultation should take place before the governing body took the formal resolution to apply for Academy status. Schools could take their time and ensure that they had carried out the process thoroughly and with due diligence. The recommendation was that the following groups should be consulted as a minimum: parents/carers of pupils at the school; for secondary, parents/carers of pupils in years 5 and 6 of any primary schools in the area; for primary, parents/carers of pupils offered a place at the school for the following September; staff working at the school and any staff due to be employed at the school from the following September; for secondary, pupils at the school; the wider local community. In addition, schools needed to consider whether there was any other organisation, person or group who should be consulted about the proposed conversion. This might include parish, town, district and county councils and councillors, the governing bodies and staff of feeder and receiving schools and any church representative, especially where schools concerned are faith schools[4].

One might have expected Castle governors to be particularly aware of this. Four years earlier, the local secondary school had had to rerun its consultation, because it had given only a very one-sided view of the costs and benefits of conversion, it had given insufficient time for consultees to consider the proposal, and the return email address for comments had been given incorrectly. Elsewhere, there had been at least one reported case of a school temporarily withdrawing its application for Academy status following a solicitor's letter which, amongst other things, challenged the way in which the school had sought parental views. The NGA had noted the judgement in R v Northumberland County Council, Ex Parte Parents for Legal Action Ltd – 18 May 2006 – which revolved around what constitutes proper consultation. The Judge commented that:

'The whole purpose of consultation is to inform the process before the public body formulates and publishes its final processes.' Although this judgement referred to statutory proposals in relation to a maintained school, as opposed to an application to convert to Academy status, it was the NGA's view that governing bodies would not go too far wrong if they bore it in mind when considering Academy status.[5]

The consultation, it was recommended, should take the form of a letter, which might refer the reader to a website for more information (but it should be recognised that access to the Internet was still not universally available). Separate meetings for parents and staff allow an exchange of views and clarification where there are queries, and some explanation and possibly consultation should take place with pupils. It was recommended that the consultation period should be open for 4-6 weeks.

---

[4] National Governors' Association. 2011. Guidance for NGA members on the Academies Act v10 180211. February 2011
[5] Ibid

Responses to a consultation *must* be formally considered before the funding agreement is signed, and the DfE requires a 'report' on the consultation to be provided prior to the signing of the Funding Agreement by the Secretary of State. This needs to be a simple account of what consultation took place and when. It is probably wise to ensure that governors and staff are not quoted in local media giving views about their own school's conversion before or during the period of consultation. The decision either way should certainly not be pre-empted by the headteacher or chair of governors – let alone by the local authority or the proposed sponsor. It is best if the consultation is even-handed and represents accurately, if not in fine detail, any points that have been raised on both sides of the argument. Consultees must be given both appropriate information and time to respond. Arrangements to collect responses must, of course, be accurate and accessible. The list of those to be consulted should probably be drawn up by the governing body. Where church schools are directly or indirectly involved, for example, local diocesan authorities should be consulted.

Thanks to the lobbying of the National Governors' Association at the time, the 2010 Act is quite unambiguous about the purpose of consultation. Section 5.2 states: *"The consultation must be on the question of whether the school should be converted into an Academy"*[6].

None of this advice, and not much of the legal requirements, appears to have been taken on board by the various authorities involved in the conversion of Castle School. Indeed, as Kulz shows: "these consultations have been criticised as toothless exercises. Former Secretary of State Michael Gove wielded this power with great controversy, publicly overriding parental opposition to conversions. Despite ninety-four per cent of parents voting 'no' to the conversion of a London primary school, it was taken over by the Harris Federation"[7]. With the senior minister of the DfE openly defying the spirit of the law, local politicians and officers were given the green light to follow suit, sometimes crossing over into blatant illegality.

What follows is a description of a procedure that provides a handbook for anyone wanting to silence opposing, or even merely questioning voices.

---

[6] DfE 2010 ibid

[7] Kulz, Christy. 2017. Factories for Learning: Making race, class and inequality in the neoliberal academy, Manchester: Manchester University Press p12

How To Block A Consultation

The key figures organising the conversion of Castle School were committed to its being done with the maximum efficiency and the minimum disruption. Those who opposed it – the governors, staff and parents – were critically hampered by a lack of information regarding their responsibilities. It seems that the governors did not formally agree to call on any experts or legal advisers except the Somerset County Council governance adviser who, of course, was employed by the organisation whose policy was to convert without delay any of their maintained schools placed in special measures.

So the field was left clear for the LA advisers, the DfE academy broker, and the officers of the Redstart Learning Partnership, the chosen Trust, the principal who became the chief executive officer of the Redstart Trust, and its chair. This last did not appear prominently in the minutes of meetings, and it seems that the initiative was very much led by the principal, soon to be designated the chief executive officer, on behalf of the Trust.

They were faced with a governing board that felt let down by the local authority, who they believed had responded inadequately to their appeals for help over the previous two years of leadership difficulties. More vocal and less restrained in the early stages, the parents and staff of the school could have presented a formidable challenge. However, they seem to have been unable to access advice on their legal status and rights. Three times, parents invoked the local press to present them as angry and let down, and anxious to protect their school. The staff chose less publicity, understandably as their jobs were on the line, but do not seem to have used professional association officers to advise them on anything other than their employment rights. The public at large played no part at all in what followed. The local paper, after a brief burst of publicity about the inspection and its outcomes around the end of the summer term of 2014, dropped the matter, perhaps as soon as the LA's position became clear. (The Western Gazette was at that time owned by the Mail group of newspapers, and avoided overtly political issues, rarely featuring local health or education and not addressing at all the increasingly swingeing cuts being imposed on local services by the new Conservative County Council).

So how did the LA, the DfE and Redstart Trust manage to neutralise the potential opposition?

1. They were well-prepared. Decisions had probably been made about the school's fate well before its Ofsted report was published (the first version having been sent back to be re-written, as it was thought to be too lenient, and did not recommend placing the school in special measures; eventually the report was published more than two months after the inspection visit). The DfE academy broker had already been speaking about possible target schools for the Redstart Trust to sponsor in June of 2014, and the Trustees had approved the process in July[8].

2. After this lengthy delay, the Ofsted report was published on the day before the end of the summer term. No timing could have been more helpful to the LA, leaving the parent movement no one to address for the best part of six weeks. The parents did their best, approaching local politicians and the constituency MP. He happened to be the Coalition government's Schools Minister, David Laws. Had he chosen to proffer support to the parents, he might have been invaluable, being on the inside track to the decision-making powers. Instead, one lobbying parent who met him suggested that Laws regarded the conversion, the identity of the sponsor and even the putative head of school, as already a done deal. Laws knew the eventual sponsor school well, as it was the nearest school to his own first constituency home, outside Chard. By contrast, the local Liberal Democrat councillor, John Bailey, an experienced governor himself, worked hard to ensure the parents got a hearing. However, his letter in the Western Gazette in November appealing for "a fair and representative consultation" seems to have been ignored.

3. This timing allowed the LA to have its act together at the very first exposure of the report to the parent and staff bodies. At a meeting for both groups, hastily called for the last evening before the end of the summer term in 2014, the LA primary adviser told the parents that there was no alternative to the academisation route: "Special Measures means academy conversion. I was there to reassure parents and focus them on supporting the school through a difficult period for the benefit of their children rather than expending time and energy on opposing the process," he has written[9]. This statement was deliberately worded to ensure that parents understood that the consultation process would offer

---

[8] Redstart Trust minutes, September, 2014

[9] email to the author

them no opportunity to express views contrary to the official policy decision. It thus undermined fatally, and at the earliest possible stage, the possibility of a consultation where any views other than those of officers of the LA, DfE and Redstart Trust would be heard.

First, it breached the requirement of the 2010 Act, that "The consultation must be on the question of whether the school should be converted into an Academy"[10]. Secondly, it stated unequivocally that any contention about the outcome would be harmful to the school and, therefore, to the children. No more powerful argument could have been made to parents and, even more so, staff. It was subsequently repeated, certainly by the interim headteacher, and probably by others throughout the following months. However, it has never been stated exactly how a reasoned and grown-up debate about the advantages and disadvantages of academy status and the identity of the proposed sponsors would have harmed the school or the children. It is a dramatic example of how the government would come to regard 'consultation'.

4. In November 2014, once the broker had put aside the governing board's grave reservations about the sponsor she had chosen, she wrote to the chair of Castle School governing board, copying in an LA officer and the Chief Executive of Redstart Trust, as follows:

"Communication to parents and staff needs to say that the governing body has decided to ask that the Secretary of State to agree (sic) to Castle joining the Redstart Learning Partnership. Please don't write anything that suggests that a decision has been made, as Ministers don't like it and both parents and staff would most likely suggest that consultation is therefore invalid. Reassure them that there will be full consultation after the SoS has given agreement in principle, and that you hope this will happen before the end of term, so that there can be consultation in January. It is also important that the message about the benefits of joining the Redstart Learning Partnership are (sic) flagged from the start and that all messages are very positive ones. Personally I would avoid the word 'sponsor' as it can be quite emotive."

This email is designed to ensure that the consultation will not meet statutory requirements, but will be a token exercise, with no opportunity

---

[10] DfE 2010 ibid Section 5.2

to discuss potential disadvantages or contrary views. It admits, in so many words, that the consultation will be invalid, because, as the broker states, the decision has already been made. It aims to coach lead officers in avoiding any possibility of participants expressing contrary views, and to stifle parents. It blatantly seeks to undermine the intention of the 2010 Act that the consultation must be on the question of whether the school should be converted into an Academy.

5. The governing board of the school gave to the public only very little, and that very generalised, information about the conversion process. The only information that was made available was put up on the school's website and comprised a general introduction to academy status from the DfE's own national website, in the form of "Frequently Asked Questions". This did not refer at all to the particular circumstances of Castle School, or to the LA policy of blanket conversion and its rationale. It did not address at all the key question of whether the school should be converted into an Academy. The governors never seem to have expressed any view about who should be consulted, although they were, nominally and legally, the body doing the consulting. Parents and the wider public were not informed about the consultation directly. Indeed, the general public were not informed at all until February of 2015, through an advertisement in a local free magazine, *after* the information meeting conducted by the CEO of the Trust, and *after* the governing board had made its decision.

6. The first 'consultation' meeting, held with the staff of the school on 14th January 2015, was conducted by the CEO of Redstart Trust. By this time, the headteacher, nominated by the CEO and previously her deputy at Redstart School, was already in post. The minutes of that meeting demonstrate that its purpose, and the purpose of the entire exercise, was not to allow the question of "whether the school should be converted into an Academy" to arise, but purely to inform the staff of the arrangements under the Transfer of Undertakings (Protection of Employment) Regulations (TUPE) document of the transfer of their employment to the Trust.

7. On the 16th January, the head of school, not the chair of governors, wrote to parents to invite them to an "information session", not a consultation meeting. There is no mention in this document of offering an opportunity

to parents to raise "the question of whether the school should be converted into an Academy". The meeting took place at 9.00 on a Monday morning – ensuring that working parents would be unable to attend. Again, the minutes of the meeting demonstrate beyond any doubt that its purpose was not to engage in a consultation, but to provide information. Again, it was conducted by the CEO of Redstart, not the school's governors. All information is given as events that "will happen", as opposed to "might happen if the conversion takes place". The public was not made aware of this meeting.

8. On and around the 1st February, 2015, an advert appeared in a local free magazine delivered to households in the neighbourhood of the school. The advert belatedly announced that "a consultation process with parents, carers and staff is currently being undertaken". It then invited anyone who "would like to be involved in this consultation process" to contact the head of the school – not the governing board. The wording appears designed to deter anyone with any knowledge of the process from engaging with it.

9. At its final meeting on the 26th February, the governing board of Castle School recorded that: "The Head Teacher set out the outcome of the consultation exercise which ran between 14th November 2014 and 26th February 2015 ... Notes of discussions and questions & answers have been made available. No issues have been raised that require further response." There are no known copies of this report, nor of the "notes of discussions", other than the information meetings noted above. There is therefore no evidence that such a report exists. The governing board is required by law to take into account, and to record that it has taken into account, the feedback from the consultation. There is no evidence that it did so.

10. A letter from the DfE in July 2015[11] reported that "The trust has undertaken that they (i.e. the sponsor) have completed such a consultation when signing the Funding Agreement". Although the accuracy of this statement was queried, the department does not appear to have conducted even the most cursory of investigations into it. It is possible therefore that an offence may have been committed by the

---

[11] DfE Ref: 2015-0028295

signatories of the Funding Agreement at this point. At this time, the DfE was struggling with the fallout of the Trojan Horse episode in Birmingham. Baxter reports that "There was a proven 'lack of inquisitiveness' within the Department of Education" regarding the origins of the scandal[12]. The habit of ignoring any inconvenient procedure that does not fit with the department's aims is well-entrenched.

What Has Happened To The 'Consultation' Since?

American novelist Alice Walker wrote that "The most common way people give up their power is by thinking that they don't have any"[13]. This appears to be true in Stoke sub Hamdon. Certainly, no one seems to have made a point of telling the governors, the parents or the wider community what rights they had when a local authority, supposedly acting in the best interests of the people, chooses to dispose of their local school. Such rights have progressively been removed from the public since the Conservative government took power after the 2015 election. One of their first acts was to put in place the Education and Adoption Act 2016. This Act removed the need for consultation where a school is to be forcibly converted to a sponsored academy. It was just the latest of an extraordinary explosion of education legislation since the Education Reform Act of 1988. As John Fowler wrote: "In 1988, the standard work on education law, Butterworths, could be found in one volume. Today, it occupies seven volumes."[14] Fowler goes on to suggest that this increasing complexity is in itself an assault on democratic participation: "Because very few people know the law, this has allowed Parliament, at the behest of successive governments, to hand vast powers to Ministers, which were previously exercised by local communities."[15]

As in the community of south Somerset, so at large, the powers that be were reluctant to make themselves available for challenge. That late section of the

---

[12] Baxter, Jacqueline. 2016. School Governance: Policy, Politics and Practices, Bristol: Policy Press p44

[13] As quoted in The Best Liberal Quotes Ever: Why the Left is Right (2004) by William P. Martin, p. 173

[14] Fowler, J. 2016. Viewpoint: Farewell Education and Adoption Bill, welcome the Act, February 26, 2016 (http://www.lgiu.org/category/education/

[15] Ibid

bill's passage where the Commons debate amendments made in the House of Lords had, in February 2016, a debating time of 39 minutes, during which the government minister introducing the Lords' amendments did not respond to the opposition front bench speaker.

It was at this point that the government made clear its view of the consultation process which had been built into the 2010 Act after the lobbying by the National Governors' Association, and which was now being discarded for 'forced' conversions. Nick Gibb, minister of state for schools, "said that people who question the government must be 'ideologically driven', and that the past practice of consultation with parents is a 'rigid approach that allowed vested interests to prevent sponsors [of academies] from taking decisive action."[16] That 'ideologically driven' members of the public must not be allowed to interfere with the smooth progress of the government's purist reforms is perhaps the most extreme example of ministers' chutzpah. It was overwhelmingly the key government line. In December 2015, Lord Nash, junior schools' minister, and himself a trust chair, stated his belief that consulting with parents on academy conversion is 'overly formal and inflexible', and that formal consultations 'unintentionally raise the temperature of debate, rather like when one gets lawyers involved in divorce settlements' and could be 'used to create delays'.[17] Instead of consultation, Nash said that academy chains "communicating" their plans to parents would provide 'robust assurances' to them.[18] I do not think it is unreasonable to suggest that the behaviour of Gibb, Nash and other ministers in dismissing any opposition to them as ideological and mischievous, and their preference for communication above consultation is redolent of totalitarianism.

This Act, seen in concert with the Prime Minister's earlier statement that the government intended to take all remaining maintained schools out of local authority control during the lifetime of the current parliament, drove many school leaders who had had no intention of converting to adopt the position of governors of Parrs Wood High School in Manchester. Against the very vocal and obstinate resistance of a well-organised parents' group, the governors argued that "the choice for a governing body is to wait to be academised or to academise on

---

[16] Ibid

[17] Whittaker, Freddie. *'Communication' but no consultation on conversion* Schools Week, 19 December 2015

[18] Ibid

its own terms."[19] The ongoing Parrs Wood debate demonstrates the impotence of the regulations around consultation:

"Yet the consultation process for Parrs Wood High School highlights the redundancy of such a process when a governing body is prepared to make decisions regardless of the opinions of those with an interest in the future of the school. A freedom of information request in relation to the consultation process revealed that 81% of staff, 75% of parents and 71% of outside agencies said no to academisation, still the decision to convert was taken. This gives a whole new meaning to the notion of forced academisation."[20]

Once again, it seems that the government's principal aim, though sometimes spectacularly failing, was to stifle opposition. This was not confined to the education sphere. In January 2016, the shadow minister for health, Justin Madders MP, tweeted in the course of a parliamentary debate on fracking: "I can't believe I am listening to a Tory MP arguing that local communities shouldn't have a say on fracking because it's controversial."[21] Clearly he had not been attending the education debates.

The 2010 Academies Act was superseded from early 2016 by the Education and Adoption Act, removing the need for consultation in the conversion of 'failing' and now 'coasting' schools. However, this was not yet the case when Castle School was earmarked for conversion.

With the publication of the White Paper 'Educational Excellence Everywhere'[22], the DfE proposed to drop any but the most cursory nod towards transparency and democratic (as opposed to professional) accountability, taking us back to before 1986, but without the protective buffer of local government. It creates a corporate provision of education, alongside similar destinations for health, transport, and the public utilities. As we saw, John le Carré suggested in 2005, "that Britain might be sliding towards fascism". Mussolini's definition of fascism was that "when you can't distinguish corporate power from governmental power, you are on the way to a fascist state."[23] In 2016, the DfE

---

[19] Ingram, Nicola. 2016. The conversation blog https://theconversation.com/forced-academisation-by-proxy-when-schools-have-little-choice-but-to-convert-56389#comment_93425) 24 March 2016

[20] Ibid

[21] Madders, Justin. 2016. @justinmadders, 18.1.2016, 19.57

[22] Department for Education. 2016. *Educational Excellence Everywhere,* London: The Stationery Office

[23] Jeffries, Stuart. 2005. *'I do give a damn',* The Guardian 6 October 2005

declared that "By the end of 2020, all schools will be academies or in the process of becoming academies. By the end of 2022, local authorities will no longer maintain schools."[24] Meanwhile, the white paper also proposed the removal of another key element in the democratic accountability of schools, by removing the requirement to have elected parent governors on school boards[25].

So What?

The Conservative government has succeeded in making education – perhaps for the first time in living memory – a significant political issue. In March, 2016, pollsters IPSOSMORI tweeted a table showing the main issues of concern in Britain.[26] Education & schooling had overtaken housing to enter the top five:

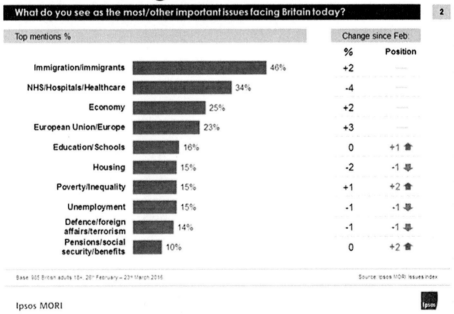

Issues Facing Britain: March

What do you see as the most/other important issues facing Britain today?   2

Top mentions %		Change since Feb	
		%	Position
Immigration/immigrants	46%	+2	
NHS/Hospitals/Healthcare	34%	-4	
Economy	25%	+2	
European Union/Europe	23%	+3	
Education/Schools	16%	0	+1 ⬆
Housing	15%	-2	-1 ⬇
Poverty/Inequality	15%	+1	+2 ⬆
Unemployment	15%	-1	-1 ⬇
Defence/foreign affairs/terrorism	14%	-1	-1 ⬇
Pensions/social security/benefits	10%	0	+2 ⬆

Base: 985 British adults 18+. 26th February – 23rd March 2016

Source: Ipsos MORI Issues Index

Ipsos MORI

---

[24] Department for Education. 2016. *Educational Excellence Everywhere,* London: The Stationery Office 4.6 p55

[25] ibid 3.30, p55

[26] Ipsos MORI, @benatipsosmori, April 2016

I have tried to show here what is meant in legal and political terms by a 'consultation'. It can be seen how, in the case of the forced conversion of Castle School, both the letter, in terms of the wording of the 2010 legislation, and the spirit, as described by David Wolfe QC, of the law were flouted, by the combined efforts of the DfE's agent, the 'academy broker', the local authority officers advising on the process, and the officers of the sponsor trust.

Against the facts of this single case study, we have seen how the intentions of the Conservative government since taking office in 2015 have been to dispense with consultation as a means of engaging the public with decisions on the provision of schooling.

Why Does The Conservative Party Hate Consultation?

The underlying thrust in getting rid of 'red tape', such as regulations and consultations, is to allow people with money to make more money, often at the social cost of the unmoneyed public. But the distaste for concepts of 'society' and 'community' is deep-rooted in many Conservatives, especially among those at the neoliberal end of the spectrum. Margaret Thatcher herself famously claimed in an interview with the magazine 'Woman's Own' in 1987 that there was 'no such thing as society. There are individual men and women and there are families.'[27]

Thatcher clearly learnt little from growing up in a small market town. More recent Conservative politicians, however, have very different backgrounds. During most of the decade from 2010, Britain has been governed by old Etonians. 65% of the cabinet in 2020 has been privately educated, many of them in boarding schools, some from an early age. One thing we know about private schools, and especially boarding schools, is that they create communities of their own. While comprehensive and grammar school pupils remain embedded in their geographical communities, their friendships, sports, hobbies, social lives and often careers are local and richly networked. Meanwhile, the moneyed create their own 'communities' with little connection with their geographical roots.

What understanding do such people have of connection to, a sense of belonging to, and a deep valuing of a town or a village, a city block or a suburb? And why, therefore, would they believe that such communities should have a say in those things that affect them, their residential areas, their commercial streets,

---

[27] *Woman's Own,* 31 October 1987

their schools and hospitals, their transport and their community services? The country's decisions become ever more centralised. Local radio and newspapers have been decimated in the course of the pandemic, with no government action to rescue them. Other community facilities are at severe risk – the places where people gather, libraries, meeting venues, theatres and cinemas, clubs and pubs. But these places serve no purpose in a nation focussed on business and on money.

The people have not so much lost their voice, as had it stolen from them.

Chapter 10
Language, Silence And
The Subversion of Democracy

One of my teachers at Columbia was Joseph Brodsky ... and he said, 'Look', he said, 'You Americans, you are so näive. You think evil is going to come into your houses wearing big black boots. It doesn't come like that. Look at the language. It begins in the language.'[1]

How The Truth Can Be Avoided

The voice of the people was silenced in the world of education through, first, the subversion of public consultation – as so plainly illustrated in the case of Castle School – and then the successive disposal of consultation and other protective regulations. These techniques were practised and developed in the Department for Education and have now been employed throughout government. Silencing opposing voices is necessary if you are to avoid criticism and leave the stage clear for you to be the only voice that can be heard.

George Orwell, writing in Horizon magazine in April 1946[2], was interested in both the conscious and the unconscious subversion of the English language. This applies to a range of words used in political writings, of which one – democracy – appears frequently in this book. In education, language has become increasingly political since the late 1970s. In Orwell's words, "political speech and writing are largely the defence of the indefensible ... Thus, political language

---

[1] Marie Howe, American poet and New York Laureate

[2] Orwell, G (1946) Politics and the English Language, in Collected Essays, Journalism and Letters of George Orwell (1968), London: Secker & Warburg, quotes from 1980 edition

has to consist largely of euphemism, question-begging and sheer cloudy vagueness"[3]

An example of the way in which education became an arena in which the language used set the tone for the political debate is given in Gann[4], and links the language to the emergence of a culture which saw success in 'failing' schools as being achievable only by exceptional individuals literally battling against the odds – Superheads and Hero Heads. That this happened towards the middle of the 1990s was no coincidence. Ofsted's inspections began in the early 1990s, the reports were published, and a debate about the 'naming and shaming' of schools burgeoned. The concept of failing schools had, until then, been rarely addressed. Where there were school scandals, they had tended to be about the school's philosophy being at odds with what the public or the media believed education should be about. Countesthorpe College in Leicestershire in the late 1960s was condemned for its democratic and egalitarian principles, not its examination results. Tyndale Primary School in Islington, the cause célèbre of the 1970s, similarly, had outraged the public and, more importantly, the media with its teaching methods, not its educational outcomes[5].

It is likely, then, that the growth of confrontational language about school achievement was encouraged by the publication of Ofsted reports and 'league tables' of school performance:

"The new focus on 'education, education, education', aspiring prime minister Tony Blair's three priorities for government post the 1997 general election, brought with it a proliferation of language previously reserved for the shock and awe of Gulf Wars. Some of the chapter headings of a book on inner London Hackney Downs Boys School, for example, are: "Gathering Clouds", "Crisis", "The 'Race War'", "Save our School", "To the Rescue", "The 'Hit Squad'" and "Picking up the Pieces" – a series of reading adventures that might be more in place in the history of a military campaign. In the final chapter of this sad account, the actual metaphor raised is one of hunting" [6]

---

[3] ibid p.741

[4] Gann, Nigel. 2016. Improving School Governance: How better governors make better schools, London: Routledge

[5] Ellis,T. McWhirter, J. McColgan, D and Hadow, B. 1976. William Tyndale: The Teachers' Story, London: Writers and Readers Publishing Cooperative

[6] Gann, ibid p117

As O'Connor et al observe: "Seeking out failing schools had, in the 1990s, become a rewarding pastime for politicians and for the media. A quarry run to ground could be publicly savaged and, if necessary, publicly done to death. The media can compete, as they did over other London schools in other boroughs, and in other parts of the country – notably The Ridings School in Halifax – to discover 'the worst school in Britain'."[7]

David (later Sir David) Winkley's account of his work at a Birmingham primary school is titled "Handsworth Revolution: The Odyssey of a School" – two somewhat mutually contradictory metaphors in one short title, but both arousing images of conflict and stress[8]. Wars and conflicts, of course, need heroes. Who better to fill that role than the rescuer of a failing school, the superhead?"

Prime Minister Blair had much to do with this – may indeed have been the midwife of confrontational education politics. During Thatcher's government of 1979-1990, the Labour Party had largely stood by the beleaguered public sector, although they hardly engaged with Thatcher's nomination of the miners as 'the enemy within', inflammatory as it was. But that historic alliance, forged in the white heat of Attlee's post-war reformation of public services, was shattered when Blair told the British Venture Capitalists Association in 1999 of "the scars on my back" from two years trying to reform the public sector. Not only was Blair engaged in a war, but he was doing so from the position of a leader receiving barely metaphorical floggings from his opponents.

The violent analogy continued to be used by the DfE. As time went on, we became used to attempts to enlist us – whoever we were – in wars on school failure, on incompetent teachers, on ineffective heads, on illiteracy and innumeracy.

Nevertheless, the years 2000-2010 were relatively quiet, as the government supported extra funding for schools and their buildings. It was the arrival of Michael Gove as Secretary of State in the coalition government of 2010 that heralded a far more combative attitude to the education profession. A journalist by trade, as we have seen – and a neoliberal Murdoch journalist believing in the efficacy of disruptive innovation – Gove was as ready to 'take on' the teaching

[7] O'Connor, M., Hales, E., Davies, J. and Tomlinson, S. 1999 Hackney Downs: The School that dared to Fight, London: Cassell p241

[8] Winkley, D. (2002) Handsworth Revolution: The Odyssey of a School, London: De la Mare

profession as Murdoch had been to confront journalists and printers in the 1980s and with, he no doubt hoped, similar radical and deep-seated impact. Taking on a trade union, though, is one thing – Thatcher had shown that that was possible. Alienating an entire profession – and one in which the public has a deep level of trust – is quite another. Gove labelled the bureaucrats, academics and teachers' unions 'The Blob', seeing them as thwarting the changes that had to be made if the UK were to have a world-class education service. The sole objective of that service, and the aspect he wished to see emphasised was, by his definition, that of competing in the international PISA league tables[9]. Gove's supporters took up the flag, with Toby Young – another journalist, and a Free School enthusiast – attacking Fiona Millar, an education writer for The Guardian, as "the blobbiest member of the Blob in the history of blobbery", for her advocacy of the abolition of tests and league tables. The apparently deliberate disaffection of the bulk of education professionals set up an irreconcilable conflict and streams of often – as above – juvenile polemic. Gove labelled his opponents "Marxist teachers hell bent on destroying our schools" and therefore "enemies of promise"[10].

Why did Gove light on this particular phrase? It originated with the twentieth century literary critic, Cyril Connolly. Connolly's 1938 work 'Enemies of Promise'[11] is a romantically nostalgic view of the self-defined decline in literary standards since his privileged Etonian and Oxonian youth. Connolly sets up a pre-First World War golden age view of English writing, and then proceeds to lambast, with limited evidence, the modernist slouches who are dragging English literature back into the Middle Ages, beset as they are by the appurtenances of wives, babies and the need to earn to eat. The self-appointed role of guardian of the culture is a mantle that Gove could adopt without a twinge of conscience. Gove cast himself, probably consciously, as the protector of educational standards, the Horatian hero defending the blob-beset bridge, the preservationist, and the conservationist. His preferences for the curriculum reflected such a position. Hence the dismissal of any teaching contrary to the heroic presentation of a beneficent British empire – a policy that would backfire resoundingly several years later in the Windrush scandal and its aftermath.

---

[9] "PISA is the OECD's Programme for International Student Assessment. PISA measures 15-year-olds' ability to use their reading, mathematics and science knowledge and skills to meet real-life challenges" https://www.oecd.org/pisa/

[10] MailOnline 23rd March 2013

[11] Connolly, Cyril. 1938. Enemies of Promise, London: Routledge and Kegan Paul

When the government's side, in what was now something like open warfare, wanted to engage with the enemy – on their terms and in their organs – they were happy to use such language. When they found themselves under attack from an articulate body often armed with hard research evidence, they retreated into banalities. It had become customary for awkward or inconvenient parliamentary questions to be brushed aside with meaningless responses. This now became common elsewhere in the world of politics. The tactic appears to be that, in answer to a question about some specific behaviour or piece of (often unassailable) data, the people in power respond with "opaque non-answers" – an example is given in the satirical and investigative magazine, Private Eye: "Treasury Minister Lord O'Neill of Gatley gave a platitudinous answer which merely recited the function and objectives of Entrust."[12]

The tactic is recognisable in an embarrassing episode when a group of senior Tory figures, including the Secretary of State for Transport and the local MP, went to visit a Cumbrian village which, in the 2015 December floods, had lost its river bridge. Turning up 20 minutes late and on the wrong side of the river, the group of (almost entirely) men in suits looked a little bemused. Later, a spokesperson, studiously avoiding addressing the real issue, said, "The Transport Secretary and Rory Stewart, Flooding Envoy for Cumbria, met local residents at Pooley Bridge during a day of visits to the area, seeing the impact first hand and how £40million of emergency government funding to repair damaged roads and bridges will help local communities recover as soon as possible."[13] While eminent visitors peered across the swollen floodwater at the villagers they had come to visit, no one quite had the guts to admit what had gone wrong, let alone to laugh about it. This kind of adult response has become quite foreign to the self-important dignity of these politicians. They must never confess to faulty decision-making, however trivial. They must never be laughed at. The only response must be an attempt, however blatant, at cover-up, and the answering of questions that have never been asked.

The DfE were to become arch exponents of this dismissive technique. In July 2016, in the midst of the greatest political turmoil for over half a century caused by the surprise referendum result and changes in party leaderships, a Labour MP asked the Secretary of State for Education, then Nicky Morgan, "whether her

---

[12] Private Eye, 18 December 2015 p41

[13] Smith, Mikey. 2016. Tory ministers branded 'plonkers' after arriving late to meet flood-hit locals on the wrong side of collapsed bridge, Daily Mirror, 4 January 2016

Department plans to publish a response to the finding of the National Union of Teachers survey published in March 2016, that 70 per cent of school leaders believed that a lack of school funding was affecting education standards in their schools." In the middle of the government-instituted chaos of enforced universal academisation and pre-Brexit government reorganisation, headteachers at least were still focusing on the basics of financing the management of schools. The Parliamentary Under-Secretary of State replied: "Funding for education is a priority for this government. As announced at the Spending Review, we have protected the core schools budget in real terms. This year the schools' budget will total around £40 billion."[14] How this funding crisis, so blithely and contemptuously dismissed by the government, continued to grow will be seen later. This was an early example of a now well-entrenched tactic of answering any question about funding with a huge figure that is being spent out of any context or meaning, with no historical comparisons and no spending 'per head' of population figure.

The government's handling of the Windrush scandal that came to light in 2017 had much more serious consequences:

"The Home Office came up with the same official response to every case I raised. The formulation was so enraging that it set my teeth on edge every time I saw it emailed through as part of a standardised reply to my queries. 'We value the contribution made by Commonwealth citizens who have made a life in the UK,' the Home Office declared in a statement about the refusal to give Sylvester Marshall free NHS radiotherapy as prescribed for his prostate cancer. 'We value the contribution made by Commonwealth citizens who have made a life in the UK,' an official statement began, in answer to my questions about why Michael Braithwaite had been sacked from his job as a special needs teaching assistant. Why was Sarah O'Connor facing bankruptcy, unable to work or claim benefits because no one believed she had a right to be here, despite fifty years in Britain? 'We value the contribution made by Commonwealth citizens who have made a life in the UK.'"[15]

Of course, as former Guardian editor Alan Rusbridger notes in his catalogue of devious behaviour from the 2019 election, there is also a place for downright lies:

---

[14] House of Commons, July 2016.

[15] Gentleman, Amelia. 2019. The Windrush Betrayal: Exposing the Hostile Environment, London: Guardian Faber pp187-188

"In an age of information chaos, you can get away with almost any amount of misleading. You can doctor videos; suppress information; avoid challenging interviews – but only after your opponents have been thoroughly grilled. You can expel dissenting journalists from the press pack or hide in a fridge. You can rebrand a fake 'fact-checking' website. In the end, none of it matters"[16]

Since the advent of Donald Trump onto the world stage, we have become almost inured to politicians who just lie. The Washington Post estimate that Trump made 13,435 false or misleading claims in his first thousand days in office. The lies about the potential of Brexit are well-known now, and Boris Johnson and Michael Gove were at the forefront of the most mendacious campaigning. The Conservative Party's opposition to immigration led to the peddling of the most egregious lies. For example, Theresa May would lie outright about the Human Rights Act and its role in protecting immigrants. "May poured scorn on the human rights-based appeals that she believed were complicating the deportation process, claiming that in one case an illegal immigrant could not be deported 'because – and I am not making this up – he had a pet cat.'" Of course, as even her colleague in the cabinet, the Justice Secretary agreed, this claim was 'laughable; complete nonsense'."[17] The then Home Secretary, responsible for the hostile environment which continues to kill innocent people years afterwards, was indeed making this up. But she never retracted it.

Once again, we are faced with a government claiming as unfortunate by-products outcomes that, like the crimes of academy leaders, were fundamentally bound up in the system as it was devised. "The Windrush scandal wasn't a mistake. It was the direct consequence of a harsh set of policies designed to bring down immigration numbers by ejecting people from Britain."[18] These blips are not blips.

So the politicians' creation and sustenance of the hostile environment, like the propaganda of the Leave campaign in the lead-up to the Brexit referendum, leant heavily on two deceits: the formulaic response, and the lie made up as evidence.

---

[16] Rusbridger, Alan. 2019. The election in the media: against evasion and lies, good journalism is all we have, The Guardian, 14 December 2019

[17] Gentleman, ibid p120

[18] Gentleman, ibid p277

What Somerset Learnt

This style of lazy evasion was replicated in Somerset by the leaders of the Redstart Trust and the officers of the local authority in response to polite but specific queries about their conduct of the public consultation and the appointment of lead staff in the run-up to the conversion of Castle School. Ignoring an email for over a fortnight, and only responding on receipt of a recorded delivery letter, an LA officer responded:

"Somerset County Council has operated a system of 'school to school' support based upon strong partnership working. This concept is based upon the original work by Hargreaves around Creating a Self-Improving School System (2010) and subsequent updates. For some time many school leaders and LA staff have worked across and beyond any differences between schools and academies to ensure that we respond rapidly and effectively to meet the developing needs of all children and young people in all Somerset settings."

The 'school to school' support cited here clearly had not been applied to Castle School when it was first needed or the school would not have found itself labelled as 'inadequate'. Not, perhaps, entirely coincidentally, the Redstart CEO, answering on behalf of both herself and the Trust's chair, replied in a similar vein:

"The Redstart Learning Partnership is committed to the principles of school to school support and is dedicated to effectively meeting the needs of all pupils within its schools."

The key elements here are a refusal to engage with a number of serious issues raised about their behaviour, in the belief, presumably, that the questioner will carry no weight and will go away if ignored or brushed aside.

Was this one of the techniques used with governors and parents in the process of the conversion? There is evidence in the minutes of meetings to suggest that this was the case, and in the wording of the public advertisement about the consultation. There is also clear evidence of the awareness of the significance of the language used. The nomination of the Redstart Trust as the sponsor trust was a decision by the DfE broker and this was to brook no opposition. The incapacity of the governors to question this was as great as their incapacity to challenge the whole conversion process. The governors were told very clearly that, if the broker's proposal were rejected, "they would be disbanded and replaced by an Interim Executive Board."[19]

The DfE broker, having then, unsurprisingly, secured the 'unanimous' agreement of the governing board to the sponsorship by Redstart Trust, despite their "grave reservations" that the Trust's ethos "in practice does not fit in with Castle School", gave the governing board the advice quoted (in Chapter 6, page 4) which is worth repeating here:

"Please don't write anything that suggests that a decision has been made, as Ministers don't like it and both parents and staff would most likely suggest that consultation is therefore invalid. Reassure them that there will be full consultation after the SoS has given agreement in principle, and that you hope this will happen before the end of term, so that there can be consultation in January. It is also important that the message about the benefits of joining the Redstart Learning Partnership are flagged from the start and *that all messages are very positive ones. Personally, I would avoid the word 'sponsor' as it can be quite emotive.*" [My italics]

Clearly there is going to be no opportunity to present the negative side of this arrangement in any consultation. There is not going to be a balanced approach in an impartial process, but an exercise, not even in persuading people, but in reconciling them to a decision already signed and sealed. In fact, this email is so neatly presented that it arouses the suspicion that it may be quoting from a DfE handbook for brokers, or at least recalling some piece of training delivered to them.

In November 2014, one of the country's eight Regional Schools Commissioners was telling the National Governors' Association annual conference that "the DfE doesn't talk about forced academisation any more" although "in reality, the pace of forced academisation was growing". As one of those involved at Castle School remarked, "There was nothing partnership about it." Staff, including teaching assistants (TAs) and other support staff, were in their own words 'summoned' to Redstart to be told how to do their jobs, however experienced and well regarded they were.

In Castle School's case, the DfE broker is actually telling the sceptical governors not to tell parents what they really think about this diktat. Far from deflecting any "emotive" content, in the November meeting at which governors

---

[19] Governing Body minutes

were the turkeys required to vote for Christmas, one governor was so upset about the whole process, and the department's behaviour, that she had to leave for ten minutes to recover herself before voting the way she was being instructed.

Is it at this point, one may ask, that the manipulation of language ceases to be a legitimate persuasive tactic, and becomes outright dishonesty? At what point does such dishonesty become systemic in a government department?

We have seen how the "full consultation" promised by the DfE turned out. But the advertisement cited by the chair of governors as representing the school's effort to engage the wider community consisted of an invitation to visit the school, and the information that the governors had voted in favour of applying to become an academy sponsored by the Redstart Learning Partnership. The request to contribute is not one to express an opinion – how could it be when the *only* source of information is the DfE's own website and its own answers to 'frequently asked questions' about its own flagship policy? – but invites people "to be involved in this consultation process". This is not, perhaps, a prospect to reassure anyone wanting to express a contrary opinion. In the event, this advert had little impact on the "full consultation in January" promised by the broker, as it did not emerge until the February edition of the local free magazine, by which time the sponsor's staff had been in post at The Castle for over a month. The die had already irrevocably been cast.

Of course, no one would be surprised to hear politicians using language tricks to persuade the public that their policies are the right ones for the country. One might wish that, once they had achieved office, they would be a tad more dispassionate, and look at evidence produced by experts to help determine their policies. Such days may be long gone. But it is something of a shock to find civil servants – even such lowly ones as academy brokers – recommending the use of such tricks to headteachers and governors of small village primary schools. The third school to join the Redstart Trust was a Church of England school, which meant that one of the trustees represented the Bath and Wells Diocesan Board of Education. It might be hoped that the ethics of that school helped the governors to avoid the most egregious examples of behaviour displayed over Castle school. As it happened, the diocesan employee who had approved the decision to 'outsource' a church school to Redstart rather than take it into the diocesan multi academy trust soon left her post with the diocese. Happily, she quickly found herself another berth with an impressive job title, as Director of Operations – at the Redstart Trust.

As we saw, despite the misgivings of its governors and the absence of any genuine consultation, Castle Primary School became a constituent member of the Redstart Trust on the 1st March, 2015, managed from some fifteen miles distance in Chard, along with a second forced conversion, Buckland St Mary Church School. Sometime in the autumn 2015 term, someone at the Redstart Trust decided that they wouldn't wait for the next Ofsted visit, likely to be some years away, to start promoting their undersubscribed school. Customarily, schools should not use Ofsted terms to describe themselves unless that was how they were graded at their most recent inspection. But Castle School bosses awarded themselves an early Christmas present by claiming, on its website and in adverts in a local magazine delivered free to houses in surrounding villages, to provide "an outstanding education for all."

Presumably this was an attempt to get parents to choose the school for their children in September, 2016, in preference to twenty other nearby primary and infant schools that were genuinely graded as 'good' or 'outstanding'. While misleading the local community, the Trust seemed oblivious to the need to keep fellow professionals onside, as the other schools, eleven of which were undersubscribed, had all forborne to use advertisements to tempt parents away from other schools. These schools even eschewed the now ubiquitous 'boaster poster', strung up outside the school to proclaim its finest qualities.

The Advertising Standards Authority had, three years earlier, been contacted about a new Free School in Suffolk which advertised itself as 'outstanding' despite not even having opened. Here in Somerset, the ASA recognised that a complainant had 'a valid point', and undertook to "instruct the advertiser to remove references to 'outstanding' unless they relate to a specific official rating that has been awarded, and ensure that they make clear that wording relating to the quality of the school is an opinion and does not imply an official rating. We will get an assurance from them that they will make these changes." The advert did not reappear and the word was removed from the website home page. Shortly afterwards, a yet to be opened local primary school had the 'outstanding' word applied to leaflets circulated in Yeovil, just down the road from Stoke -sub Hamdon. This was being sponsored by an already 'outstanding' primary school, the leadership of which must have assumed a right to apply it to any school it had anything to do with. Of course, state-funded schools are new to advertising, and the words "legal, decent, honest and truthful" may have yet to gain a meaning for them. This leaflet arrived in the offices of the local paper, who quickly involved the ASA, despite the headteacher somewhat disingenuously denying "that the use of the word was meant to have any reference to Ofsted."[20]

Five years on, the Home Office was forced to remove a promotional post describing "the department's efforts to deport people with no right to remain in the UK and attacked 'activist lawyers' for frustrating the process, prompting a furious response from barristers and solicitors."[21] So the government was still trying it on in the Covid-19 summer of 2020. Anyone opposed to its policies and anxious to ensure the rule of law, is an 'activist' or, in education, has a 'vested interest'.

Those challenging the DfE in 2015 based much of their argument on the evidence that "there is no link between academy status and automatic school improvement"[22], showing a touching faith in the idea that evidence might impact on policy-making in the Department for Education. In the Lords debate, the former Labour Education Secretary, Estelle Morris, "said the trend over the past twenty years had been towards 'giving parents a louder voice', and warned that the government would have to make a 'strong case' to exclude them from the decision-making on converting schools."

Apparently not. But in the next section, we will look at whether Estelle Morris was right to make this claim or whether, in fact, the rowing-back on the democratic accountability of schools has been happening over a much longer period.

The Power Of The Job Title

"Glittering prizes of dameships and knighthoods, some to be later ignominiously stripped, became common. When the Independent Academies Association met (in 2013), there was hardly a plain headteacher to be seen among the principals, executive heads, chief executives and operating officers."[23]

The term 'executive headteacher' began to be used widely from 2010 onwards, usually, but not exclusively, to describe headteachers of more than one school, often with a local 'head of school' in place on site. But the National Governors' Association, in January 2016, found that the term could also describe

---

[20] Western Gazette, 26 April 2016

[21] Grierson, Jamie. 2020. Home Office wrong to refer to 'activist lawyers', top officials admit, The Guardian 28 August 2020

[22] Academy plans survive Lords challenge, BBC website, 17 December 2015

[23] Gann, ibid p119

a head of a single school or a head responsible or accountable to more than one governing board. During negotiations with Castle School in November 2014, the headteacher was described as the Principal of Redstart Primary School. After conversion, she became a Chief Executive Officer – a rather grand title perhaps for a head of schools with around 700 primary age children. Castle School's near neighbour, Stanchester Academy, the local secondary school, which converted to academy status in 2011, had taken, by March 2016, to referring to "Principal Beardmore" – an American approach which may not have been used before in this country. Since staff of an East Anglian-based academy chain headed up by a Dame claimed that she insisted on the title being used at all times, it may be that, in a profession with a long history of not taking its leadership too seriously, some self-regarding leaders may find themselves subjects of ridicule rather than fawning admiration.

The End Of The Consultation

What this series of events demonstrates is that, while rhetoric may be the power to persuade, officialese has become the power to evade. Following the meagre Tory majority established in May 2015, any pretence about community participation in their schools was dropped. Parents were now to be told about, not involved in, their children's schools.

The DfE has now dispensed with any but the most cursory nod towards transparency and democratic (as opposed to professional) accountability, taking us back to before 1986, but without the protective buffer of local government. It is creating a corporate provision of education (and health, transport, public utilities, etc.) where it has become difficult to distinguish between corporate power and governmental power. As Russian Bolshevik politician Nikolai Bukharin projected and Mussolini observed, once that happens, you are on the way to a fascist state.

Using Silence And Secrecy: A Footnote To Language

The 1970s witnessed powerful movements for democracy and transparency, including the growth of the consumer movement, and demands from an increasingly better educated and informed public that politicians be more open and consultative. Until that time, the right of central and local government to get on with its business uninterrupted, other than by the occasional need to hold an election, had been challenged only rarely. "But, irrespective of the political

144

complexion of the government, there was an underlying culture of secrecy that permeated the state apparatus in the 1970s, founded upon the twin assumptions that the vast behemoth of government was there to benefit the people, and that it was not for the people so benefited to question its mysterious workings. It was certainly not for journalists to challenge those assumptions or to pry into those workings."[24] Thomas Grant is writing of the notorious ABC case of 1978, where two journalists and a low-ranking former soldier, were charged with high-level espionage offences for revealing 'secrets', all of which were available from published sources. The use of phone-tapping and jury-vetting were addressed by the government-selected counsel for the prosecution as being 'normal in cases of this sort', while the judge agreed that checks such as jury-vetting were 'perfectly proper in cases like this'. It is the use of language such as 'normal', 'proper' and 'cases like this'[25], based on untested assumptions about what is normal or proper, that offers such threats to anyone challenging the status quo.

This held true at this time at the local as well as the national level. Governors and parents in 1970s schools largely knew their place, and governors were appointed anyway in an opaque way, and could be removed similarly if they rocked the boat. It now seems possible that we are returning to those days in education, though the significant decision-making bodies are not governmental, and therefore no longer subject on occasion to some electoral accountability. Instead, they are now corporate and answerable only to themselves.

We have seen how officers of the DfE and Somerset County Council sought to silence any potential opposition by the robust use of language. The chair of Castle School governors had been extremely helpful in the early stages of this research, quite properly supplying minutes and other documents. Once the Redstart Trust had taken over, he became chair of the new local governing board, which is effectively a committee of the Trust's Board of Directors. There were to be no representatives from the two schools joining the trust on this decision-making body. He stood down altogether soon after but, when asked in December 2015 if he would take part in a discussion about the conversion process in retrospect, he replied: "As I do not represent Redstart I have been asked not to comment to ensure confidentiality is maintained." It is of course unclear what confidentiality he is trying to protect here. The chair knew about the Castle perspective, and was aware of what had been published, so Redstart officials had

---

[24] Grant, Thomas. 2015. Jeremy Hutchinson's Case Histories, London: John Murray
[25] Ibid, pp 312-3

no right or power to restrain him. At the time he would have been speaking about, he was the chair of a democratic body responsible for a school maintained by the local authority. He could not be restrained from speaking truthfully about what had taken place, provided he did not breach the regulations governing the confidentiality of certain items in governing body minutes such as matters concerning individual staff or pupils. Indeed, he was subject to the DfE's guidance, that every school "decides its policies and conducts its day-to-day operations in a way that stands up to public scrutiny"[26]. This is underlined in Ofsted's guidance, where governing boards are required to be "transparent and accountable, including in recruitment of staff, governance structures, attendance at meetings and contact with parents."[27]

This could be another worrying trend. Maintained schools have a duty of transparency to the public, along with their local authorities, but trusts have used the argument that they have to protect commercial sensitivities as corporate bodies, and therefore cannot be required by Freedom of Information laws to release certain documents. Even the LA, when presented with a formal complaint based on evidence that there may well have been breaches of the law in this conversion process – evidence which it had taken months to collect – decided that, since "Somerset County Council will normally only consider complaints that fall within 12 months of an incident ... (this) complaint does not fall within the Council's timescale, so we are unable to deal with your complaint."[28] That a suggestion of possible legal impropriety might be regarded by the LA as 'normal' is, perhaps, remarkable.

Despite requirements of transparency, the LA, the DfE, and the Redstart Trust all used secrecy, usually branded as 'confidentiality', in order to keep governors and parents in the dark. This reached such an extent, as we have seen above, that governors were unclear when and how a sponsor had been decided on by the DfE, despite being promised participation in an open discussion. Neither were they told how a new head of school had been lighted on, with no advertisement, no application process and no competitive interview, despite

---

[26] Department for Education. 2015 The governance handbook: For trustees of academies and multi-academy trusts and governors of maintained schools, November 2015, p110

[27] Ofsted (Office for Standards in Education, Children's Services and Skills). 2015. School Inspection Handbook (issued 28th August 2015), London: The Stationery Office

[28] Letter from Somerset County Council 'Head of Outcomes and Sufficiency' [sic], 22 June, 2016

having explicitly been promised that they would have a say in a "fair process". Parents were more than once warned that exercising their lawful rights might harm the school and the children, without explaining what this harm might constitute. In fact, the school did lose a number of children to other local schools that autumn, which suggests that the secrecy might have rebounded on the school. Parents on the whole seem to value being confided in and told the truth, not sheltered from it in a patronising way. It was presumably this drop in numbers that led to the decision, taken we do not know where, to publish the mendacious advert leading to admonishment by the Advertising Standards Authority.

Secrecy surrounded the writing and publication of the original Ofsted report, and how it was rewritten, the process leading to the broker's choice of sponsor, the sponsor's choice of headteacher as well as the conduct of the consultation, and this all contributed to a perception of conspiracy. Secrecy and silence are weapons of power. They include a favoured few and exclude everyone else. This paternalistic style of management, being explicit about who knows best, has the power to raise quite atavistic emotions. Secrecy pleases those people inside the tent and frustrates those outside. People half inside, like governors, perhaps, might have felt slightly privileged by knowing more than parents, but were intensely frustrated by knowing considerably less than the actual decision-makers – hence presumably the unwillingness of so many to discuss it afterwards. So secrecy and silence here were used to push people away but, when it suited decision makers, it could be used to recruit and enfold those whose knowledge might damage the process or the people manipulating it[29].

It is therefore possible that the use of secrecy and the manipulation of language as weapons of power are not aberrations of the multi-academy trust system, used only by those wanting to pervert it to their own ends, but are endemic to its structure and included in its design to achieve the outcomes aimed at by its creators. It is a characteristic of corporatism, rather than of local, democratically accountable government.

When language and silence are used as weapons, power is enhanced, and transparency and accountability are threatened. The next chapter looks at how democratic accountability in our schooling system is being diminished in the interests of centralised decision-making and corporate authority. The final

---

[29] See, for example, Costas, Jane & Grey, Christopher, 2016 Secrecy at Work: The Hidden Architecture of Organizational Life, Stanford, Stanford University Press

chapters consider the exercise of power and powerlessness, and what corporatisation may mean for the future of English schooling.

Chapter 11
Democratic Accountability in Schools
Whose School Is It Anyway?

The last thirty years of the twentieth century saw substantial developments promoted by the various governments in the public's participation in state education, and in schools' accountability to parents. What was this for? Why did it happen? And now, why has it been snatched away by a neoliberal Conservative government which disdains the public and prefers the embrace of big business? How did people and communities lose any say in how their schools are run?

Formal public involvement in our schools is an issue that has been around since the beginning of the state funding of education in the nineteenth century. It runs parallel to, and often merges with, the history of school governance. Conservatives, capitalist marketeers and neoliberals have seen it as the exercise of consumer rights over a paid-for commodity; socialists might see it as the exercise of state control over a nationalised provision for the public good; radicals, perhaps, see it as the engagement of communities in one of their own support services, reflecting the ultimate ownership of the provision and the right to determine its shape and purpose. From 2010, the party in power in England chose to see the public as customers paying for a privatised product in which they could expect to have little personal investment.

In the customary British constitution-less muddle, the history of public participation in educational governance displays an almost complete absence of rationale and principle, the predominance of compromise and the grasping of any convenient (or sometimes inconvenient) zeitgeist.

In the absence of coherent philosophies of public engagement, the three major political parties of the nineteenth and twentieth centuries toyed with various cautious models as suited their political convenience, until a consensus around a perceived national need for global competitiveness formed in the early 1990s. Since then, public involvement has been whittled away, as the views of politicians on that shape and purpose have drifted further away from those of parents and teachers.

The political consensus on the need for the ever-improving 'performance' of young people from two to twenty-two now appears embarrassingly distant from the priorities of the general public and most education professionals. The politicians' answer to this is to, as far as possible, remove lay people from educational governance and to replace them with utilitarian 'skilled' (and if necessary, paid) practitioners who accept and unquestioningly pursue the current political definition of 'quality' schools. In January of 2016, the first academy chain to openly embrace this position was E-ACT. Previously known mainly for losing control of ten of its schools for poor management, and for a 'culture of extravagant expenses' for its trustees, directors and staff[1], E-ACT decided that the 'challenge' part of the job description for its local governors should be passed back up to the national board, and that local governors would now be 'academy ambassadorial advisory bodies'. Removing the planning, monitoring and evaluating roles from governors means that they can no longer really be called governors. As ambassadorial advisers, they become unofficial "supporters' clubs"[2].

In 1999, it was suggested that a governing board which displayed democratic accountability could show that it was "managing itself fairly and equitably, and encouraging stakeholders to hold it accountable for its actions and the performance of the school"[3]. Accountability is a word much used but more rarely defined. In 2014:

the then chair of the parliamentary select committee on education told a conference of governors and academics that he was 'less interested in democratic accountability than in quality'. This apparently throwaway

[1] Burns, Judith. 2013. 'Culture of extravagant expenses' at academy group, BBC News, 17 May 2013

[2] Coughlan, Sean. 2016. Academy Chain to scrap governing bodies, BBC News, 19 January 2016

[3] Gann, Nigel. 1999. Targets for Tomorrow's Schools: A Guide to Whole School Target-Setting for Governors and Headteachers, London: Falmer Press

comment, however, betrays a commitment to centralised thinking and planning that undermines the whole accountability process of school governance. Quality in schools, as we see, is effectively defined outside the democratic process. There was no public commitment in 2010 by either of the coalition parties to a policy about the widespread academisation of the schooling system. No-one – neither lay, professional nor academic – was invited to express views about this and, indeed, those opposed to it were characterised as 'the Blob' and as 'enemies of promise'.

Governance of schools appears to hold both democratic and professional accountability, by the process of election to the board by stakeholders, and by accountability for the performance of the school, upwards to the Secretary of State, and downwards to the headteacher. But much of this accountability is spurious. Academy chains and stand-alone academies have largely internally appointed and potentially self-perpetuating trustees and boards of governors, and Ofsted, the DfE and, for maintained schools, local authorities have the powers to remove governors, to remove schools from trustees, and to remove headteachers from schools. How sustainable is this model?

As Wilkins suggests[4], perhaps: "The definition of good governance should be expanded to take account of the different mechanisms by which schools aim to enhance local accountability through greater stakeholder engagement and the creation of student-, teacher- and parent-led feedback systems, including councils, forums and Friends' Associations" (though we might want to expand 'teacher-led' to staff-led')[5].

Not only had no party committed to wholesale academisation in any manifesto, even the 2015 Conservative manifesto went no further than promising to "turn every failing and coasting secondary school into an academy and deliver free schools for parents and communities that want them"[6]. As we saw in chapter 1, the decision to require all schools to become academies was announced by the

[4] Wilkins, Andrew. 2014 Governing Schools: The Role of Community and Professional Volunteers
https://www.academia.edu/8901867/Briefing_Paper_for_ESRC_SASE_project_-_findings_and_recommendations

[5] Gann, Nigel. 2016. Improving School Governance: How better governors make better schools, London, Routledge 2nd edition p192

[6] Conservative Party manifesto, 2015

then chancellor of the exchequer in March 2016, confirmed in a white paper later that month, and then withdrawn less than two months later.

This chapter addresses some ideas about democratic accountability in general, and how they might apply to school governance in England. At the end, I will suggest some specific behaviours that we might expect to see in a governing board that seeks to make itself democratically accountable.

The concept of a public service responding to democratic accountability – that is, being answerable to all or some members of the public intended to be recipients of that service – was addressed in 1942 by the politician most associated with the founding of the National Health Service, Aneurin Bevan: "Representative government itself was government of the experts by the amateurs and always had been."[7]

A Brief History of The Democratic Accountability of Schools

Governance has been a major arena through which state-funded schools have been accountable to their communities. Between 1870 and 1902, local school boards were directly elected (by a limited electorate), and responsible for the appointment of governors for schools, except where the church took this responsibility. But from 1902, when local councils became the local education authority, they became ultimately responsible for school performance. They reserved the right to appoint all school governors, except in church schools, and as time went on, usually did so according to the ratio of the representation of political parties. And so this continued to be the case until 1980, when the new Conservative government started to become exercised about the rights of parents. As Joan Sallis, a member of the Taylor Committee on the government of schools[8] later wrote: The 1980 Act "was a delayed and diluted response to the Taylor recommendations."[9] But the act made statutory for the first time some elements of the accountability of schools to the public that the more enlightened local authorities had been applying for some years. It reduced the amount of grouping of schools under one governing body; it required two parent governors and one

---

[7] Foot, Michael. 1997. Aneurin Bevan 1897-1960, London: Victor Gollancz p182

[8] Department of Education and Science (DES). 1977. A New Partnership for our Schools (The Taylor Report), London: HMSO

[9] Sallis, Joan. 1988. Schools, Parents and Governors: A New Approach to Accountability, London: Routledge, p.133

or two teacher governors (and later, non-teaching staff) to be elected by secret ballot; it allowed headteachers, if they wished, to be governors. In the attached regulations, governors were required to elect a chair annually, and any governor could be a chair, except employees of the school. Governors could no longer serve on more than five boards, governors could request special meetings, and agenda and minutes had to be available to parents, staff and pupils. "Finally, the regulations made it clear that governors should only be constrained from taking part in any discussion by direct pecuniary interest ..."[10]

Sallis sums up this act and its regulations by underlining its significance, for all its shortcomings, in shifting the relationship between schools and their public: "The Act and the Regulations were clearly intended to bring in a more open and participatory style of school government, and there is no doubt that there was an increase in awareness of the ways in which things were done"[11].

Around this time, an in-depth study of the operation of governing bodies was undertaken at Brunel University. Kogan et al[12] identified four main views of governing body function – the accountability model, the supportive model, the advisory model and the mediating model. The report suggested that the governing bodies studied moved uneasily between these four models – perhaps because, before the 1986 and 1988 Acts, there was little definition of their role, and, without local management of schools, little meaningful for them to do. Keith Joseph's 1984 Green Paper for the Conservative government[13] contained the most radical proposals yet, suggesting that parents should have an overwhelming majority on governing bodies. Hardly anyone liked this – it projected a view of the governors as, as Sallis suggested, "a sort of consumer council"[14]. Even active parent groups rejected the idea as they accepted the view proposed by the Taylor Report, of governing boards as stakeholder partnerships, with parents, staff, local authority members and the local community working together in relative harmony. Joseph's model seemed to encapsulate the worst elements of what could happen in the governance of public sector organisations. It assumed an

---

[10] ibid p134

[11] ibid p134

[12] Kogan, M., Johnson, D., and Packwood, T. 1984. School Governing Bodies, London, Heinemann

[13] Department of Education and Science. 1984. Parental Influence at School, London: HMSO, May 1984

[14] Ibid, Sallis p 135

adversarial relationship between consumers and providers, while offering the consumer only an advisory role with no real or effective power.

In the event, the Taylor stakeholder model was more or less the one selected for enactment in the 1986 Act, strengthened considerably as it was by the 1988 Act establishing, following pilots in local authorities such as Hertfordshire and Cambridgeshire, the local management of schools, and giving the new governing bodies significant powers.

But were these stakeholders meant to be 'representative'? It seemed that much of the discomfort of professionals and politicians with apparently handing over real power to the stakeholder partnerships centred around the fact that parent and staff governors were to be elected by their constituencies. Politicians, professional associations and many headteachers, fell over themselves to deny that these governors might be there to *represent* the bodies that elected them although, of course, the very process of election suggests – indeed, determines – that the elected person may represent the views of their electors. If not, why go through the process? Those working with governors spent many wearisome hours explaining the difference between representatives and delegates – governors necessarily, whether elected or appointed from a constituency, being the former while not being the latter. It does not seem to be a difficult concept to grasp – after all, the model offered by members of parliament is pretty easy to assimilate. What it assumes is that the successful candidate will communicate with the electoral body after election, sharing with them the topics being discussed and, in some circumstances, taking their views to the governing body, expressing them, and feeding back the results. It does not imply that the elected governor should support those views, let alone vote for them. The key is this – that the governor always acts and votes in what *they* see as the best interests of the school and the children, while ensuring that their governor colleagues are aware of the feelings, and the strength of those feelings, of people who are going to be affected. So it's not complicated, and the fear that seemed to be engendered by the mere use of the word 'representative' seemed quite disproportionate.

When you are invited to vote for someone – a politician, national or local, for example, or a school parent or staff governor, a police commissioner, a trade union official – in preference to someone else then, unless you are particularly perverse (or playing a tactical game, perhaps), you are going to choose someone who you think is going to vote for things and say things in ways nearest to how you would vote or speak if you were there. In other words, you choose them as the candidate more likely to represent your views than any of the other candidates. When this happens – even for those people who did not vote for them (that's democracy) – this person becomes a representative. It therefore becomes that elected person's responsibility to ensure that they know what the people who could have voted in the election are likely to think about key issues, take responsibility for communicating those things and reflecting them in discussions, and for feeding back information – not, of course in every fine detail, but in key strategic decisions, and usually in general terms rather than in particular. This is a major (but not the only) way of ensuring that governors know what a parent or a staff body might make of their decisions, even if they disagree with them. This is what happens in a representative democracy. The clue is in the word 'representative'. It's what we expect of our members of parliament, and the voting process goes some way towards ensuring that more people in the voting body are likely to be happy with the way the successful candidate behaves than not. The representative is not a delegate and should not attempt to vote as the majority of their electors would want to, but should reflect the range of views so that, when the governing board makes a decision, it does so in the best knowledge of its impact on that body.

The whole process of voting is designed to ensure this relationship between a body and its 'stakeholders'. Elected governors are now rarer beasts. They provide a key assurance between the people who are responsible for an organisation and the people who use it or work for it, that the voices of the latter will be heard by the former. Otherwise, we are left purely with 'advisory' or 'ambassadorial' bodies – courtesy bodies who can be ignored or who can end up in an adversarial relationship because they have no absolute right to be heard at the main table where sometimes confidential matters are discussed and often important decisions are made about the strategic direction and priorities of the organisation. Their very exclusion from this arena becomes a source of suspicion and possible antagonism, separating those with power from those without.

Voting also makes more likely another key characteristic of an accountable body – that it embraces dissenting views. Trusts who largely, or perhaps entirely, comprise appointees, may be tempted to avoid awkward or opposing members. But such people offer the very essence of debate, that different views are reflected from different perspectives. Democracy requires strong oppositions as well as representative governments, and schools benefit from a similar approach.

So voting is important for most school governor positions. And there is a clear link between the act of voting and the expectation of representation.

Why is it important? Its significance predates the current debate and goes back to the earliest days of stakeholder governance in schools. Wary as they were of parents and staff having a say in the oversight of schools, some headteachers, and many LA officers, were determined to emasculate non-professionals. So the best way to do this was to deny them any right to speak for their constituencies. In fact, of course, the power of speaking for the body of parents, or for the body of staff, was often the factor that gave lay governors their legitimacy. They were likely to be inexperienced compared to LA politicians, in both the subtleties of educational management and the various obscure rituals of meetings and organisational conduct. Subverting the voices of parents and staff became common practice for some professionals, especially when they colluded with local politicians. This has become less common as more senior school leaders have come to recognise that most – not all – parents are likely to be allies, not adversaries, where politicians are most likely to be the common enemy. Indeed, the leading headteacher and school staff associations and unions, faced with widespread enforced academisation, happily joined together with governors and parent representative groups to attack the anti-democratic intentions of the government: "We believe the (2016 Education and Adoption) Bill focuses too much on school types, and will silence the voices of parents, governors and local authorities in respect of both school standards and the right to a voice over the future of their local school."[15]

To deny the representativeness of parent and staff governors is to undermine the capacity of governors to embody the democratic accountability of the governing board.

Accountability in Schools

So how were schools accountable in the 1990s, and what is the current situation?

- They were subject to regular and systematic inspection.
- Inspection outcomes were published.

---

[15] NAHT, ATL, NUT, UNISON & NGA. 2015. The Education and Adoption Bill, http://www.naht.org.uk/welcome/news-and-media/key-topics/organisational-structures/education-and-adoption-bill-briefing/ October 2015

- Test and examination results were published, and league tables of schools' performance were created.
- Parents could complain according to a formalised procedure, and complaints could be passed on to the local authority on appeal.
- Parents of excluded children could appeal to their local authority.
- Admissions in all but grant-maintained and voluntary aided schools were controlled by the LA according to DfE regulations.
- Local authorities could hold governing bodies and headteachers of all types of state-funded schools to account for poor performance.
- The Department for Education established laws and statutory guidance for the ways schools, their governing bodies and individual governors should conduct themselves.
- Governors were elected or appointed from the parents, staff, local community and local authority to hold the school to account for its conduct.
- Governing bodies were required to report to parents annually and to hold a public meeting at which they could be held answerable for the school's conduct.
- The local authority audited the finances of all LA schools.

How did these accountabilities change as the privatisation of schools got under way through city technology college, grant-maintained and foundation status, then transformed into 'corporatisation' in the sponsored academy, academy trust and free school?

Certainly, and despite the DfE's line of greater autonomy for schools alongside freedom from the local authority, academies and free schools found themselves subject to a mighty corpus of regulations imposed by the Department and the Education Funding Agency, amidst a general confusion always likely to be inevitable with the creation of more than three thousand independent state-funded schools.

- Not all academies are subject to DfE regulations on admissions – but some are.
- Academies have individual funding agreements with the DfE/EFA and it is difficult to track the individual responsibilities of academy and free schools.

- There is frequent uncertainty about which DfE regulations are applicable to all state-funded schools; which only to maintained schools; and which to some academies and free schools, but not to others (note the proliferation of websites explaining which regulations might apply to which schools).
- With every school that is a member of a multi academy trust subject to a scheme of delegation, the responsibilities and powers of the MAT directors (legally the responsible authority) and any local governing board will be governed by internal documents not always accessible to the public.

How Accountable Are Schools?

- The rules on which schools are subject to inspection, how often, and to what detail, are constantly being changed.
- While parents of children in maintained schools can still apply to their local authority with any query or complaint against the school, academy parents, if dissatisfied with the governing board's handling of the complaint and an independent panel review, have recourse only to the secretary of state via the EFA.
- In the case of excluded pupils, academy parents can appeal to an Independent Review Panel.
- Academy admissions are required to conform to DfE regulations but appeals against decisions are conducted by the school itself. The Office of the Schools Adjudicator is established to ensure that schools abide by the DfE Code, but only councils and local parents have access to it, so oversight is limited. As the adjudicator noted in her 2015 report, "the admission arrangements for many schools that are their own admission authority are unnecessarily complex and lack transparency, especially those with numerous subcategories within individual oversubscription criteria. Such arrangements are difficult to understand and limit parents' ability to assess the chance of their child being offered a place."[16]

---

[16] Office of the Schools Adjudicator. 2015. Office of the Schools Adjudicator Annual Report September 2014 to August 2015, November 2015

- Local authorities still have a responsibility to promote high standards in education throughout their area, but have no powers or funding to intervene in academies; the DfE can require MATs to transfer schools where performance is less than good, and stand-alone academies can be required to join a MAT.
- Governing boards/boards of directors/trustees of academies, are responsible to the secretary of state, and practice varies widely in terms of conduct, conflicts of interest, payment of expenses and so on. There is little effective oversight of non-maintained school governing boards, other than through Ofsted inspections.
- Academy boards need have no more than two elected parent governors, and all other appointments are made by the board itself; some MATs have the power to select and appoint all members (A handbook published in 2014 by The Institute of Chartered Secretaries and Administrators and endorsed by the then chair of the National Governors' Association, noted uncritically that "Generally, the first port of call for academies looking for governors is the connections of those already on the board").[17]
- There are currently no requirements for governing boards in any state-funded school to report on their work to parents or to hold meetings for parents.
- Finances in academies are overseen by the Education Funding Agency, which issues a warning notice when concerns come to their notice.
- Governors are required to report on the school's website on board attendance and members' pecuniary interests.

This summary of changes over the last ten years or so to the accountability of schools, both professional and democratic, seems to suggest a hardening of professional accountability and a loosening of democratic accountability. So what are the elements of democratic accountability that we might look to in a state-funded school serving the community in which we live, whatever its legal status?

---

[17] Paxton-Doggett, Katie. 2014 How to Run an Academy School, London: ICSA p105

Elements of Democratic Accountability

The following elements are necessary in an organisation and in a national structure which values its accountability to the public it serves. These elements not only go towards ensuring that the public values, sees the value of, and is therefore likely to offer its support to, the service provided; but that the service is more likely to be effective if it contains these elements, because it will be more efficient, having a wider set of views to be taken into account, and more responsive, in that it will be more likely to provide the service that is needed and wanted.

Representativeness

It seems likely that the model of stakeholder governance introduced in 1986 was intended to ensure that the various elements concerned in a school – parents, staff, local authority and the community served by the school – would have representation in a school's leadership. This, as we have explored already, implies a duty on the school to be aware of the feelings and views of the people who have elected or appointed them. It also implies that the governing board will make some effort to be 'representative' of the community served by the school in terms of gender, race, culture, beliefs and so on. While no one would seek to replicate precisely the make-up of the community, we would probably agree that a girls' school in which the majority of governors and senior staff were male would not be a good thing. Similarly, a coeducational school serving a predominantly south Asian community, such as the academy on the board of which I was asked to serve by the DfE, should at the very least acknowledge that, and not have an exclusively white, predominantly male governing board (as it did). If there is no other reason, it is difficult for a public body to have the confidence of the people it serves if it does not to some extent reflect the key characteristics of those people. It becomes a 'provision for' rather than a 'provision with'. Then, if it does not enlist the loyalty of the community, it is unlikely to convince the members of that community that it is always seeking to work in their best interests. These, I think, are the two meanings of the word 'representation', and two strong reasons why we should seek representativeness in the leadership of our community's organisations.

For similar reasons, there is some resistance – now acknowledged by the DfE – against school governance having no geographical coherence. Certainly, some of the more widespread academy chains such as Academies Enterprise Trust

(AET) and E-ACT have found themselves criticised by Ofsted for a failure to improve failing schools sufficiently quickly. There appears to be a recognition that working effectively with schools separated by huge distances is logistically problematic, and the absence of local leadership and governance seems to contribute to that.

Certainly, the issue of the creeping undermining of the concept of the local management of schools – at the heart of the 1988 Act – has not been openly addressed by the DfE. Is it that locality is no longer valued in school governance? Is it that the centralisation of education is now a key policy of government – centralisation by stealth, because it has never been declared as a good thing, even though it is at the heart of the corporatisation of schools and the removal of local authority oversight?

There are a number of elements underlying the concept of 'representativeness' which are rarely reflected in the move towards skills-based, as opposed to stakeholder, governance.

Diversity

One of the key elements of representativeness is the capacity of the school's leadership to reflect some of the characteristics of the population it serves. It is not to the academy system's credit that its schools are considerably less likely to be led by members of the black, Asian and minority ethnic (BAME) communities. An analysis by Schools Week in 2018[18] could find only two such chief executives of the seventy-two academy trusts with fifteen schools or more. But at the same time, there was not one director of education from a minority ethnic group in the country's twenty largest councils. Both women and ethnic minority leaders were under-represented in senior education roles in 2018, and the government "laid out plans to improve diversity under a new statement of intent."[19] But this does not seem to have yet had any impact. Schools Week repeated the exercise in 2020 and found that "The proportion of black, Asian and minority ethnic (BAME) leaders of England's largest academy trusts has fallen, with ninety-eight percent of the top chains now run by white bosses."[20]

---

[18] Staufenberg, Jess. 2018. Revealed: the lack of diversity in education leadership roles, Schools Week, 2 November 2018

[19] Staufenberg, ibid

[20] Carr, James. 2020. Investigation: diversity of education leadership roles fails to improve despite DfE pledge, Schools Week, 21 June 2020

Meanwhile, the state sector had very marginally improved the diversity of its senior leaders. It does not seem that academisation is doing anything to develop diversity in educational leadership.

Transparency

The carefully wrought process of crafting, publishing, debating and enacting government legislation of the twentieth century appears to have gone by the board over recent years. The transparency that this provided in terms of identifying a government's priorities was helpful. We could understand what a government sought to do and, often, throughout the process, its motives became clear. Rationale and evidence in support of legislative change could be identified too. But the use of emergency legislative processes, introduced to facilitate law changes in the face of increasing terrorist risk, for the 2010 Academies Act by Michael Gove, suggested that careful and rational debate was not to be embraced by the coalition government.

Over recent years, legislation seems to be only rarely preceded by a Green or White discussion Paper, leaving educationists and political commentators to guess at what might be planned by government ministers, or even extrapolated from chance remarks. For some months in 2015-16, until the publication of Educational Excellence Everywhere[21], the best guess had been that the Conservative government would soon enact legislation to require all remaining maintained schools to become academies by the end of their term of office in 2020. But the finer detail of the DfE's preferences in the terms of present conversions was not always clear. At one time, in 2013-14, one growing MAT reported that, when visiting the DfE, on one side of the corridor they would be called in to discuss why they were expanding so slowly while, on the other side, officials would warn them that they would soon be advised that they had reached their optimum size. For a long period, good and outstanding schools were encouraged to convert singly. Then rumours went around that outstanding schools would be required to adopt other schools if they wanted to retain that grading. A little later, and it became clear that stand-alone academies would no longer be approved by the DfE, and some of the bigger MATs had schools taken away from them as they were failing to improve sufficiently quickly. Meanwhile, some Church of England schools found another layer of obfuscation in their

---

[21] Department for Education. 2016. Educational Excellence Everywhere, London: The Stationery Office

diocese, where practice varied across the country about the formation of one large or several small MATs, and about the possibility of joining in MATs with non-Church schools.

Much energy was expended, and wasted, by headteachers and governors in trying to second-guess what the DfE was up to, and this opacity turned out to be catching.

Public bodies spending taxpayers' money, whether they are government departments or the governing board of a 130-pupil village school, have become less subject to scrutiny about their practices. While academy boards are required by law to make their agenda and minutes available to anyone with an interest, just as maintained school governors have been for years, there may be some evidence of increasing unwillingness to open their discussions to public scrutiny. Again, perhaps, government plans to limit the Freedom of Information (FOI) legislation may be setting a trend. Certainly, publications such as Schools Week find all sorts of obstacles put in their way when asking for documents about, for example, the tenders for free schools. This writer had to resort to the Information Commissioner's complaints procedure to get any sort of acknowledgement of an FOI request regarding an academy broker's earnings out of the DfE, and an answer was only reluctantly forthcoming several weeks after the supposed statutory deadline. When a government's own departments are so secretive about policy and about information, it is unlikely that other organisations are going to feel it incumbent on them to be transparent. This attitude appears to have 'trickled down' to universities. Private Eye reported in 2016 that the University of Birmingham wrote to its staff about planned job cuts in its modern languages department, saying that "No one's interests are served by open discussion", and "staff have been told not to discuss the matter without written permission from the change management group"[22].

The other common tactic which appears to have trickled down from government practice to some governing boards and trusts is touched on in the section on language – the use of a bland statement of broad policy to answer specific questions about past and current practice. This is done in parliament in responses to opposition questions, and has been used by the Redstart Trust, the Local Authority and the DfE.

---

[22] Private Eye, 19 February – 3rd March 2016, p7

The word 'transparency' was used twenty times in the Education Select Committee's report on the Regional Schools Commissioners[23]. The DfE's own governance handbook is clear about the responsibilities that governors have in this regard: "Governors should be mindful that in exercising all their functions, they must act with integrity, objectivity and honesty and in the best interests of the school; and be open about the decisions they make and the actions they take and be prepared to explain their decisions and actions to interested parties. This is required in maintained schools by legislation. Similarly, governors should be aware of and accept the seven principles of public life, as set out by Lord Nolan and applying to anyone, locally and nationally, who is elected or appointed as a public office-holder. They are: selflessness, integrity, objectivity, accountability, openness, honesty and leadership"[24].

Transparency in school leadership can be hard work, but it, perhaps more than any other element, can develop parental engagement and improve parental relationships to the benefit, most of all, of the children. Transparent schools provide regular newsletters, put meetings' agenda & minutes prominently on their websites and notice boards, offer invitations for views, make their accounts understandable and invite challenge, provide regular and comprehensive governor profiles, refer frequently to their academic and moral purpose, and demonstrate how operational decisions match their vision and their ethos. They provide a coherent and consistent organisation.

It is particularly notable how the leadership of Redstart Trust, the Castle School and the local authority failed to meet their obligations here, and fell back on 'confidentiality', although, as is clear, there are no rights to which they could possibly apply this principle. Currently, some of this can be tackled with use of the Freedom of Information Act, 2000.

---

[23] House of Commons Education Committee. 2016. The role of Regional Schools Commissioners: First Report of Session 2015-16, London: The Stationery Office, 20th January 2016

[24] House of Commons. 2013 The School Governance (Roles, Procedures and Allowances) (England) Regulations 2013, DfE 2013; Statutory Instrument 2013 No 1624: The School Governance (Roles, Procedures and Allowances) (England) Regulations 2013, coming into force 1.9.13. Lord Nolan, who devised these principles, should not be confused with Liam Nolan, the headteacher admired by Michael Gove and banned from teaching.

Answerability

While governing boards are required to hold their headteachers to account for the performance of the school – the second in the list of the three core functions that the DfE requires of the governing board – there is substantially less opportunity for the public to hold the governors to account. Trusts may be geographically as well as structurally distant from schools and their communities, while a local governing board may be purely advisory, and certainly has no statutory powers. Annual parents' reports and meetings are long gone in most schools; elections for governors rare. Complaints can no longer be directed at local councillors, and it was possible for the headteacher/chief executive of a small trust like Redstart, meeting the governors of its first member school, to admit that she had no idea of the school's ethos, and therefore could not guarantee to preserve it.

There is no longer any formal mechanism of answerability to parents or to the local community in any state-funded school.

Another form of answerability is "Who takes the blame when things go wrong?" Naturally we expect the professional leaders to carry the can if they have been failing in the operational areas where they have delegated responsibilities. But decision-makers – politicians, trustees, governors – also have to consider the responsibilities they have. While the heads of headteachers roll readily in the aftermath of school failure, we should expect trust leaders and chairs of governors to carry the can occasionally. In government it has been long established that ministers accept liability for decisions that emanate from their office. 2020 seemed to be seeing the end of this truism. In August, the number one civil servant in the DfE was summarily removed in the wake of the A Level results fiasco. Yet, almost certainly the debacle was caused by the secretary of state's insistence that the algorithm developed by Ofqual should not allow any grade inflation. It was far from being a 'mutant algorithm' as described by the Prime Minister. But the civil servant, not the minister, had to go. This appears to be a result of Dominic Cummings' reported warning in June "that a 'hard rain' would hit the civil service"[25].

---

[25] Stewart, H and Weale, S. 2020. Civil servants 'fall guys for No 10', say critics as education chief removed, The Guardian, 27 August 2020

Access to Decision-Makers

The physical distancing of a school's management and leadership from the building where the children are taught undermines the concept of local management of schools. This attack on the concept introduced in 1986-88 has rarely been articulated, but it is inevitable that parents will find it more difficult to access the people who really make the decisions about schools.

If by chance a parent does get to meet with the decision-makers in their child's school, the five questions that Tony Benn formulated, and shared in his final parliamentary appearance, might be useful:

"In the course of my life I have developed five little democratic questions. If one meets a powerful person – Adolf Hitler, Joe Stalin or Bill Gates – ask them five questions: 'What power have you got? Where did you get it from? In whose interests do you exercise it? To whom are you accountable? And how can we get rid of you?' If you cannot get rid of the people who govern you, you do not live in a democratic system."[26]

Participation in decision-making.

As we have seen, there has been a significant reduction in the elected membership of governing boards, and boards of academy trustees may be required only to have two elected parents. All other members are appointed by the board itself, bringing about the danger that membership of such boards can be self-perpetuating. One notorious example is that of an East Anglian free school where the chair of governors unilaterally sacked all current members, and appointed her husband, her father, her best friend and her best friend's husband to the board.

Free schools – widely advertised to be the places where parents might run their own schools – are now dominated by existing academy trusts. In early 2016, the DfE seemed to favour groups with experience of education. In a Tweet, the department announced: "Free schools: we've revised the application process for applicant groups who have a strong educational track record". Of the twenty-two free schools announced by the secretary of state in February 2016, only one would be run by a parents' group, while familiar names like Harris and Dixons

---

[26] Benn, Tony. 2001. Hansard Debates for 22nd March 2001 Pt 13

featured among the sponsors of others to be opened. By 2021, parents opening Free Schools had become an extinct species.

The growing absence of parents and the local community from decision-making, as opposed to advisory or celebratory roles, is a significant threat to the democracy in schools that had been developing throughout the 1990s. The point about democratic participation is that it provides the possibility of dissent within an organisation's leadership. As we saw above, this is not only democratic, but also it is likely to make the organisation more efficient, by ensuring that it considers a range of viewpoints and possible actions and decisions. Statutory guidance makes it clear that governing boards can remove any appointed governor, though not an elected governor, so the increase in the proportion of appointed governors gives further concern about the overarching powers that boards have to stifle dissent.[27]

Code Of Conduct

The DfE, as we have seen, believes that governors should subscribe to the seven Nolan principles of public life – selflessness, integrity, objectivity, accountability, openness, honesty and leadership – and that all governing boards should publish a code of conduct ensuring such behaviour, from individual governors and the board as a whole. This code should be published to parents and the public and ratified annually to ensure governors understand and meet their obligations.

Dealing with Complaints

We have already seen how the complaints process in academies is largely internalised, and how difficult it is to appeal if the parent is still unhappy. Parents still approach their local authority about schools which are outside their jurisdiction and find themselves being referred to the Secretary of State. Parents could have had recourse to the review procedure, as the decisions of local authorities in the exercise of their duties can be subject to it. The BBC described judicial review as "Arguably ...the most important and effective way in our democracy of holding the government and other public authorities to account."[28]

---

[27] Department for Education. 2015. The constitution of governing bodies of maintained schools: Statutory guidance for governing bodies of maintained schools and local authorities in England, The Stationery Office, August 2015

[28] BBC News 2014 http://www.bbc.co.uk/news/uk-30226781, 1 December 2014

Nevertheless, the procedure continues to be under threat from the government, as is the human rights legislation to which judicial review is linked. Similarly, the extent of public access to freedom of information is again under consideration – a commission set up by the government to review the act back in 2015 "issued a consultation paper which suggested it is considering sweeping restrictions to the legislation, including:

- Imposing charges for requests.
- Making it easier to refuse requests on cost grounds.
- Making it more difficult to obtain public authorities' internal discussions, or excluding some from access altogether.
- Strengthening ministers' powers to veto disclosures.
- Changing the way the Act is enforced."[29]

These changes are still on the table. So many of the structures designed to protect the public from arbitrary or illegal acts by public authorities are currently under threat. In addition to judicial review – still very much at risk in Johnson's government – these include the scope of and access to the Freedom of Information Laws, the Human Rights Act, the 1951 Refugee Convention, the Electoral Commission and the jury system.

Clarity of Vision, Ethos and Strategic Direction

This is the first core function of governing boards in all state-funded schools[30]. We should be able to find these prominently on a school's website. While vision and ethos are often easily found, a statement of strategic direction is usually more difficult to locate. The problem may be that governors of schools, unlike charity trustees and non-executive directors of companies, have very little freedom in identifying strategic objectives. It is the DfE and Ofsted, usually with little or no consultation and often at short notice, who decide what success is, what quality looks like in state funded schools, and what measurements will be used to define good and outstanding schools. Governors have little if any elbow room in determining a school's priorities. In addition, the uncertainty of future

---

[29] Campaign for Freedom of Information (2015) Stop FOI restrictions https://www.cfoi.org.uk/campaigns/stop-foi-restrictions/

[30] Department for Education. 2015 The governance handbook: For trustees of academies and multi-academy trusts and governors of maintained schools, November 2015

government policy and funding makes strategic planning unpredictable and, in some areas, impossible. This uncertainty is significantly greater than it was in the, in retrospect, comparatively stable 1990s and early 2000s.

This was brought starkly into the spotlight in the middle of the 2020 pandemic. Rarely, a Secretary of State for Education, in this case Gavin Williamson, declared the major purpose of education as he saw it: "We must never forget that the purpose of education is to give people the skills they need to get a good and meaningful job."[31] This seemed to be endorsed by the leader of one of the country's largest Trusts, CEO of Harris Academies Sir Dan Moynihan, when he was reported to have spoken of the need to narrow the secondary curriculum in the pandemic: "I do not think they [the pupils] will be pleased to look back when they are 40 and see that, because of a bit of art or French…they did not get the qualification in English or maths they needed to get a job."[32] It is quite remarkable to hear such an influential figure in education, first, be reported dismissing elements of a broad and balanced curriculum as 'a bit of art or French' – the heads of those departments and their staff in the forty-nine Harris schools around the country must have been thrilled to read that. But to suggest that studying languages and the arts can be an obstacle to high achievement pushes this contemptuous – and contemptible – remark to another level. Perhaps the fact that he works for a Trust whose hereditary ownership is written into its articles of government, endorsed by the government Department for Education makes it less surprising. But no less disturbing.

'Who, then, shall conduct education so that humanity may improve?' (John Dewey[33])

---

[31] (Speech to the Social Market Foundation, reported in FE Week, Thursday, 9th July, 2020)

[32] Private Eye, 11th July 2020

[33] Dewey, John (1916; this edition 2011) Democracy and Education, New York: Simon and Brown

The Castle Captured; The Future of English Schooling Foreseen

Castle Primary School has been captured by the academy movement, against the wishes of its governors, its staff and the parents of its children. The school had been consistently 'good' and stuttered only when experiencing a change in leadership – a period during which it had every right to expect the support of its local authority. It became an academy because the local authority wanted to wash its hands of demanding schools, so that it could reduce its school support staff to a bare minimum, but also because the LA believed in the privatisation agenda in education, an agenda which squeezes out local engagement in, and the democratic accountability of, village schools.

This took place in the constituency of the then Schools Minister, David Laws – an elected representative on an education manifesto in which academisation played no part – a frequent visitor, as it happened, to the sponsor school. Parents who lobbied Laws were unable to get any practical help from him. David Laws went on to hold a senior post with Ark academy chain (the chair of whose trustees donated £15,000 to Laws' failed general election campaign in 2015. He presumably thought that Laws might be an influential voice in a new government – a miscalculation that makes you wonder about his powers of foresight, or possibly just his common sense). Ark does not believe in giving its local 'governing' boards any powers. It appoints the chairs of its Local Governing Boards (LGBs) and has a 'central team member' present at every meeting. Laws now heads up the influential Education Policy Institute.

ARK Schools looks "to US networks for inspiration, including the Knowledge is Power Programme (KIPP) and Uncommon Schools."[34] The 2017 appointment of chief inspector of schools went to Amanda Spielman, whose background is in corporate finance and management consultancy. She is closely associated with Ark schools. The chair of Ark received a knighthood in the 2016 birthday honours: "He is the co-founder, with Ian Wace – chair of Ark's global board – of Marshall Wace Asset Management Ltd, a big hedge fund. Of the eight trustees of ARK Schools, five are hedge fund managers. None have any

---

[34] Department for Education. 2014. ARK Schools: In-depth sponsor profile, April 2014 p5

background in education."[35] KIPP is a curriculum produced by a corporate provider of American Charter schools. The circle of commercial corporate provision of state-funded education is complete.

All the evidence points to the continuing corporatisation of English schools on the American charter schools model. Despite reaching an apparent peak of 'disruptive innovation' in schools in the spring and summer of 2016, the formation of a new Conservative government, with little apparent opposition in the wake of the EU referendum outcome, heralded a prolonged period of uncertainty. In schools, headteachers and staff grappled with constant change in pupil expectations and testing regimes, creating ever more workload pressures on adults and children alike.

Meanwhile, both the ethical and qualitative bases of academisation come increasingly into question, and consideration of the purposes of education is side-lined or simplified. Teachers continue to improve children's schooling as assessed by tests and examination in both maintained and academy schools, while the goalposts are continually shifted farther and farther from achievability.

How will schools survive the next years? How will adults working in schools survive them? How will educational historians look back on the first quarter of the twenty-first century?

---

[35] Bennett, Matthew. 2016. Ark Schools: An example of philanthrocapitalism Local Schools Network https://www.localschoolsnetwork.org.uk/2016/06/ark-schools-an-example-of-philanthrocapitalism

Chapter 12
Power and Powerlessness in The Lay Governance of Education

This quote from Alice Walker: "The most common way people give up their power is by thinking they don't have any"[1] reminds us that power is not a simple one-dimensional concept. Here we briefly explore why it is that people so often vote, speak and act against their own best interests – and how this phenomenon can be exploited.

What Has Schooling to Do with Power? Or with Democracy?

It may be a truism – it may be arguable – but it is possible that people in the western world now know more about what their governments are up to than ever before and yet have little or no power to do anything about it. We feel as if we have very little control over anything much around us except over our very nearest circumstances. For many, work is precarious, unrewarding and underpaid, with little possibility of medium-term improvement or long-term security. In the UK, schooling, health and social care have been underfunded for ten years. Transport, manufacture, communications are provided, or not, with little regard to need or input. Even basic utilities such as power and water are subject to competitive providers whose competition has no discernible impact on cost. The value of our houses increases by around five per cent every year, while the real value of wages has remained static for the last ten years. We live in a country where property is doing better than people.

Local government, designed to be the closest form of democracy to the voter, is emasculated by central government regulation and impoverishment. All of this

---

[1] See Chapter 10 p83 notes (13): As quoted in The Best Liberal Quotes Ever: Why the Left is Right (2004) by William P. Martin, p. 173

was true even before the pandemic of 2020 struck. Now the concept of community itself is under threat. As we saw in Chapter 9, the local communities that are so crucial to 'ordinary people' may have little meaning to the moneyed classes. Some of the key elements of localism are already disappearing. John Harris, writing in The Guardian, described the "drastic changes to local commercial radio, and the broadcasting giant Global getting rid of around sixty local breakfast and drive time programmes, remodelling local news bulletins and closing studios. Now, the radio company Bauer is folding almost fifty local stations into a national radio network branded Greatest Hits that will carry programmes made in London …A month ago, the BBC confirmed that it was cutting 450 jobs from its regional news operations. Meanwhile, the demise of local newspapers continues apace. Reach, the UK's largest publisher of local and regional news, is shedding hundreds of jobs. More than 245 British papers have closed in the last fifteen years."[2] How can people engage in local political processes when the organs they use to communicate about them no longer exist? It is not likely that social media will be able to plug that gap.

Binarism – typified by what is in practice a two-party, first-past-the-post (FPTP) system, and reinforced by an either/or referendum and dualistic post-referendum negotiations – has the frequently realised potential to disempower 49% of the electorate. Britain and Belarus – in turmoil throughout 2020 – are the only two European countries using FPTP voting, disenfranchising all those who live in any but the most marginal constituencies. The Manichaean struggle exemplified by the simplistic referendum question requiring an irrevocable choice of light or darkness has entered other arenas, particularly, perhaps, state schooling. So Twitter resounds with the clash of arms between traditionalists and progressives; children's champions and 'zero tolerance' school disciplinarians ; between the proponents of knowledge and the advocates of skills.

So who, to take up John Dewey's question of a century ago, "shall conduct education so that humanity may improve? …Is it possible", he asked, "for an educational system to be conducted by a national state and yet the full social ends of the educative process not be restricted, constrained and corrupted?"[3] How can knowledge, he suggests, mean anything without experience: "It is not enough to

<hr>

[2] Harris, John. 2020. How the Tories are working to create a cookie-cutter country, The Guardian, 17 August 2020

[3] Dewey, John. 1916; this edition 2011. Democracy and Education, New York: Simon and Brown, p.55

insist upon the necessity of experience, nor even of activity in experience. Everything depends upon the *quality* of the experience which is had."[4] Whatever knowledge accumulation took place in the primary classrooms and the streets of Stoke sub Hamdon in 2014 and 2015, what did the children and the parents actually learn about the world, about local education officials, about politics, about the elected and the non-elected in power? However proficient the children are now at their times tables and at identifying fronted adverbials, what did they learn about 'life'? That adults could not be trusted. That whatever worthwhileness existed in their small and protective community, it could be trampled on by people from far away whose opinions, at that moment in time, were the only ones that counted.

At one time, public service counted.

Education as A Public Service in The Twentieth Century

As the academy broker representing the Department for Education met with the governors of Castle School in the autumn of 2014, in order to impose the wishes of a bureaucracy far, far away, a gathering of what was termed by their host as "an educational Valhalla" took place at the Institute of Education in London. The event was called to celebrate the centenary of the birth of Harry Rée, advocate of cradle-to-grave community education, professor of education at York University, grammar school headmaster, war hero and conscientious objector.

Rée was one of a number following in an honourable tradition of British middle-class, mainly privately-educated, men who believed that education – and a particular type of life-enriching, cultural-centred education embracing the arts and the humanities – is a right to which everyone, whatever their origins, is entitled.

It is a Romantic tradition, and its earliest manifestation lay probably in Matthew Arnold (1822-1888), the schools inspector, poet, and son of Rugby School's famous headmaster, Thomas. We know where Arnold would have stood today on SATs, the Early Years Curriculum and the Progress 8 and Bold Beginnings culture, because he wrote a not very anonymous pamphlet on the introduction of Payment by Results in 1862. Payment by Results, he argued,

---

[4] Dewey, John. 1938; this edition, 1997. Experience and Education, New York: Touchstone, Simon & Schuster p 27

would lead to "cutbacks which would 'lower the standard of popular education', at a time when schools were beginning to make progress in their wider aim of compensating for deprived educational backgrounds. By focusing on a narrow cost-cutting yardstick, the proposal treated a school as 'a mere machine for teaching, reading, writing and arithmetic' rather than 'a living whole with complex functions, religious, moral and intellectual'. Arnold wanted to meet 'the strong desire of the lower classes to raise themselves' by giving them the means to acquire a full share in cultural life rather than just a few basic skills."[5]

Numbers followed in that tradition, following the introduction of universal free elementary education. Edmond Holmes, another schools inspector/romantic idealist, with his seminal reflection on the meaning of education "What Is and What Might Be" was one. He too contrasted two educational paths: the path of mechanical obedience and the path of self-realisation[6]. His nephew Gerald was another, the 'Omes' of Teddy O'Neill's Prestolee, arguably the first urban community school in the Lancashire of the 1920s onwards[7].

The vision was picked up by Henry Morris, Director of Education for Cambridgeshire from 1922 to 1954, and founder of the village college model of lifelong education. Morris' Sunday walks with groups of young men are reminiscent of the great hikes undertaken by the romantic poets of a hundred years before[8]. Morris was Harry Rée's mentor when he showed an interest in education administration while he was at Cambridge University in the early 1930s.

In the 1960s and 70s, the tradition was represented by some great comprehensive headteachers who were themselves educated privately, but who saw the redemptive possibilities of a lifelong non-selective, liberal education rooted firmly in the community. These were people like the Leicestershire upper school comprehensive heads hand-picked by Director of Education Stewart

---

[5] Murray, Nicholas. 1996. A Life of Matthew Arnold, London: Hodder & Stoughton p193

[6] Holmes, Edmond. 1911. What is and What Might Be: A Study of Education in General and Elementary Education in Particular, London: Constable

[7] Holmes, Gerard. 1952. The Idiot Teacher: A Book about Prestolee School and its Headmaster E. F. O'Neill, London: Faber and Faber

[8] See, e.g. Rée, Harry. 1973. Educator Extraordinary: The Life and Achievement of Henry Morris 1889-1961, London: Longman; and Daube, Jonathan. 2017. Educator Most Extraordinary: The life and achievements of Harry Rée, 1914-1991, London: UCL Institute of Education

Mason, such as Tim McMullen of Countesthorpe and Tim Rogers of Bosworth College – idealists, democrats who valued the widest possible participation in educational decision-making. Many others came from this 'officer class' who committed their lives to providing a transformative lifelong education from cradle to grave. Michael Duane of Risinghill School in Islington, north London, made it clear that a commitment to public education also assumed a commitment to democracy – indeed, that such a commitment must be democratic by its very nature. Democracy, therefore, must be embedded in the school experience from the first days.

That does not mean, though some thought it did, that schools must always be run on pluralist lines. But it does mean that the engagement with, and ownership, of, their own learning that we hope to engender in children must permeate the organisation of the schooling structure. This involves most significantly the accountability of professionals in schools to the public they serve. Where there is no formal link between a community and the school that serves its members, education becomes an imposition to be endured. Where children, their parents and the wider community are not allowed to be part of the school's accountability, the system becomes a tool of politicians and professionals to meet the indeterminate ends of the nation, not of the people who attend them and indirectly pay for them.

So schools have a dual responsibility here, to both engage with democracy and to help people learn how to practise it. Michael Duane wrote: "Democracy, like language, needs practice from infancy if it is to become as much part of our natures as language is"[9].

Democracy is by its very nature comprehensive. We can no longer, as the Athenians did, as most imperial powers did, exclude slaves or women or uneducated males. So for a school system to call itself 'comprehensive', it must not only take all children into its neighbourhood schools, but it must engage their parents and offer to everyone the opportunity to realise the possibilities within them. It can only do that if, in turn, it offers not only its assets but its governance to the community it serves.

That there are difficulties in doing so does not mean it can be left untried.

---

[9] Duane, Michael. 1991. Work, Language & Education in the Industrial State, London: Freedom Press

School Governing as A Democratic Engagement – And the Government's Responses

The reintroduction of stakeholder school governance offered such an opportunity in the years following the 1986 and 1988 Education Acts. These two pieces of legislation placed schools legally in the hands of their local governing bodies, with powers over spending, employment and, to a limited extent, the curriculum. Some of those who advocated for universal comprehensive education saw this as a potential threat to their ideal, but the enactment, even though perhaps unwittingly, held the seeds of a community-led schooling system with sufficient checks and balances to ensure a significant degree of equality of service throughout the country. From that base, and with an inspection system focussed on school improvement over and above judgmentalism, we might have moved towards a national education service addressing the worst manifestations of unequal funding and staffing, while retaining the precious and growing engagement of the community.

But many governing bodies found themselves disempowered from the outset by their limited capacity to confront the massed ranks of an education service within local authorities resolutely determined to withstand the ambitions of ordinary but committed local people. Local politicians got onto the new boards and filibustered themselves into the chair. Officers refused to engage with anyone other than professional teachers, regarding it as beneath themselves to be subject to the accountability of lay people. Many headteachers too saw governors as a threat, not a promise. Emasculating governing bodies before they had had the chance to prove themselves turned out to be an easy task in many authorities. And it could be seen as 'helpfulness'. Officers wrote policies so that schools wouldn't have to. They prepared the meetings' agendas and clerked the meetings, resolutely fending off any attempt by governors to address genuinely strategic issues and pushing the board towards 'bikeshedding' – where a group spends hours on operational matters because it doesn't have the knowledge or confidence to tackle the big questions. In such schools, headteachers always had the right answer to any issue raised by governors and could ensure that agendas focussed on the simple and operational, rather than the complex and strategic. If all else seemed to be failing, they could fall back on their professional status, blinding governors with too much information or assuring them that whole realms of school business were outside their remit.

Of course, this was only true of some of them. Noble exceptions saw the potential of lay school governance to create a strategic level of school leadership alongside the senior professionals, supported by far-sighted education officers. The number of these grew throughout the nineties, as good headteachers who understood that they couldn't run the school by themselves at strategic or operational levels worked in partnership with increasingly confident governors.

But this was resisted by some at every level. True – the teachers' unions cottoned on quite quickly to the potential benefits of an alliance between school and community. So did many local authorities. But the government, of whatever hue, went on undermining its own structures, mainly because not one senior politician seemed to believe that local people, working with their own council staff, could lead a school. So the plethora of control features came into being, each one designed to stifle the weak seeds of local engagement into a system rigorously regulated to cater for the lowest common denominator. A supportive inspection system disseminating best practice across the country became a quality compliance procedure, pitting inspectors against teachers and school leaders to achieve quotas of failure. A broad and balanced national curriculum became a series of compulsory tests whose outputs would determine the careers of both teachers and children. And school governance became a grind of reports, policies, data and rubber stamping.

What seems to have been happening here is that education governance, as noted by Clarke[10], "concerns the struggle to maintain control in the face of 'contradictory systems, contested positions and contentious subjects'". These positions include such delicate and vote-endangering themes as favoured learning patterns, behavioural issues, the range of parental aspirations, hostility to or acquiescence in governmental priorities and, perhaps most strongly emotive, school closures. It is important that government at both local and national levels can wash their hands of, or at worst shelve, such uncomfortable decisions. "But rather than concede incomplete and imperfect control, governments typically pursue techniques and strategies that may enhance their capacity to govern at a distance. In some cases, the generation of attrition and compliance through inspection, managerial deference and high-stakes testing is

---

[10] Quoted in Wilkins, Andrew and Olmedo, Antonio. 2018. Conceptualising Education Governance: Framings, Perspectives and Theories in Wilkins and Olmedo (eds) Education governance and social theory: Interdisciplinary approaches to research, London: Bloomsbury

monitored and regulated by third-party organisations and agents to strengthen accountability to the centre."[11]

In the terms of governing boards, while 'bigging them up' in the sense of giving them significant powers and creating a sense of self-importance and worthiness by close engagement with government powers, the DfE simultaneously undermined their capacity to subvert government policy direction by, for example, encouraging them to become smaller. DfE attempts led by then education minister Lord Nash – himself chair of a small academy in Pimlico –to underline the greater efficiency of small governing boards, was nevertheless unsupported by any objective evidence, as shown by Balarin et al. Their report "shows that there is no significant or substantive relationship between the size of a governing body and aspects of its effectiveness."[12] So, with the help of the educational establishment – Gove's Blob – school governors could thwart some of the government's attempts at emasculation.

Nevertheless, by not addressing the obvious weaknesses of multi academy trusts covering large geographical areas, the DfE also enabled governing boards of trustees to be physically distant from the schools for which they were responsible, and continued to encourage them to adopt the habits of business boards with "constant demands over twenty-five years that schools be more 'business-like' and learn skills from business models …"[13]

"The techniques and strategies that may enhance (the government's) capacity to govern at a distance …" using monitoring and regulation "by third-party organisations and agents to strengthen accountability to the centre"[14], may have been evident in the evolution of the representative body for school governors, the National Governors' Association (NGA). Formed in 2006 from the merger of previous representative bodies, the NGA was a membership charity with the purpose of lobbying for more effective governance structures and support. In the heterogeneous pattern of local authority, largely not-for-profit landscape of governor support of the early 21st century, the NGA provided a valuable and cohesive national voice for school governors.

---

[11] Wilkins and Olmedo ibid

[12] Balarin, M, Brammer, S, James, C, McCormack, M. 2008. Governing our Schools: A research study commissioned by Business in the Community, University of Bath p66

[13] Gann, Nigel. 2016. Improving School Governance: How better governors make better schools, London, Routledge 2nd edition p191

[14] Ibid Wilkins and Olmedo

The NGA became a major source of governance knowledge and experience. It was governed by mainly lay governors. It provided regional and national conferences with renowned speakers, materials and consultancy. And then it found itself to be the place where politicians went to learn about governance. State schools had certainly had their share of feisty, non-compliant lay governors who saw LAs and the Department of Education in its various manifestations as the enemy – bureaucrats who didn't understand the importance of the lay voice in schools, and who provided ineffective support and few resources. However, with the corporatisation of schools outside the LA, the governor role began to drill further down into something dangerously close to operational leadership. Governors found themselves managing budgets instead of overseeing them, appraising senior staff, writing policies, managing health and safety and child protection. In particular, secondary governors (because secondary schools were at least three times more likely to academise than primaries) found themselves working closely with heads on the academisation process, a legal and financial minefield with no LA to act as a buffer between them and the DfE. So the support that governors needed became more functional, more utilitarian, more pragmatic, and more legalistic. In amongst the jungle of regulations, and with increasing professional accountability for the minutiae of the school's performance, there was less time for governing boards to be truly strategic – considering the aims and objectives of the school, overseeing its values and ethics, supporting and challenging the senior staff.

The blizzard of regulations from the DfE provided an environment where compliance was almost all. Ensuring compliance is an operational function, not a strategic one. Furthermore, compliance reached into all the legal and financial areas as well as the increasingly data-led (and therefore most likely to be dominated by professional educators) performance of the school. And the NGA seemed, at some point, to change direction. The organisation started formally to provide consultancy and training to governing boards in 2013. But from 2015, there was a development in relationships with the DfE and with parliament. The DfE had already used much NGA material for its governance handbooks and there was some useful cross-fertilisation. From around 2015 on, the relationship became much closer.

Staff clerked the All-Party Parliamentary Group and hosted a site for it on the NGA website. They acted as representatives on the DfE's Education Forum, Advisory Group on Governance, and School and Academy Funding Group. The chief executive was on the DfE's Expert Group on the review of the National Professional Qualifications in leadership. The NGA had already performed one research contract for the Department – an exercise in 2016 defining what makes an effective governing board. In January 2018 it advertised for a training and consultancy director, part of whose job was defined as being to negotiate new governance development programme contracts with the DfE. It went on to promote the delivery of free training in governance throughout the country, all paid for by the DfE.

Of course, explicitly or not, the training delivered in this scheme will fit the DfE's views of what governance should look like. Importantly, it raises the question: How does an organisation designed to represent and lobby for its members become so enmeshed with the organisations and finances of the government department it is presumed to be lobbying?

So the National Governors' Association for member governors and trustees became the National Governance Association, a third-party organisation working with DfE funding to enable compliance with models of governance backed by the Department for Education.

How Corporatisation Speeds Up the Centralisation of Power

We have seen how there has been a historical struggle for power between the various parties engaged in education, and how that was exemplified in the curious tale of the conversion of Castle Primary School. Education officers, politicians and ambitious school leaders all had their own agenda which was served by the conscription of the children and parents of the village. School performance in itself became an irrelevance against the political demands of corporatisation which coincided happily with the personal agenda of senior educators. *How* they got what they wanted has been explored earlier. *Why* they got what they wanted is the history of English schooling since 2010, although its roots sit a great deal deeper.

A Very Brief Look at Power

It is possible that the characteristics of powerlessness and the weakness of protest are amplified in rural communities like Stoke sub Hamdon. John Gaventa, exploring power, powerlessness and acquiescence in the scattered coalmining communities of the Appalachian mountains of the eastern United

States, considered that the non-participation of communities in political and social movements, and their silent consent to the activities of large corporations (many of them British) which were impoverishing them, was particularly intrinsic to their situation: "While the possibilities for effective action by a relatively powerless group may be limited in any situation …the difficulties may be even greater for the non-elite of a rural community attempting to bypass the local elite and to influence an absentee target."[15] Villages not only lack numbers in school protests, but they may lack easy communications with local and central government and have few community members with experience of political action and protest. Further, the complex multi-role relationships in rural communities, where the teaching assistant may be your neighbour, the teacher your customer, the vicar your school governor, make contentiousness a risky business which cannot be compartmentalised. In Somerset, a parents' meeting will probably comprise of a number of people employed by or for the school – cleaners, lunchtime supervisors, teaching assistants as well as teachers – suppliers of food, and single traders offering maintenance skills. Even a small village school will most likely be one of the larger employers in the community. The decentralisation of power effected by local community school governance, in this case, was quickly overturned. Meanwhile, some similar protests in urban areas have proved, and continue to prove, successful.

We have seen that many governing boards have been disempowered by their limited capacity to confront the representatives of local authorities, whether elected members or officers. Members have their own political agendas to follow, not to be overridden by community feelings. Officers have their own careers to consider, unlikely to be advanced by opposing the governing party politicians who employ them.

If the NGA fulfils the role of a third party organisation designed to strengthen accountability to the DfE, then the way in which local authorities have lost their key position in the English education system can be explained by the need of central government to replace them with organisations more likely to provide that accountability. In place of the seriously powerful local education authorities, often led by charismatic and opinionated directors of education steeped in sector knowledge and connections – those very un-acquiescent twentieth-century men –we now see multi academy trusts led by businessmen with little understanding

---

[15] Gaventa, J (1980) Power and Powerlessness: Quiescence and Rebellion in an Appalachian Valley, Chicago: University of Illinois p.ix

of the sector and looser ties with its influential networks. Lords Harris, Nash and Agnew are slight figures against the best leaders of the second half of the twentieth century, but they sit well with a meritocratic government populated with and supported by businessmen, bankers and hedge fund investors.

Some governing boards were, or felt they were, disempowered by their limited capacity to confront local authority officers and politicians. It is likely that trustee boards free of the strictures of regular elections and very public scrutiny, with their experienced and comparatively time-rich chief executives, some of them geographically very distant from their schools, are proving even more resistant to challenge.

Indeed, corporatisation in some instances (by no means all) resembles the adoption of distant regions by colonial powers. Keeping your local governing boards in place (if you even have such a structure) when you are fifty or a hundred miles away from your trustees and their offices, if your CEO rarely visits and is difficult to access by phone or email, and if you are separated from them by a punitive school improvement process which focuses on performance, you are not going to feel that your voice is heard. Traditional LA governors who never developed a sense of history or entitlement in their position may find their lack of understanding being used against them to embed the power of the MAT's complex structures.

Some MATs have taken on this disempowerment agenda with enthusiasm. The author experienced governance in one early city academy established under the Labour government:

"A modernistic temple to education as business, sited in the middle of one of the country's most blighted areas, with an ethnic minority population of around 80%, the academy's governing body comprised sixteen governors, all relentlessly white, all with one exception male, with one Lord, one Dame and one Sir. The academy stuck to the letter of the law, and there was just one (white) parent."[16]

If a MAT wants to make sure the local voice is inaudible, it gets rid of local governing boards, it makes them 'ambassadors' rather than governors, it makes sure that the CEO sits on the local board. At the time of writing, "Sir Daniel Moynihan, chief executive of the Harris Foundation, whose salary last year was £440-£450,000, sits on thirty-five of its schools' local governing bodies

---

[16] Gann, Nigel. 2011 Academy Conversion: a view from the governing body, in Forum Vol 53 No 3, Didcot: Symposium Books Ltd p379

...Carolyn English, Harris' director of secondary education (serves) on the governing bodies of fifteen of its schools. And third is another academy superhead: Rachel de Souza, chief executive of the Norwich- based Inspiration Trust. The DfE's academy governance records, which extend to 79,040 lines of governing data and feature 33,235 governor names, show that de Souza sits on the local governing bodies of all fourteen Inspiration Trust schools, including serving as chair of one governing body which covers four of the schools in Norwich."[17] In the maintained system, the grouping of schools under one governing board was scrapped in 1986.

Is this remarkable level of involvement with individual schools designed to extract the maximum accountability of CEOs to local governors? Or is it to ensure that LGBs remain firmly in line with MAT principles? Even better if the leading lights of corporate academy governance can put together a voluntary organisation with a name with which no one can disagree, but which has an agenda with which many parents and teachers are understandably uncomfortable. A third-party agency of an almost unique type provides a further level of compliance to MAT principles. Parents and Teachers for Excellence is "a new movement to promote reforms within the education system and to spread good practice to help deliver excellence in schools across the country ...Supported by parent activists and some of the most respected people working in education (sic), we believe in autonomy for schools, the knowledge based curriculum, rigorous assessment, cultural enrichment and effective behaviour policies"[18]. PTE was founded by a familiar name – Rachel Wolf. Wolf was adviser to Boris Johnson when he was shadow minister for higher education; adviser to Michael Gove when he was shadow education secretary, working with Dominic Cummings. She founded (with help, we assume, and a lavish grant from the government) the New Schools Network which advised Free School starters. PTE started off with some lavish funding too, from the venture capitalist Jon Moynihan. Wolf was "a founding partner of Public First, a strategy and communications firm"[19] and advised on the 2019 Conservative party manifesto. This is a tight-knit group, these friends of promise. Almost, if one might dare say it, a new blob.

---

[17] Mansell, Warwick. 2018. Education Uncovered, 19 March 2018

[18] http://www.parentsandteachers.org.uk/

[19] Staufenberg Jess. 2019. Features: Rachel Wolf, SchoolsWeek, 23 July 2019

CEOs, Executive Principals and 'government advisers' figure prominently in the leading membership of PTE and it is easy to guess the kind of agenda being pursued by Michael Gove's favourite adviser and his pet headteacher. One of Inspiration Trust's schools, with more than thirty pages of rules such as no slouching, look your teacher in the eye and, if you feel poorly, vomit in a bucket rather than leave the classroom, started off by losing pupils at a worrying rate.

The drive for 'autonomy', then, is not a drive for localism. It is not a drive for responsiveness to local need. It is not a drive towards greater parent and community participation. On the contrary, it is a drive towards uniformity and control unrecognisable to any of the old local education authorities. And it appears to demand a level of obedience to a purist view of curriculum and behaviour management that is unlikely to acknowledge the rich variety of parental views that most schools respect and absorb into their working methods.

There can be little doubt that such a model of corporatisation has been enabled in order to further a unified view of schooling impervious to local participation and engagement. But it also enables a system in which a number of highly undesirable qualities are integral. That corporatisation has led to the vices we will be looking at in Section IV. That the majority of headteachers and governors, in secondary, primary and special schools are profoundly well-meaning and committed to the wellbeing of children and staff; that many LA officers are models of dedicated local government servants, is little comfort. For when good people are able do nothing, the field is left clear for the politically ambitious and the venally acquisitive.

The system then, has been developed in order to incorporate into it high levels of self-interest and organisational participatory dysfunction.

So Why Don't People Participate More?

"One of the most important aspects of power is not to prevail in a struggle but to predetermine the agenda of struggle – to determine whether certain questions ever reach the competition stage"[20]

What are those questions that it is so important for the governing classes to suppress?

---

[20] Parenti, Michael. 1970. Power and Pluralism: A View from the Bottom, Journal of Politics, 32 (1970) pp 501-3

Perhaps the simplest version of them is that set of questions – questions that can only be asked in a democracy – that we were encouraged to ask by Tony Benn (chapter 11, p161):

- What *power* have you got?
- Where did you get it from?
- In whose interests do you exercise it?
- To whom are you accountable?
- How can we get rid of you?[21]

When those questions are not being asked – or when they are asked but those in power refuse to answer them – we see the absenteeism from democratic engagement that characterises so many fields of activity today, including voting:

"Absenteeism reflects the suppression of the options and alternatives that reflect the needs of the nonparticipants. It is not necessarily true that people with the greatest needs participate in politics most actively – whoever decides what the game is about also decides who gets in the game"[22]

This approach broadly describes the three-dimensional approach to power developed by Steven Lukes: "In so extending the concept of power, the three dimensional view offers the prospect of a serious sociological and not merely personalized explanation of how political systems prevent demands from becoming political issues or even from being made"[23]. So, "In the three-dimensional approach is the suggestion of the use of power to pre-empt manifest conflict at all, through the shaping of patterns or conceptions of non-conflict."[24]

The individual conflict in the enforced conversion of Castle School was between village parents and school 'authorities'. These proved to be the local authority, mainly personified in its officers, the DfE, through its academy broker and, eventually, the professional staff of the selected sponsor school trust. Each of these had interests in the outcome above and beyond the good of the children of the school, in the retention or advancement of their career. The school's

---

[21] Chapter 11, note 26

[22] Schattschneider, Elmer. 1960. The Semi-Sovereign People: A Realist's View of Democracy in America, New York: Rinehart and Wilson p105

[23] Lukes, Steven. 1974. Power: A Radical View, London: MacMillan p38

[24] Gaventa, John. 1980. Power and Powerlessness: Quiescence and Rebellion in an Appalachian Valley, Chicago: University of Illinois p13

governing board and the parents were actively encouraged not to engage – indeed, they were told that any engagement would be first, futile and secondly, actively damaging to the interests of their children. They had had at that time a perfectly legal and democratic right to engage, using the local and national press, mobilising local opinion, holding professionals to their legal duties. In some other schools in the country, communities did this. Sometimes they won. But rarely. We can guess that similar tactics were employed by the authorities elsewhere, although some communities had the legal knowledge, the practical skills and experience, and the self-confidence to challenge. But in general, the authorities succeeded in getting their way.

The authorities' continuing dominance, except for a few rare outbreaks of open conflict, has been embedded in the system by the change in the law forbidding governors from challenging conversion to sponsored academy status where the school is required by Ofsted to convert. More significantly, perhaps, the continuing and probably deliberate confusion created by successive secretaries of state between Gove's departure in 2014 and the present has led many schools to submit to what they saw as the inevitable. After all, when the messages from the DfE become so mixed that, one minute, schools are told they will all be academies by 2020, the next, that there will be no legal enforcement because there seems to be a natural drift towards 100% academisation anyway, governors and headteachers can only put up with so much. Largely, it depends on the school's geography. Once a tipping point has been reached, all schools in an area will submit. But where the majority of primary schools have stood firm, mainly in urban areas, there is still a way to go – or not to.

These two tactics together appear to have inoculated most communities against protest and towards submission. Small outbreaks around the country continue to appear but are eventually put down. That, anyway, might be the obvious conclusion.

Or Is Something Else Happening?

What are we witnessing in the early 2020s? The beginnings of the final domino push that will take all state-funded schools into the corporate utopia of 'autonomous' business-run schools? The victory of neoliberal education politics – performance-orientated, knowledge-centred, socially divisive schooling, with education seen no longer as a public good, but as a servant of post-industrial capitalism, feeding a low-tax, low-employment, gig service economy? With around one-third of the country's children living in poverty, the writing would seem to be on the wall. The direction of travel seems clear.

Perhaps this is a moment of what Paul Mason calls "system mutation".[25] Maybe there is a shift away from an industrial capitalism based on the productive output of the mass of the working population, their early lives suitable preparation for it, as Willis[26] identified forty years ago in a differentiated but largely functional education designed to teach the necessary skills to be deferential and conformist. Meanwhile, the system discouraged participation in the social and labour organisations that shape our lives. If industrial capitalism is unable to meet people's economic and spiritual needs – the need for purposefulness, worthwhileness, congregation, interdependency – then it is possible that the population may sink into a barely-managed anomie punctuated by occasional social disruption like the 1981 inner city riots, the widespread protests of 2011 and the peaceful but powerful demonstrations of Black Lives Matter in 2020.

But maybe people will demand some kind of meaning to their lives, and maybe those working in the essential public services – essential even to the privileged 1% who still rely on the provision of food and roads and hospitals and educated working people – will demand some respite from the daily grind, or they will just stop turning up.

And what impact will the 2020 pandemic have on society, on labour patterns and on our expectations of our politicians?

Whichever of these alternatives emerges, the so-called winners of neoliberal capitalism might begin to be afraid.

Are There Early Signs That the Schooling System Is Tottering?

- 30% of children in the UK in poverty before the pandemic and benefits still being cut.

[25] Mason, Paul. 2016. Postcapitalism: A Guide to Our Future, London: Penguin Random House p70

[26] Willis, Paul. 1977. Learning to Labour: How working class kids get working class jobs, Farnborough: Saxon House

- Schools and individual teachers increasingly paying for children's food and clothing.
- School governing boards tackling endemic poverty and destitution in their communities.
- The exposure of the growing inequality in educational outcomes, not created but exacerbated by school closures during the pandemic.
- DfE lack of control over its own funding.
- Continuing headteacher 'disappearance'.
- CEOs of MATs on £250k plus salaries defending breaches of financial rules.
- Threats to the continuing cronyism of political appointments.
- That two-thirds of primary schools have still not academised.
- That the academy system cannot progress without people engaged by acquisitiveness for money and/or power being persuaded to take on economically unviable (e.g. PFI) schools – unless the DfE takes on the debts. (eventually, Michael Gove's chronic overspending will come home to roost)
- The continuing absence of evidence of school improvement being significantly – if at all – greater in corporate schools.
- And similarly the absence of evidence that grammar schools do better than comprehensive schools.
- The challenging of modes of acquisitiveness and venality which have been inherent in the system – especially with the continuing stagnation of wages for school staff.
- Councils and parents continuing albeit sporadically to challenge academisation.
- Signs of public exhaustion with conventional local and national politics.
- The revitalisation of teaching and school staff unions, through the newly amalgamated National Education Union, Unison and the GMB.

Is There an Alternative?

Subsidiarity offers an alternative to the current all-dominating centrism; decisions in all public services taken at the most local level that can realistically be sustained, counter-balanced by national expectations in all services. In education, this means a localised, democratic, participatory system within a national education service setting overall expectations but allowing prioritisation responsive to local need.

This may be the true path towards enabling the people to "catch the vision of their own powers"[27].

---

[27] Chapter 8, Note 8

Section IV
Corporatising Our Schools

Chapter 13
The Castle Captured
The Corporatisation of
English Schools

In this chapter, we sum up where we have reached in this account of English schooling since 2010. We introduce the idea that certain 'sins of commission and omission' have become endemic in the system, before we go onto explore what we might do about it.

"There was a rift in American life that was now coursing through American government. It wasn't between Democrats and Republicans. It was between the people who were in it for the mission, and the people who were in it for the money."[1]

The context in which the events described here occurred, as we have shown, as part of a national movement inspired to a large extent by similar movements in Sweden, New Zealand and the United States. In these countries, there is currently a rowing-back on the concept of providing state education through independent, corporatised schools. It has sometimes been described as the privatisation of state-funded schooling, in that it takes schools out of the public sector[2]. However, it actually hands the control – that is, the governance and leadership – of schools to corporate bodies in the form of trusts, which are exempt charitable companies limited by guarantee. They are registered with Companies House but are not required to register with the Charity Commission. It is the Department for Education whose duty it is to ensure that they are compliant with charities law. The Secretary of State for Education is the

---

[1] Lewis, Michael. 2019. The Fifth Risk, London: Penguin 2019, p191

[2] Meek, James. 2014. Private Island: Why Britain Now Belongs to Someone Else, London: Verso

'principal regulator' for academies[3]. I therefore prefer to call this process one of 'corporatisation'.

For the most part, in huge numbers, schools are led and worked in by leaders and other staff whose first interest is the welfare and education of children and young people. The vast majority of schools, surely, still contain such conscientious, ethical – and overworked – adults. The system supporting them, being managed by professionals as part of the public sector, and aligned with all the other public services provided, not just for the benefit of the economic health of the country, but also for the welfare of its citizens, assumed that. It did what it could – often imperfectly and certainly underfunded but largely with the best of intentions – to reflect those standards. These assumptions, which have served us well for some one hundred and fifty years, are now open to question.

That is not to say that the academy system is rotten throughout. The Castle School, at its first inspection as a member of the Redstart Learning Partnership, is now a 'good' school. Ofsted called it 'rapidly improving'. Of course, it was a 'good' school until 2014. It is claimed that most parents and children are happy there and that they are learning. Whether or not this would have happened if the LA had decided to turn the school around themselves – or, indeed, if it had intervened the moment that weaknesses in the leadership succession appeared four years before – is impossible to say. The dedication of the new leadership and their staff is unquestioned. Like all good school staff, they daily demonstrate their commitment to the children of the village.

As they do in all schools. The same teachers, teaching assistants and support staff, by and large, serve in academies as in the remaining maintained schools. Many of the leaders and governors of such schools hold to the same beliefs and standards. The new system is constantly under scrutiny and subject to government efforts to improve it, in both its efficiency and its probity. There are models of academy trust schools, such as co-operative trusts, that replicate the very best in democratically organised, popularly accountable, community-centred education.

Also, there is ongoing work towards adjusting those parts of the academy system that tend towards abuse or corruption. There continue to be significant changes in the requirements laid on the governance of stand-alone academies and multi academy trusts. New demands are made, for example, on the

---

[3] Paxton-Doggett, Katie. 2014. How to Run an Academy School, London: ICSA , 2014 p3

publication of governance arrangements, schemes of delegation, and relevant business and pecuniary interests of accounting officers; the robustness of evidence-based decisions on executive pay (an issue that continues to resist resolution); the declaration of the interests of trustees; establishment of a national database of trustees, local governors and senior staff; and the adoption of a whistle-blowing policy in all academies[4].

So the following sections are not meant to be Luddite about any new system of schooling. Indeed, the disruptive innovation[5] has been coming from the government. But academies continue to be judged predominantly on Ofsted ratings and published performance measures (of progress, achievement and improvement), before they will be allowed to expand (casting some doubt on the system's capacity to achieve an all-academy system by 2022). The success of all schools is dependent on a set of largely quantitative assessments, with little room for qualitative judgments.

What Now?

So what are the questions that need to be addressed about the corporate provision of state education in England?

The four key questions posed in this section are:

What risks are there in school provision in England under the new arrangements that were not significantly present in the LA system?

How do these arrangements compare with the government's handling of the corona virus crisis of 2020?

Do the benefits of academies and multi academy trusts outweigh the costs of ten years of structural change?

If not, what might a coherent model of school provision and governance look like in a post-pandemic state?

---

[4] Education Funding Agency (EFA)
https://www.gov.uk/government/organisations/education-funding-agency

[5] Gann, Nigel. 2016. Improving School Governance: How better governors make better schools, London: Routledge 2nd edition p181

Corporatisation in Education

Corporate management made its way into local government, and therefore into the administration of public education, in the 1970s, and appeared in schools themselves following the introduction of local management of schools in the 1988 Education Act. Since that time, it has manifested itself in two main ways:

- The engagement of business/quasi political people with corporate backgrounds in educational organisations (e.g. ARK, Harris Federation, Future Academies, the appointment of an accountant as HMCI) and administration (e.g. Theodore Agnew, John Nash, James O'Shaughnessy), and;
- the requirement that people working in education must behave in business-like ways (target-setting; bottom-lining; using business labels – CEO, Executive Head, Principal, Chief Operating Officers; recruiting governors from 'business').

This process has resulted in a schooling system far more liable to media and public criticism. So one issue we need to keep in mind as we look at the fallout of the last ten years is whether similar criticisms could have been made of the LA-dominated model between 1902 and 2010.

Academies and Free Schools have been subjected to considerable scrutiny in educational circles[6], often exposing both ineffectiveness and various forms of corruption that constitute perversions of the ideals of public service. These ideals reflect the belief that public goods should focus on the interests of users, and turning users into consumers involves a set of processes that are more akin to 'business'.

The first issues to resolve, then, are whether the new models enable, or even encourage, a set of behaviours and characteristics that are incompatible with the ideals of public service; and whether the new models are more effective, less effective or about the same in achieving the desired outcomes of a schooling system. Of course, these behaviours were not entirely absent from a local

---

[6] See, for example, Johnson, Martin & Mansell, Warwick. 2014. Education not for Sale: A TUC Research report. London: TUC; Gann, Nigel. 2014. Educating Ethics: The Probity of School Governance, in Forum Vol 56 No 3, Didcot: Symposium Books Ltd; Boffey, Daniel and Mansell, Warwick. 2016 Are England's academies becoming a cash cow for business? The Guardian, 12 June, 2016. Also the work of Stephen Ball, Andrew Wilkins and Andrew Allen

authority-led service. Not for a moment should we think of the past as a golden age of unblemished professional conduct. But LA oversight seems to have provided some constraints on the poorest leadership behaviour, while having other precautionary measures built in – national pay scales managed largely by in-house LA services, national regulations on expenditure under local management of schools, complaints and accountability systems which led directly to local council members as well, perhaps, as a culture within the public services where the user's entitlement to a certain standard of treatment was implicitly accepted.

We should also bear in mind that the emergence of social media means that the breadth and depth of public scrutiny of services from national provision to individual private traders is unrecognisably different to how it was in the twentieth century. Even so, the history of academisation suggests that it has brought about a significant change in the culture and the conduct of public education.

A study of the literature of opposition to and judgment on the academy model suggests these behaviours and characteristics can be categorised as in the next seven chapters. They mainly, but by no means exclusively, relate to the academy sector. But they also demonstrate the capacity of the developing culture in corporate schools to infect others across boundaries. Each also raises some questions about the values and tactics driving the government's management of the 2020 pandemic. The question that will hang at the end of this list is whether these behaviours and characteristics represent the emergence of a set of dominant values that are endemic in or aberrant to the schooling system.

The seven potentially deadly sins of the corporatisation of schools are:

1. Venality
2. Deceit
3. Secrecy
4. Centralisation
5. Cronyism
6. Isolationism
7. Precariousness

Chapter 14
The Seven Deadly Sins of the
Academy System: No 1 Venality

The independent sector, to which all academised schools now legally belong, is no stranger to the concept of greed. Indeed, one eminent representative of privately-funded education in England broke ranks in 2018 to attack his former colleagues and, in particular, their governing boards:

"The greed that has driven fee increases lies at the door of poor governance, and too many governors whose eyes rarely take in more than the good lunch they get at a Governors' meeting." He said that while the greed of public schools has previously been associated with corruption and a "desire to line one's own pockets", this no longer applies. The former private school headteacher wrote that nowadays, "private greed has been replaced by corporate greed", as schools seek to lure their potential clients with state-of-the-art facilities and raise fees to "astronomical heights" for overseas students. It is "the greed of those who see a market and people willing to pay more and more for their child's education without asking too many questions", he said[1].

Has the desire to line one's pockets penetrated state-funded schooling, where in the past a vocation had rarely been associated with greed?

Leadership Salaries

Perhaps the most persistent of complaints about academies, from the Parliamentary Select Committees on Public Accounts and on Education downwards, has focussed on leadership salaries and resultant pay inequality. The

---

[1] Turner, Camilla. 2018. Private schools' corporate greed is driving out middle-class families, former St Pauls' headteacher says, Daily Telegraph 14 May 2018. www.telegraph.co.uk/education/2018/04/14/private-schools-corporate-greed-pricing-middle-class-families/

revelations of double-figure percentage increases for growing numbers of senior administrative staff, at a period of zero increases and deteriorating working conditions for teaching and support staff in schools are now an annual event[2]. They are accompanied by repeated, but impotent, requests from the DfE to Trusts to rein them in[3].

"Before academies, we paid one local authority children's services director £132,000 to lead 50,000 pupils. Now we pay eight multi-academy trust chief executives £143,000 each to lead 50,000 academy pupils between them. Total £1,144,000. A staggering waste of resources"[4].

In March 2018, the Education and Skills Funding Agency wrote to eighty-seven academy trusts requiring them to justify CEO salaries of more than £150,000. After some years of headlines in both the educational press and mainstream media about excessive leadership pay, the government revealed the names of academy trusts of varying size and reputation that were being challenged about their CEO's salary[5]. This was picked up by some local papers[6] identifying the 14-school Inspiration Trust, where Rachel de Souza, now the Children's Commissioner for England, was CEO and Lord Agnew, DfE minister, is a founder and former trustee, as one local recipient, along with the Creative Education Trust (thirteen schools, including five in Great Yarmouth) and the four school Norfolk Academies, where three leaders including a former CEO have been paid £323,000 between them. The CEO of the National Academies Transformation Trust with twenty-two schools was paid between £225,000 and £250,000, an increase of some 20%, at a time when teachers' salaries continue to be held to one per cent annual increases. Transforming Lives Education Trust increased its headteacher's salary by £50,000 to a salary of between £270,000 and £280,000, despite the Trust having accepted only its second school in September 2017.

---

[2] See, for example, Staufenberg, Jess. 2018. Named: The 92 academy trusts with multiple staff on £100k+, Schools Week, 30 April 2018

[3] Department for Education 2018 & 2019 List of trusts receiving letters from ESFA about high executive salaries, https://www.gov.uk/government/organisations/department-for-education 6 July 2018 & 24 May 2019

[4] Courtney, Kevin. NUT leader, Twitter twitter.com/cyclingkev, 10.12.17

[5] See, for example, Schools Week, 28 March 2018

[6] e.g. Eastern Daily Press, 28 February 2018

In a time of increasing austerity, with school staff being laid off and, as we shall see, enormous pressure on budgets, the generous remuneration to CEOs and headteachers in trusts is bound to cause real concern.

Thus the largest salaries, such as Daniel Moynihan's at Harris Academies, amounting to at least £420,000 in addition to pension contributions of at least £50,000, receive considerable publicity, as do those trusts where earnings are boosted by other perks – generous pension contributions, BMW cars (for four senior leaders at Swale Academy Trust, with ten schools), and lavish expense accounts – listed by one website as including "Marco Pierre White meals, broadband at holiday homes, luxury flats and sex toys" (the unauthorised examples resulting in disciplinary action). Much of the concern arises where the trusts themselves are in straitened circumstances or even in deficit – The Kemnal Academies Trust, for example, had eight schools in the red, while paying its CEO more than £170,000. Other 'senior' staff also benefit. At the Durand Academy, a caretaker was paid £100,000 in 2016-17[7].

"Neo-liberal models of public services were supposed to bring private efficiency and public integrity together. Instead we got private sector inefficiency and a government without integrity."[8]

Parliament's Public Accounts Committee's report on the DfE's lack of control over, or even apparent interest in, this expenditure of money intended for children is thought-provoking: "(The Education and Skills Funding Agency) told us that where it identifies that an academy trust is in financial difficulties and this is partly due to staff salaries, *it will encourage* the trust to reduce pay accordingly"[9] (my italics). Similarly, the government continued to try to regulate to control breaches of financial regulations, such as inappropriate and excessive spending on non-essentials, and to limit related party transactions. But as long as access to trust funds is controlled by a small number of individuals often self-appointed, sometimes in perpetuity, this will continue to cause problems.

In short, the provision of state-funded schooling in England has been monetised. It can be seen by a significant number of players as an opportunity to have more power, and to make more money, in a statutory provision than can ordinarily be made by the provision of goods or services. If that were not the

---

[7] Santry, Charlotte. 2018. Times Educational Supplement, 11 January 2018

[8] Voices, https://www.independent.co.uk/voices/carillion-academies-conservatives-deficit-financial-scandal-education-a8186751.html 31.1.18)

[9] Public Accounts Committee. 2018. House of Commons, March 2018

case, why would senior staff of businesses like Harris Carpets and Babcock International, as just two examples, want to play a larger role in the organisation of schooling than the mere selling of their specialist products?

Breaches of Financial Regulations and Related Party Transactions

Parliament's Public Accounts Committee reported in March 2018: "A related party transaction is a business arrangement between an academy trust and an organisation or a person with whom those responsible for the governance of an academy trust have a personal connection. This can include family members. In 2015–16, academy trusts undertook over 3,000 of these transactions worth a total of £120 million. The Department asserted that related party transactions can be beneficial to schools, as they may receive goods or services for free, or at reduced cost. It recognised, however, that it is important that related party transactions are transparent and properly procured. The Department told us that 40% of academy trusts have related party transactions that involve either the academy's Headteacher or governors."[10]

This degree of consanguinity between trustees responsible for the impartial strategic oversight of a charity and service providers who have a business relationship with it, however well dressed-up it might be, is remarkable by any standards. The first finding of the committee's report is that "The Department for Education's rules around party-related transactions are too weak to prevent abuse."[11] These transactions are required to be only 'at cost' – that is, the provider of the related services should be making no profit from the arrangement. It is difficult to believe that trustees and CEOs are contributing such an amount of financial goodwill to their organisations with no benefit to themselves.

Examples of these breaches include:

- Lilac Sky Schools Academy trust: repeated breaches of financial rules including staff severance payments before re-employing the staff the following day; a £1.3m deficit while paying "extortionate and expensive" chief executive consultancy costs (at more than £900 a day

---

[10] ibid

[11] ibid

for two-thirds of a year, paid to the chief executive whose partner was a trustee)[12].

- The head of Perry Beeches Academy Trust in Birmingham being paid £120,000 salary while receiving a further £160,000 as CEO of a company providing management services to the trust, with no proper tendering process, while the trust had a deficit of £2.1m; this headteacher left his job after an EFSA investigation, and was subsequently appointed to the headship of a school in the Gorse Academy Trust from September 2017. However, in January 2018 it was reported that this appointment was brought to an end after three months[13].

- In December 2017, police were reported to be investigating the collapse of the twenty-one school Wakefield City Academies Trust (WCAT). "The trust transferred millions of pounds of its schools' reserves to centralised accounts before admitting that new sponsors would need to be found for them ... In October 2016, it emerged that the trust had paid almost £440,000 to IT and clerking companies owned by its then chief executive and his daughter[14]; police were still investigating WCAT in March 2018.

- The Collective Spirit Multi-Academy Trust, with just 284 pupils in two schools, paid over half a million pounds in 2014-15 to a company set up by, and whose only shareholder was, the trust's chief executive[15].

- At Aspirations Academies Trust, the co-founder and chair of trustees was paid more than £3,000 a day for consultancy services, a total of nearly £180,000 over two years, including travel, accommodation and meals – the travel bills for six trips amounted to £38,300[16].

- The chief executive of the seven school EMLC Academies Trust engaged a consultancy firm over two years at a cost of almost £1.5m – a firm of which she was a director and shareholder, where her daughter is

[12] Dickens, John. 2017. The Lilac Sky Scandal: Accounts reveal Astonishing Financial Impropriety, Schools Week, 16 June 2017

[13] Local Schools Network. http://www.localschoolsnetwork.org.uk/2018/01/disgraced-superhead-liam-nolan-leaves-one-year-principals-job-after-just-three-months

[14] Perraudin, Frances. 2017. The Guardian, 6 December 2017

[15] Mansell, Warwick. 2016. The Guardian, 16 August 2016

[16] Ibid

also a director and her daughter-in-law an employee. The CEO's husband is a trustee on the EMLC board[17].

- Cumbria police were investigating Bright Tribe Trust in March 2018[18]. Bright Tribe received £1m to establish a 'northern hub' of schools in 2015, but funding was exhausted by the end of the following year, leaving four schools without sponsors. The 'embattled' chief operating officer left her post in November 2017[19], while two months later the trust was revealed to have paid three companies owned by one of its trustees £681,000 in 2016-17 for staffing issues including secondments of staff[20];
- In February 2018, Schools Week reported that five schools, three of them stand-alone academies, one a Bright Tribe school, made large severance payments to staff without having gained the necessary permission from the ESFA[21].
- The Galileo Multi-Academy Trust was investigated by the ESFA in the summer of 2019, just a year after its opening. The trust "broke rules over a 'for-profit' contract with a firm linked to one of its directors'[22]. Galileo Trust seemed to have close links with the Diocese of York but lost all of its trustees and its chief executive in post at the end of August 2018.

Other Perks

There seems to be a substantial amount of junketing going on for staff and trustees in some academy trusts. Silver Birch Academy Trust "that runs four primary schools spent thousands of pounds on overseas trips for its leaders, more than £1,000 on two hotel rooms for two nights and almost £10,000 on Facebook adverts for a free school that has not yet been set up", according to allegations in a draft investigation seen by the Observer[23]. This turned out to include a trip to

---

[17] Robertson, Alix. 2018. Academy Trust Boss defends £1.5m in Payments to Family Firm, Schools Week 19 January 2018

[18] Schools Week, 16 March 2018

[19] Times Educational Supplement, 29 November 2017

[20] Ibid. 31 January 2018

[21] Schools Week, 23 February 2018

[22] Dickens, John. 2020. 'Supersized' trust investigated by government just 14 months after opening with 10 schools, Schools Week, 6 July 2020

[23] Mansell, Warwick and Savage, Michael. Silver Birch Academy Trust in spotlight again over spending, The Guardian, 12 May 2018

Shanghai and New Zealand by the trust's chief executive and his deputy costing over £12,000. Trustees at the now closed Schools Company Trust paid just under £4,000 for a "psychic workshop" given by a South African woman with 'extrasensory observation'[24]. A stand-alone special school in Brent "paid hundreds of thousands of pounds to consultants, including one who served as its chair of trustees and chief finance officer"[25], a practice strictly forbidden under charity regulations. Meanwhile, the ESFA found it necessary to advise MATs against spending money on alcohol and 'excessive gifts' for its staff and trustees[26]; and an executive headteacher was reported to have spent just short of £56,000 on his office refurbishment[27].

These practices seem to have become so widespread that in May 2020, a director at Rachel Wolf's *Public First* and Head of the Education Practice, felt able to publicly praise an old Eton and Oxford mate of Boris Johnson in a tweet for turning AET into a viable business, it having been "synonymous with early MAT overreach+financial profligacy"[28]. So success in academy leadership is now measured by the capacity to stop them throwing money around.

Very little of this would be possible in a maintained school.

However, these practices, especially the related party contracts, have become well-established in the government before and, particularly during, the pandemic. The emergency powers associated with that have inflated exponentially the opportunities for directing money towards one's mates and financial supporters. Reports emerged in May 2020 of how an artificial intelligence start-up that had worked on the Vote Leave EU campaign with Downing Street adviser Dominic Cummings – Michael Gove's key adviser at the DfE in his period of office there – was awarded "at least seven government contracts worth almost £1m in the space of eighteen months"[29]. Theodore Agnew (see above), a key Gove associate, minister and academy facilitator and leader, had a £90k shareholding in this company, while holding office as a Cabinet

[24] Schools Week, 12 October 2018

[25] Allen-Kinross, Pippa. 2019. Academy rapped over consultancy payments to chair of trustees, 1 February 2019

[26] Roberts, John. 2018. Don't buy booze, funding agency tells Mats, TES, 8 June 2018

[27] @nohandsup, 16 June 2018

[28] TES; @jonathansimons, Twitter, 5 May 2020

[29] Evans, R and Pegg, D. 2020. Vote Leave AI firm wins seven government contracts in 18 months, Guardian 4th May 2020

Office minister – "responsible for the government department that promotes the use of digital technology within public services"[30]. He was eventually reported to be relinquishing the shares in the autumn of 2020.

Some colleagues of Michael Gove and Dominic Cummings even managed to monetise the A Level results fiasco of 2020. Public First, founded and run by James Frayne and Rachel Wolf, advisers to Gove alongside Cummings, was contracted by the Cabinet Office, run by Gove, to "work on 'insight on public opinion for this year's exam arrangements'. The spokesperson added: Public First is currently assisting Ofqual's small communications team with an unprecedented amount of media interest in a complex policy area'"[31]. The reader might wonder what unique insight might have been provided by Public First that in some way detoxified the scandal and upset following the declaration of manifestly unfair exam results. How might the disaster have been worse without Public First's, no doubt expensive, intervention? At the time of writing, how much Wolf and Frayne made from this contract has not been published. But we do know, from the Daily Mirror, that they also had a contract from the Department of Health and Social Care for £116,000 to "lock in the lessons learned" by the government during the pandemic[32]. Locking in the learning – whatever that actually means – is a lucrative business. Even more so when you have old mates in the government department with authority to dole out the contracts without tender or competition.

This toxic mix of engagement with a state-funded provision, control of the government department responsible for the provision, and financial interest in its promotion, translated seamlessly from the DfE of the early 2010s, through the various EU campaigns, and into the era of the pandemic.

Pay Inequality

Since 2003 the School Teachers Pay and Conditions publication has provided the framework for teachers' pay in England and Wales. However, this does not apply to the independent, though state-funded, academies. So much of the inflated pay awarded to senior academy leaders – all public money provided by taxpayers – is taken at the expense of both the children attending the schools

---

[30] Ibid

[31] Conn, David. 2020. Firm linked to Gove and Cummings hired to work with Ofqual on A-Levels, The Guardian, 20 August 2020

[32] Daily Mirror, 19 August 2020

and the lower-paid staff of the schools. Pay differentials, therefore, which are regulated in maintained schools, have no limitations in academies.

"Seven of England's larger multi-academy trusts paid one of their employees – probably their chief executive officer – at least double what anyone else in the organisation received, their latest published accounts reveal. In two cases, the *gap* between the top-paid and the second-highest remunerated in a single trust was considerably higher in itself than the highest possible salary that a headteacher operating in England's non-academy sector could usually earn."[33] In the Transforming Lives Education Trust, a trust with only two schools (see above), "the accounts show that the headteacher is paid around £200,000 more than any of her fellow employees"[34].

Academies may also be more inclined to increase central office staffing costs at the expense of front-line staff. Delta Academy Trust, named by the DfE as their preferred sponsor to take over four of WCAT's academies (see above), with forty-four schools in the north of England, cut its overall wage bill by 11% in 2016-17, including a cut of 13% in the number of full-time equivalent (FTE) teachers, while increasing its management and support team from sixty to seventy-eight FTEs. The CEO received a salary of between £180,000 and £185,000, doubling his minimum pay of the previous year[35]. By 2019, the average disparity between the pay of academy leaders and classroom teachers was significantly greater than in maintained schools.

Schools Week's analysis of CEO pay in the year 2016-17 also revealed a significant gender pay gap. Across the twenty-four trusts with twenty or more schools, those headed by men show an average CEO salary of £174,765; in those headed by women, the average salary was £139,800. The Guardian's analysis of data from the government's national survey on the gender pay differential suggests this is a widespread problem, and specifically a problem arising from corporatisation: "Women working in a number of academy chains are paid less than half of their male counterparts. Schoolsworks Academy Trust in West Sussex, which runs six schools, has a median hourly pay gap of 62% in favour of men, while the Wakefield City Academies Trust, which managed twenty-one schools before folding last year, had a figure of 52%. Of the 50 companies with

[33] Mansell, Warwick. 2017. Education Uncovered 15.12.17
[34] Schools Week, 12.3.18
[35] Schools Week, 24.3.18

the worst gender pay gap, twenty-four happen to be multi-academy chains."[36] 80% of teachers are women and they appear to bear the brunt of the deregulation of schools and the cutting of costs.

The Monetisation of Schooling

These issues, of excessive and unequal pay, and of profiteering from a public sector service, are new in schools. Very occasionally before the turn of the century, newspapers would run items about a rogue headteacher who had somehow, often through negligence of governance or collusion of a finance officer, got their hands on money or goods intended for the school. This was very rare. Before local management of schools came along in the early 1990s, it was barely heard of at all. Misconduct in public service in the teaching profession was much more likely to be about inappropriate sexual conduct or bullying of staff. Most likely, it would be about poor management. Any rows about money would almost always be about teacher pay and would be a national issue.

The introduction of performance-related pay in the early years of the twenty-first century, however, for the first time brought pay under the supervision of school governors. While many heads rightly saw the opportunity to achieve salaries worthy of their responsibilities, for the first time, a very small number of headteachers saw flashing £ signs when they sat down with a weak and malleable governing body. And the next stage – lay governors making decisions on the advancement of all staff through a range of pay scales – opened the floodgates for those who thought that money was the only real motivation for people who work in schools.

It has proved impossible to come up with any hard evidence that performance-related pay works, while there is considerable research which suggests the opposite, as the website of the National Union of Teachers shows[37]. Performance-Related Pay:

- Does not improve teacher or pupil outcomes.
- Does not motivate teachers.

---

[36] Okolosie, Lola. 2018. The Guardian. 27 March 2017

[37] National Union of Teachers https://www.teachers.org.uk/edufacts/performance-related-pay-in-schools, 2018)

- Undermines and disrupts effective school improvement, encouraging competition above cooperation.
- Ignores the success of collaborative models such as City Challenge.
- Encourages teachers to work with the best classes.
- Does nothing to assist the measurement of good teaching.
- Assumes the ending of pay progression based on length of service, so making teaching a less attractive career choice at a time of a growing teacher recruitment crisis.
- Is an unnecessary and bureaucratic burden.
- Can often lead to discriminatory outcomes.
- Is unpopular with teachers.

PRP, of course, is an essential part of the salary structure in all English state-funded schools. However, the way it has been practised in some academy trusts demonstrates how pernicious its impact can be.

Chapter 15
The Seven Deadly Sins of
The Academy System: No 2 Deceit

Any regime that depends on competition and punishment rather than collaboration and support to improve performance will see an increase in cheating. Professional educators know that encouragement and confidence are needed to help children learn, that carrots always work better than sticks. The Conservative-led administrations from 2010 seemed unaware of this basic facet of human nature – perhaps their leaders had never come across it in their rarefied but often emotionally deprived upbringing – and tried pretty well every trick in the book to ridicule and demean those they disagreed with and to punish those who failed to match up to their objectives. In most recent times, this became an assault on the civil service, with the departure in 2020 of five senior officials within a few months. As you might expect, as the government's own performance worsened and it looked ever more incompetent, the casualties fell wherever blame could be laid.

It seems certain that the use of deceit in the education sector has grown. This may be true of all school sectors, due to the increasing demands on school performance. Between 2013 and 2017, incidences of cheating in the performance and reporting of tests and exam outcomes quadrupled[1]. We had seen few reports of teachers cheating on examination and test results until relatively recently:

"The number of teachers caught cheating to obtain better GCSE and A-level results for their pupils has risen fourfold in the past four years. A total of 388 penalties were issued for the offence last year, as a sharper focus on tests, league

---

[1] Allen-Kinross, Pippa. 2018. Doomed Schools Company Trust 'double-counted' GCSEs Schools Week, 4 July 2018; Staufenberg, Jess 2018 Second Harris academy has SATs results annulled, Schools Week, 21 September, 2018; Schools Improvement. 2018 Britain's best school has its SATs results ruled null and void in cheating storm, schoolsimprovement.net, 23 July 2018

tables and inspections forced them to choose between helping their pupils and helping themselves", research from the Royal Society of Arts found[2]. Ninety-seven penalties were issued for 2013 in England, Wales and Northern Ireland. "Considering how hard some forms of cheating are to detect, this is likely to understate the true scale of the problem," the report said. Even the venerable Harris Academies fell foul of this. The Standards and Testing Agency found that teachers at Harris Academy Philip Lane, the former Downhills Primary that Michael Gove had ensured would close and be transferred in north London in 2012, had 'over aided' pupils in their SATs in 2018, a similar accusation to those made against NETAT staff drafted into Waltham Holy Cross. A few weeks later, pupils at the 'outstanding' Harris Primary Academy Kent House in south London had some of their results annulled[3]. Schools Company Trust, before it walked away from its three Devon Pupil Referral Units and a secondary school in Kent in 2018, seems to have reported 'unreliable' GCSE figures, double counting some GCSEs and overvaluing entry level BTECs and certificates[4]. Even at a school lauded as the TES (Times Educational Supplement) School of the Year, "the results of two SATs tests taken by pupils at Broadfoot Primary School in Romford, East London, have been annulled following an investigation by Government inspectors"[5]. The Gove curse on the hero head had struck again.

In some cases, inflating SATs results was just one deceit amongst a much wider range of bad behaviour. In July of 2018, in addition to fiddling the grades, the headteacher of Willowpark Primary Academy in Oldham also "had a stack of porn images on her phone …" and took "her partner on a paid-for school trip to Manchester United and bought computer kit with school funds, the Teacher Regulation Agency found"[6].

That year saw a growth in such incidents: "Provisional key stage 2 data for 2018 …said 2,688 test results were suppressed while the government investigated, compared to just 723 in 2017."[7]

---

[2] Bennett, R. 2017. The Times, 16 November 2017

[3] Staufenberg, ibid

[4] Allen-Kinross, ibid

[5] SchoolsImprovement.net: https://schoolsimprovement.net/britains-best-school-has-its-sats-results-ruled-null-and-void-in-cheating-storm-after-superhead-takes-failing-primary-to-top-award/, 23 July 2018

[6] BBC News website. 2018. Oldham phone porn head teacher banned for life, 2 July 2018

[7] ibid

Maybe those that live by the league tables also die by them.

The practice of 'off-rolling' and informal exclusion has grown to be a significant issue[8]. Reports of 'informal' exclusion, mostly by 'invitation', where it is suggested to a pupil's parents that their child's school record would look better without a formal exclusion, are inevitably difficult to prove and so are largely anecdotal. Similarly unprovable are the occasions when schools suggest that parents keep their ADHD child at home during an Ofsted inspection. The focus on pure results is bound to have such outcomes. Questions have often been raised about the performance of academies in Ofsted inspections, for example, by bringing in more experienced teachers from other schools during an inspection[9].

The behaviour of some leaders in academy trusts leaves a lot to be desired. One businessman became chief executive of The Education Fellowship Trust on the strength of spurious claims to have been "high up in John Lewis" and "been put on the board of the British Airports Authority". By the time he had completed 6 years at the trust and been paid around £160k a year for running twelve schools, he had driven the trust into a deficit of millions of pounds, producing poor results and failed inspections[10]. The 6,500 pupils of the trust had, we presume, no compensation for the combined negligence engineered by the DfE and the trust over a period equivalent to a pupil's whole secondary education.

Some academy leaders find it difficult to keep their fingers away from social media and their mouths shut when silence would be a wiser option. "The chief executive of a trust whose schools were rated 'inadequate' was criticised by parents after a post that said 'F**k Ofsted' appeared on his Instagram account." Not content with that, the former primary school headteacher and president of the National Association of Head Teachers posted a "picture of a yacht …with the caption: Sod all you bl**dy peasants. I'm having one of these and cruising the Adriatic – because I'm worth it."[11]

---

[8] Weale, Sally. 2018. 300 schools picked out in GCSE 'off-rolling' investigation, Guardian 26 June 2018; Adams, Richard. 2019. 'Off-rolling' hides true extent of disadvantage gap in schools, Guardian, 5 December 2019

[9] Youle, Emma. 2018/19 Top Academy Chain Accused of 'Cheating' During Ofsted Inspection, HuffPost, 19 September 2018, updated 12 July 2019

[10] Hackett, Geraldine. 2020. John Lewis salesman lied his way to £1m job running schools, The Times, 21 February 2020

[11] The Times. 2019. Instagram post lands school chief in hot water, The Times, 16 October 2019

At the Victoria Academies Trust, the chief executive was incensed by a whistleblower's letter to Ofsted "raising issues relating to safeguarding, trust expenditure and treatment of staff"[12]. Sadly, he went on to deliver a tirade to staff at the school, and "threatened to uncover and 'deal with' the anonymous whistleblower who had behaved in a 'treacherous', 'underhand' and 'pathetic' way". His services dispensed with in May 2020, Andrew Morrish now runs his own educational consultancy "that provides strategic support and consultancy for system and school leaders, CEOs especially."

However, academy chief executives are not the only ones to breach the rules around whistleblowing. In February 2020, it was revealed that the DfE's response to an FOI request about the forced conversion of Waltham Holy Cross Primary School (see p104) published the names of three whistleblowers at the school five times in a 164-page report. While initially it was thought that this was the result of an oversight, it turns out "that the DfE actively opted not to redact the names"[13]. The DfE's bullying behaviour here and its collusion with the NET Trust is evidence that its behaviour has not changed since the days of Gove and Cummings. That may reflect the nature of the incumbent at that time, who legendarily kept a Tarantula spider in a jar on his desk when he was Chief Whip, and a whip on his desk when he was in charge at Sanctuary Buildings.

Meanwhile the DfE has become ever more mendacious itself under a succession of politicians notable only for their commitment to their own advancement within their party. Back in late 2014, the then Secretary of State for Education, Nicky Morgan, was told by the UK Statistics Authority to "reconsider her comments" when she claimed that "one in three pupils left primary school unable to read or write under Labour"[14]. This was the second time in a week that the chair of the authority, Sir Andrew Dilnot, had criticised the use of the statistic. The Education Policy Institute attacked figures presented by longstanding Schools Minister Nick Gibb for three years running which purported to show increasing numbers of pupils attending 'good' and 'outstanding' schools; a concurrent investigation into Damian Hinds' persistent mendacious assertions about school funding led to admonishment by the UK

---

[12] Allen-Kinross, Pippa. 2019. "I'll deal with this treacherous whistleblower" Schools Week, 5 April 2019

[13] Mulholland, Hélène. 2020. DfE in 'serious data breach' after naming whistleblowers, Schools Week, 14 February 2020

[14] BBC News website, 19.12.14

Statistics Authority. Gibb achieved the honour of his own hashtag on Twitter in 2020 as '#FibbyGibby.'

In the autumn of 2017, analysis of statistics used by the DfE to proclaim the effectiveness of free schools was challenged in the TES. Even the number of free schools claimed to have opened to date had been bumped up from the 305 shown on its own website to 500, by including university technical colleges and studio schools – and even free schools that had subsequently closed! But when the (very unreliable) statistics on the free schools' performance claimed to show much better outcomes, the results of the 195 less successful non-free free schools, and the now-closed schools, were excluded. In the new push to open more grammar schools, there appears very little evidence to show better performance without taking into account the nature of the entrants to the system. Grammar schools take in very few children from disadvantaged neighbourhoods, even when they are successful in primary school. Grammar schools take very few free school meal pupils – 0.4% of grammar school pupils, against 4% nationally.

In early 2018, three claims made by the DfE were demonstrated to be false in less than a month. New Secretary of State Damian Hinds, in an otherwise quite unremarkable term of office, engaged the interest of the current chair of the UK Statistics Authority, Sir David Norgrove, in claiming that school funding was being increased when it was demonstrably only being maintained. Even Hinds' correction was shown to be incorrect. He falsely claimed that all schools would see at least a small cash increase, when some would be seeing cuts. Less than a fortnight later in the middle of March, Hinds found himself again on the naughty step when he announced that there would be £26m to support breakfast clubs in schools, but later had to admit that this commitment had first, already been announced months earlier and, secondly, was to be spread over three years, not one. The total amount provided for primary school breakfasts turned out to be equivalent to 1p per pupil per day. In April, following claims that around 500 Sure Start centres had been closed since the Conservative-led government took office in 2010, the Sutton Trust showed that, in fact, the number was double that, at least 1,000.

In 2019, teachers' unions claimed that four in five state schools would be financially worse off in 2020 than they had been five years earlier, "despite promises by Boris Johnson's government of a multimillion-pound funding boost"[15]. And in 2018, David Laws at the EPI argued that "the government should drop a 'misleading' statistic that suggests up to 1.9 million more pupils in England attend good or outstanding schools than in 2010"[16]. Many of these pupils, it emerged, were in schools that had not been inspected for at least eight years.

So it has been very difficult to take the DfE's word for anything. The row around the appointment of Free School founder Toby Young's appointment to the Office for Students resulted in a damning indictment of DfE practice, this time in the politicisation of public appointments. The former and current ministers, Jo Johnson and Sam Gyimah, had already decided who they wanted to appoint, and went on to do it, despite the attempts of civil servants to ensure a fair process conducted according to due diligence procedures. Even during the Commissioner for Public Appointments investigation, the department failed to produce the documentation requested. It is difficult to think of a more blatant disregard of due practice or a greater contempt for transparency and fairness. In the end, of course, because of the sheer incompetence of those involved, the process collapsed. No one among those responsible lost their job.

But most pertinent to this book is the revelation in February of 2018 that the DfE continued, four years on from the Castle saga, to pre-empt the process of transition to academy status of failing schools.

"Education Uncovered found twenty-eight cases in the past two years in which the school is listed as having been approved by the DfE for academy status before the day on which the latest report, which in all cases gave the school an 'inadequate' or failing rating, was published …In one case, where there was a six-month gap between a school's Ofsted inspection and its report being published, the school's conversion to an academy was approved three months before its official report confirming it was 'inadequate' with serious weaknesses was published."[17]. The DfE was not able to respond to queries about the procedure followed in these twenty-eight cases, likely to be the tip of a large iceberg.

---

[15] Weale, Sally. 2019. School cash boost 'leaves most worse off than in 2015', The Guardian, 1 October 2019

[16] Burns, Judith. 2018. Drop 'misleading' statistic, government told, BBC News, 2 July 2018

[17] Mansell, Warwick. Education Uncovered, April 2018

The DfE sets an example which will worry and distress most schools. But others seem to have taken their lead as an example to follow. As the death toll of corona virus in the UK surpassed all others in Europe, the information made available in early May 2020 about testing and the availability of personal protective equipment for health care professionals was often highly questionable. The use of numbers and statistics and graphs often showed very poor performance by the UK against international comparisons, while being greeted as a series of triumphs – "world-beating" according to the Prime Minister – by government spokespeople and ministers. Meanwhile, the behaviour of government figures during the Brexit referendum and later throughout the 'negotiations' reached almost Trump-like proportions.

Chapter 16
The Seven Deadly Sins of the Academy System: No 3 Secrecy

It seems unlikely that anyone at any time could have complained that a government was giving us too much information. But in a world of judicial reviews, freedom of information and data protection, the Department for Education during the 2010s stood out as extraordinarily opaque. We have already seen its response – or rather lack of response – to any matters about the conversion of Castle School. This was hardly exceptional. The parents, governors and community of Stoke sub Hamdon were routinely ignored and dismissed, not just by the officers of the local authority, but also by some of their political representatives, the academy broker and others in officialdom who had anything to do with the case.

Secrecy can be a form of deceit, and it breeds suspicion and discontent. While confidentiality is an important element in organisational management and in dealing with individuals, it is now used routinely in many areas of educational governance to avoid trouble. Readers will be reminded of the tortuous mess that officers engaged in during the conversion of Castle School[1], and the then junior Schools Minister's extraordinary claim in parliament that consultations "unintentionally raise the temperature of debate, rather like when one gets lawyers involved in divorce settlements" and could be "used to create delays" (p122). The DfE's efforts to save us from ourselves could be commendable. Or not.

In the spring of 2017, Schools Week revealed the contents of the minutes of the DfE board. This board is the governing authority of the department. Little was known (or probably cared) about it until one of its lay members resigned early the following year due to a connection too close for comfort to a

---

[1] Chapter 6

particularly seedy event organised by the now defunct Presidents Club. David Meller, a non-executive director of the department, turned out to be co-chair of the club responsible for the louche evening.

At that time, the last available minutes of the board were from January 2015. They comprised the following:

Department for Education Board: Summary of Meeting
27 JANUARY 2015

Welcome
The Secretary of State opened the meeting by welcoming all members

Note of Discussions
The Board held discussions on the work of the department during the Parliament.

It is fair to say that no school governing board or trust would get away with such a contemptuous attitude to transparency. Indeed, Schools Week's chasing seems to have had a result, as the minutes of the 2-hour meeting on the 12th September 2017 stretched to 2 pages. Neither transparency nor communications, though, are listed as agenda items. (When in 2020 the DfE did at last publish its most recent minutes, it was revealed that the Board had not discussed the inevitable A Level results fiasco, so in that case, perhaps it would have been better if the departmental dog had eaten them.)

But it is a pity, because investigations by the Times Educational Supplement in the first two weeks of that very month in 2017, reveal a raft of occasions when the DfE appears to have deliberately set out to keep its actions and decisions secret:

"1 Sep. : The government *tried to hide* its scheme to build free schools in 'mixed use developments' such as retail parks. Private property developers will share any "rewards" from free schools that will be built in retail parks and leisure developments, under plans the government *wanted* to keep *secret*.

5 Sep – The DfE attempted to suppress the fact that an academy trust it wanted to take over a school had been under investigation for payments it made to its directors.

The case is one of a series of revelations about secret inner workings of the academies programme that the Department for Education was only persuaded to disclose after an intervention by the Information Commissioner.

6 Sep. 2017: The government *tried to hide* the fact that "quick growth and capacity" had become an "issue" at an *academy* trust where a schools minister had encouraged rapid expansion only two years previously,

7 Sep. 2017: The Department for Education *tried to hide* the fact that an unofficial Ofsted inspection that was not designed to hold schools to account was used to justify transferring an *academy* to a new sponsor.

8 Sep : The investigation of a multi-academy trust (MAT) for payments to directors, the use of an unofficial Ofsted report to justify an academy transfer and the "issues" caused by a minister encouraging the rapid expansion of an academy chain …are all aspects of the running of today's state school system (by) the Department for Education."[2]

Sometimes, the DfE claims that what we call secrecy is ignorance – which may or may not be a comfort. When the TES asked them how many people work for the regional schools commissioners – a structure created by and directly responsible to the secretary of state – "it was told: 'we don't hold this information readily available due to restructuring to the RSC team over the years.'" The current cost of the commissioners in 2018 was £31.2m[3].

Even friendly parliamentary questions fail to extract any worthwhile information. In January 2018, Schools Week reported: "Today (Schools Minister Nick Gibb) is asked by fellow Tory MP Henry Smith about the discussions that have taken place between him and the chancellor about the impact of cash on school outcomes since 2010. Gibb writes: 'My rt hon friend the secretary of state for education routinely discusses matters of shared interest with cabinet colleagues, including my rt hon friend the chancellor of the exchequer. Pupil outcomes are, of course, at the heart of the Department's decision-making'"[4].

---

[2] TES, 1-8 September, 2017

[3] TES, 16 February 2018

[4] Schools Week, 19 January 2018

In a seminal but little-publicised case, Geraldine Hackett's disclosures about the debacle at The Education Fellowship Trust (TEFT)[5] got to the heart of the DfE's attempts to keep the public in the dark about the most egregious cases of misbehaviour and its own poor oversight. Freelance journalist Hackett put in an FOI request for information about the vetting of CEO Johnson Kane and how his total lack of experience in education had not been spotted by the DfE, what sort of communications had taken place between the RSC for the region and TEFT, and what measures the DfE might have required to deal with the Trust's underperformance. Lord Agnew rejected this request, using an obscure exemption in the FOI Act which protects the free and frank provision of advice and views, and seeks to avoid the possibility of prejudicing the effective conduct of public affairs.

The Information Tribunal, to which Hackett had recourse after the Information Commissioner supported Agnew's position, unanimously and roundly rejected the DfE argument. The DfE's contempt for openness and transparency was cruelly exposed in the Tribunal's judgment. So was its incompetence: "If proper checks had been carried out and Mr Kane's background was as he stated in his CV (which is on TEFT's website), then disclosure would have no adverse implications. If proper checks were not carried out …then there was a clear public interest in knowing that."[6]

Agnew had, of course, never been elected to any of the enormously influential posts he has held in government since 2010 under the sponsorship of Michael Gove, from education to the cabinet office. Nevertheless, his entry on the government's own website declared in 2020 that "There is no experience to show"[7].

Agnew's relaxed attitude to vetting seems to have travelled to the cabinet office with him. You may remember Dominic Cummings' attempt to attract "an unusual set of people" into 10 Downing Street in early 2020. By the summer, two of those unusual appointments had come croppers. Andrew Sabisky lasted hardly any time at all after his appointment to the PM's office. "No. 10 refused to answer questions about how he had been recruited and whether he had been

---

[5] See Chapter 15, note 10

[6] Mansell, Warwick. 2020. DfE sets out in detail its reasons for cloaking academy decision-making in secrecy. But legal tribunal rejects them, Education Uncovered, 26 February 2020

[7] https://members.parliament.uk/member/4689/experience

properly vetted."[8] His suggestion in his writings that "black people on average had lower IQs than white people" presumably hadn't been spotted in the recruitment process. Five months later Will O'Shea, another toiler in the vineyards of No 10, posted a comment about the Black Lives Matters protesters, suggesting that it could be "Time to get out the live rounds"[9]. It is reported that O'Shea had applied through the Cummings 'advert' and was interviewed by Ben Warner, Cummings' close associate. Of course, he said that he didn't mean his tweet to be taken seriously. He was initially appointed to "the No 10 project to reshape the government's use of data, which would involve breaking free of the controls each department has. 'So basically they wanted to see how they could break governance rules', he said."[10] When the project was suspended as the pandemic hit, Warner was able to call on his "friends in the Cabinet Office" to take O'Shea on in Theodore Agnew's Government Digital Service. A spokesman said that "All standard vetting processes were carried out for a contractor role through a commercial framework."[11] Whatever that means. Whatever it does mean, it doesn't seem to have been very effective. To appoint one employee given to posting potentially racist comments on social media might be unfortunate. To appoint another advocating the shooting of black protesters looks like carelessness.

Leaders and governors of English schools and multi-academy trusts may goggle at the dismissive attitude of the DfE to questions which they will have been asking themselves about their own institutions for several years. Regional Schools Commissioners, though, have learnt different lessons. In a case dealing with more schools in Somerset, Hannah Woodhouse, whom we met over dealings with Sexey's School, gave permission to Swanmead Community School in the market town of Ilminster to become an academy. There was an immediate problem here. Somerset CC had for years been trying to sort out the fact that this part of the county had, unlike its neighbours (which included Stoke sub Hamdon and Stanchester Schools), a three-tier structure with first and middle schools. Swanmead was one of these. The granting of Swanmead's application would have "severely curtailed" the LA's options to re-organise schooling in this

---

[8] Shahid, Nimra. Conn, David. Goodley, Simon. Cutler, Sam. 2020. Cummings recruit was fired after BLM tweet The Guardian 3 September 2020

[9] Ibid

[10] Ibid

[11] Ibid

area[12]. The LA had pleaded with the RSC to wait until its own review affecting a whole tranche of schools had been completed, but Ms Woodhouse ignored the request. The high court judge "issued a stinging verdict on those involved, saying it's in 'nobody's interests for time, money and effort to be spent challenging one another in legal proceedings in this way'". He ruled the permission to convert unlawful. The Bridgwater and Taunton College Trust (BCT) was seeking to expand its influence in the area, having already got permission for another former middle school, Maiden Beech in Crewkerne, to join it in December. This was a complicated case, with injunctions and requests for judicial review flying back and forth – BCT "threatened a judicial review in April after the council allowed Hinton St George school to expand from accepting pupils in year 1 to 4 to include years 5 and 6. Hinton was a 'feeder' school for Maiden Beech, which was now part of BCT"[13].

The chaos engendered here can do little to give confidence to parents and children – the very opposite of what Somerset officials warned Stoke sub Hamdon parents about. In a similar case, Dickens reports, the then RSC for the West Midlands, Pank Patel "allowed a school in Redditch to expand a two-tier school despite concerns it would 'decimate' the town's three-tier system. In 2019, the school consulted on reverting back to becoming a high school, saying it should have listened to the local community"[14]. A novel concept indeed.

To the DfE, there seems to be little interest in counting the cost of its failed attempts at secrecy. The TEFT case cost around £50k. The Swanmead case, up to £60k.

An interview with Warwick Mansell reported on his Education Uncovered site[15] sums up the remarkable lack of discipline and order within the DfE and the ESFA. It was seen before that trust leaders visiting Sanctuary Buildings in Gove's time in charge could find themselves greeted on one side of the corridor with invitations to grow their school numbers as quickly as possible, while on the other side they were warned that they would not be allowed to expand beyond, say, twelve. The former executive principal/chief executive of

---

[12] Dickens, John. 2020. High Court judge slams pricey legal rows as RSC's academy conversion ruled unlawful, Schools Week, 30 June 2020

[13] Ibid

[14] Ibid

[15] Mansell, Warwick. 2020. Government operating 'almost feudal', dysfunctional system of oversight and influence over academy trusts, says ex-trust CEO, Education Uncovered, February 2020

Shrewsbury Academies Trust said that "having experienced both the system of local authority oversight of schools and the DfE's academies structure, it was clear to him that both were 'flawed' …What's been put in the LA's place [there was a note almost of incredulity here], some of the 'rebrokering' and the deals that are being done are …extraordinary. From my perspective, it's almost like a feudal system where some people are favoured and some are not. This trust might get offered this deal, but this other trust might not get offered the same thing. It's a bizarre system, not remotely fair, open and transparent. It's a system of smoke-filled rooms, and behind-the-scenes deals …I think there's a lack of clear strategic direction and a lack of morale within the organisation. There's a lack of continuity of staff. When I was having conversations with the ESFA or DfE over two to three years, every single person, from the junior officers to the senior people, would change. Every single layer of personnel changed, more than once."

There could hardly be a better description of the chaos and disruption that Gove, Cummings, Agnew and their colleagues imposed on the DfE and that still reigns there, although the main players have moved on to a bigger stage.

It is therefore not surprising that the academy movement itself can also be prone to secrecy. Secrecy, that is, as a culture, not an occasional resource. The author has heard more than one chair of governors introduce a meeting by telling everyone that the entire meeting would, of course and as usual, be confidential (hint: the full minutes, excluding any confidential items, of governing board meetings must by law be available to any interested party).

Despite these outriders, transparency is widely accepted as being the norm in state schools. But corporatised academies and academy trusts seem less likely to accept this accountability of their governance of state-funded organisations. The running disaster of the Wakefield City Academies Trust, handing over its twenty-one schools to eight academy chains before closing in 2018, "had been planning to give up some of its schools nine months before the announcement."[16]

In moves more than reminiscent of Castle School's forced conversion, the Norfolk-based Inspiration Trust seems to have agreed a locally very unpopular merger of two of its schools "months before a public consultation began, emails seen by the BBC suggest"[17]. Here, the trust decided that a free school it had

---

[16] Whittaker, Freddie. 2017. Bright Tribe to give up struggling Whitehaven Academy, 30 November 2017

[17] BBC News 23 November 2017

opened just a year earlier would be merged with the local high school it had just taken over – a school labelled as having "the worst GCSE results in the county" (ibid). The maybe more aspirational parents, who had favoured the new Trafalgar College in September 2016, advertised by Rachel de Souza's Inspiration Trust as "a brand new free school for Great Yarmouth, bringing a fresh focus on high academic standards to the town", may have been a tad disappointed when, just over twelve months later, they discovered that the trust committed to "delivering academic excellence for the young people of East Anglia, pairing the highest quality teaching with the widest possible opportunities" was effectively closing the Trafalgar site and sending the pupils to the Great Yarmouth High School that they had carefully avoided. It may be no surprise that the trust was at the time chaired by its founder Theodore Agnew.

Early in 2018, the parliamentary education committee took the issues raised by this and similar manoeuvres to the newly appointed minister. "Lack of transparency" in the Wakefield case led to parents, staff and pupils being left "in the dark over who is running their schools" and claimed decisions were being taken "behind closed doors"[18]. The letter continued: "The lack of transparency is particularly evident in the relationship between regional schools commissioners, Ofsted and the Education and Skills Funding Agency." There is also a strong suggestion that the secrecy maintained by the RSC and the DfE about Wakefield, dating from a year before the trust announced its closure, enabled bosses to make "significant and unwarranted transfers of assets" up to the time of the trust's collapse. So the culture of secrecy not only kept the community in ignorance about what was happening to their schools, but allowed a year's-worth of asset-stripping.

Sometimes, the secrecy strikes very close to home. The senior staff of a school are likely to be seen by pupils and parents as the day-to-day embodiment of the school's values. While the complexities of trust and governing boards may pass them by, the headteacher is the face of the school the children attend for five or more years, and often they are the reason why parents choose one school over another.

Parents at Cyril Jackson primary school in Tower Hamlets, in the east end of London, were astonished to learn that their headteacher had simultaneously held the post of Director of Education at the University Schools Trust (UST) – which

---

[18] Schools Week, 19 January 2018

as you may remember from Chapter 7 became involved in the long-running John Roan Secondary School debacle in 2018. Geraldine Kemp, according to a letter of complaint from parents of the school, "was UST's co-chief executive officer. And subsequently she has been appointed UST's CEO, effective from 7 October 2019 and announced just fourteen days after the governors' announcement to commence due diligence for the school to become a UST academy. Given Mrs Kemp's central professional role in UST, and her clear trajectory toward becoming its CEO, we have no confidence that her career and financial interest has not influenced her decision to favour the conversion of Cyril Jackson to a UST academy."[19] It then emerged that the meeting at which the governors had decided to start down the academisation path had been labelled 'confidential'. Its minutes had therefore never been released to parents and staff – another gross abuse of the legal provision of confidentiality in the event of a matter vital to individual staff or pupils[20].

Some headteachers seem to have benefited enormously from academisation and the attendant secrecy. Others have not. The growth of the academy system has seen an increase in the summary dismissal of school leaders.

This is not specifically an academy issue. Kent LA was reported to be 'disappearing' headteachers back in 2014:

"The Kent Messenger has discovered, via a Freedom of Information request, that twenty-one headteachers of Kent schools were removed from their posts since September 2012. Of these, fifteen were told to go due to performance reasons, five on grounds of conduct and one for an issue not disclosed. These will be mainly primary school heads, but would include secondary heads like the head of the North School, Ashford, a Kent County Council run school, who resigned after the school was placed in Special Measures in December. It will not include the additional ones removed from academies, such as Castle Community College in Deal and Molehill Copse Primary in Maidstone. Neither does it include those who 'voluntarily' gave up their posts, rather than face the

[19] Mansell, Warwick. 2019. How could a local authority primary school headteacher simultaneously be working as director of education for an academy trust? Education Uncovered, 31 October 2019

[20] Mansell, Warwick. 2019. Governing body refuses to release minutes of meeting where it decided to start academisation process, deeming it 'confidential', Education Uncovered, 15 November 2019

stigma of removal. I hear that in total some forty heads have given up or 'lost' their posts since September 2013."[21]

Similar 'disappearances' have happened in many other LAs.

This is a remarkably short-sighted practice, as it not only leaves a school leaderless, but discourages anyone else from taking up similar challenges. The Messenger goes on to describe how a new head was appointed to run an 'at risk' CofE primary school in 2012 and found herself dismissed when Ofsted placed the school in special measures in November 2013. How an LA can expect a headteacher to turn around a school's results in just over 12 months – and how a diocese can collude with such a move – is incomprehensible.

We have seen how the interim headteacher of Castle School was improperly dismissed by the chair of governors before Christmas in 2014, so that the CEO of the new sponsor – not due to take over until March – could immediately put in her own deputy as head. This was a minor shortcut compared to the steps taken by academy trusts:

"It was like a bomb dropped on me. I was shocked, numb," says James Wiggins, a former headteacher, recalling the day, two years ago, when his academy trust chief came in out of the blue and ordered him to clear his office. "He said the governing body had had a vote of no confidence in me – which I later found out was a lie – and that I needed to leave and couldn't make contact with anybody."[22]

So reported the Guardian of one case among "a growing number of headteachers who are summarily sacked or forced to 'resign', and who cannot talk openly about the brutality of their treatment because of gagging clauses they are compelled to sign as part of their settlements." Very often, as in the Kent case, these are heads given impossible targets. In Wiggins' case (his name has been changed due to the gagging clause), he was given the task of achieving 'outstanding' in his primary school's Ofsted, when he had made it clear that this would not be possible. In the event, he was sacked within days of the publication of the Sats scores.

The Guardian reports ten Kent schools starting the 2017-18 school year without a headteacher, and a "noticeable increase in sackings" throughout England reported by the National Association of Head Teachers: "The union has seen a tendency for a particular type of dismissal. 'Over the past three years

---

[21] Kent Messenger, 16 June 2014

[22] The Guardian, 24 October 2017

we've seen a rise of 'some other substantial reason' dismissals ...' This means an employer does not need to provide evidence of underperformance or a conduct issue, but can simply assert that there is a breakdown in trust and confidence."[23]

Such treatment of professional staff – in a profession struggling to recruit both beginners and senior leaders – is not only immoral but self-defeating. The harm it does to the mental health of people who commonly have been working 70-hour weeks, and to the confidence of the school's community, is immeasurable. It fits with a corporate mindset, but when it has happened in the public sector it has only lately become acceptable.

Another weapon of the commercial world, non-disclosure agreements (NDAs) seems to be creeping into usage in the world of education. The process of agreeing a financial reward in exchange for total confidentiality in the event of 'resignations', thus ensuring that the organisation does not get the bad or embarrassing publicity it might deserve was, of course, widely used in the US to protect Harvey Weinstein, serial harasser and rapist of women, from the consequences of his behaviour over many years. Some of this usage of NDAs seems to cover up criminal behaviour, in which case it is probably illegal. Within educational organisations, the use of these 'gagging clauses' seems particularly inappropriate. Teachers are not able to report colleagues to the Teacher Regulation Agency without the risk of being exposed, as the TRA is not on the list of bodies to which they can confidentially whistleblow. Teachers can report concerns direct to the DfE, but we have seen how that turned out in the Waltham Holy Cross case. "Trustees of academies, or governors, are, unbelievably, not required under any guidance or legislation to be informed about NDAs or check how they are used."[24]

Secrecy was at the heart of government practice during the early months of the pandemic. Was achieving 'herd immunity', recommended by some scientists and spoken of approvingly by the prime minister, really an aspiration? Who was leading government policy-making, while the PM missed five critical COBRA (Cabinet Office briefings) meetings? And who exactly was 'on' the SAGE (Scientific Advisory Group for Emergencies) group of advisers? Who attended, and who was allowed to participate? What figures were being used to report the number and proportion of infections and deaths, and how did they compare with

[23] Ibid

[24] Staufenberg, Jess. 2019. This is oppression: Non-disclosure agreements used to muzzle teachers, The Guardian, 6 August 2019

others in Europe? And as the management of the pandemic became more localised, what figures were used to produce the rate of infection (R) numbers that were used to determine the lockdown of towns, cities and, indeed, whole countries? In fact, much of the issue here was about the way in which the government maintained a tight hold on data, disabling city, county and district councils from what would have been a more effective localised response. So secrecy goes hand-in-hand with centralisation.

Chapter 17
The Seven Deadly Sins of the
Academy System: No 4 Centralisation

One thing politicians and school leaders have in common is that no one ever accused either profession of being shrinking violets. That is why it is so important to have in place robust systems of accountability. Until the appearance of local management of schools in 1988, there was a tendency to see headteachers as the captain of their ship, and directors of education likewise.

Such an attitude does no one any favours. While it might initially seem attractive to be able to rise above the petty carping of junior staff and an ignorant public, some element of professional and public accountability is a safeguard for both the public and the leader. It not only ensures open challenge to questionable decisions, but it enables groups to come to better decisions on behalf of the service provided – decisions which take into account a range of perspectives and expertise.

School autonomy has been an attractive mantra for the government, but autonomy has turned out to be the property not of schools but of the trusts that lead them, and in particular of the CEOs who run them on a day-to-day basis. One such leader in an educational charity eyeing the early academies in 2003 rubbed his hands in glee at the thought of having "our own train set". As education journalist and blogger Warwick Mansell writes: "the MAT reforms kill school-by-school autonomy, whatever its merits, stone dead."[1] "School autonomy is 'difficult' to justify according to the chief executive of one of England's largest multi-academy trusts", Rowena Hackwood of the David Ross Education Trust[2]. Yet it was on the promise of *school* autonomy, not Trust

---

[1] Mansell, Warwick. 2017. Education Uncovered blog, 7 December 2017

[2] George, Martin. 2018. Exclusive: 'It's hard to argue for school autonomy,' says academy chief, TES, 17 August 2018. David Ross is sponsor, member and trustee of his

autonomy, that the idea of academisation has been sold to thousands of eager headteachers and governors.

As it happens, the pandemic exposed some of the downsides of 'autonomy'. Ross' trust found standardisation harder to apply when Unison and the GMB reported it to the Health and Safety Executive. The unions representing support staff across the trust claimed that it went ahead with an "unsafe increase in pupil numbers" when schools reopened after the first lockdown, in June 2020[3]. While small local trusts could negotiate with their headteachers, a number of larger trusts found it difficult to apply procedures across schools which were often geographically widespread and varied in type. Harris Federation primaries experienced problems with its teachers, as union members suggested it wasn't safe to reopen in June[4]. The pandemic raised a number of interesting questions about who would make the final judgment about the safety of schools, especially when those lockdowns became localised: the head of school, or the trust CEO? Or the unions? The chief executive of United Learning, the largest trust in the country, is reported as saying that "union advice to its members over reopening is 'counter-productive'"[5]. Yet union advice for many heads was the only practical and digestible advice they were getting.

The average academy school in a MAT is now considerably less free to choose its curriculum, its staff, its teaching methods, and its entire ethos than it has been for the last 150 years. The DfE's regulations reinforce this centralisation towards MATs. In all, "Many academy heads seem to have swapped local authority and government bureaucracy for strict trust controls", concludes the executive head of a federation of maintained schools in Lambeth, south London[6]. He went on to cite the areas where he has more discretion than the head of a

---

own trust. He is "a close friend of Boris Johnson, known for providing the PM and his partner with free holidays in Mustique." (Private Eye, 23.10.2020) He is the founder of Carphone Warehouse. A private venture of his, Nevill Holt Opera, was the only country house opera to benefit from "the first round of handouts from the government's Culture Recovery Fund" in 2020 (ibid)

[3] Whittaker, Freddie. 2020. Coronavirus: Unions report academy trust to health and safety watchdog over 'unsafe' return of pupils, Schools Week, 2 June 2020

[4] Mansell, Warwick. 2020. Education Uncovered, 8 June 2020

[5] Ibid

[6] Toye, Christopher. 2017. The false freedoms of becoming an academy, Schools Week, 15 May 2017

school in a multi academy trust: decision-making, behaviour policies, choice of suppliers, school improvement strategies among them.

There is no longer a requirement for parental representation on a trust board and in any local governance arrangements – only one or the other. So parents are taken out of the decision-making level of governance. Boards run their own budgets with accountability only to the EFSA – not to any local body. Individual school headteachers can be subject to an academy board often miles – sometimes hundreds of miles – away. One such was the Chapel Street Community Schools Trust, with seven schools, based in south London, which had as its chief executive a man who doubled up as headteacher of a primary school in Bolton, Lancashire[7]. Meanwhile, local governing (or 'advisory') boards find themselves with no powers, little influence and, in one extreme example, in a trust of just seven schools in Staffordshire, the inability even to meet, let alone discuss strategic issues with, their own chair of trustees. Elsewhere, some trusts see no role at all for parents or members of the local community in their leadership or governance[8]. The government's boast that academisation offered local communities, and parents in particular, the chance to run their own schools was always, of course, laughably hollow. As the National Governance Association reported in 2019, "The evolution and promotion of Mats without sufficient thought to governance has produced a [democratic] deficit that requires debate, one that must not be ignored any longer"[9].

As we saw in Chapter 6, regional schools commissioners report to ministers but have no obligation to talk to the schools and communities for which they are responsible. Their headteacher boards are elected only from heads of 'outstanding academies' "by *existing* academy leaders, even though they advise regional school commissioners (RSCs), who now oversee *all* schools and whose decisions affect everyone in the country."[10]

MATs continue to grow larger, meaning that fewer people are school governors with legal powers, and fewer schools have formal links to their local

[7] Mansell, Warwick. 2020. Education Uncovered, 27 February 2020

[8] Coughlan, Sean. 2016. Academy Chain to scrap governing bodies, BBC News, 19 January 2016

[9] National Governance Association, quoted in The Guardian, 28 June 2019

[10] McInerney, Laura. 2017. These Boards are corrupt, self-serving and secretive, Schools Week 5 May 2017

communities. So the twenty fastest-growing academy trusts accumulated between 23% and 700% more schools in the year 2016-17[11].

Even the MAT trustees can find themselves out-manoeuvred by the trust's members. The regulatory structure of MATs has always been problematic. In the early days of the rush to academisation of secondary schools between 2010 and 2015, the DfE provided a model based on company law, rather than the usual membership-based structure for charities, which provided for a small group of members to appoint a larger board of trustees. The self-appointed members took up their positions in, if they wished, perpetuity. It was clear to some from the word 'go' that this could cause problems down the line.

The most obvious abuse was the idea that the then headteacher, or a CEO in a multi-academy trust, might be a member. Clearly some of these people saw themselves as the founding mother or father of the academy idea and had done much of the work in persuading the governors and putting in the legwork. But wise governors saw that it would be highly unsuitable for the governing board to be accountable for its performance to a small group containing the CEO. Others had less foresight. In 2017, "the chief executive and founding member of the Academies Transformation Trust (ATT) was put on temporary leave by (the chair) ... over finance concerns. Forecasts showed the trust will have £26,000 reserves next year, compared with more than £5 million in 2014. But Cleland [the CEO] used his powers as a founding member of ATT to sack Tilsley [the chair] and appoint four new directors, one of whom was appointed chair. Those trustees reinstated (the CEO)."[12]

The centralised model is leading some MATs back to what Tim Brighouse has called the bad old days "reminiscent of the worst of the old-style LEAs"[13]. Again, it was perhaps inevitable that the removal of the individual legal status of member schools of a MAT would lead some MATs to replicate the old LEA style of centralised budget-holding. "E-ACT, for example, is typical of the growing number of such organisations that pool individual school budgets,

---

[11] Robertson, Alix. 2017. The Expandables: Academy Trusts are supersizing, Schools Week, 15 September 2017

[12] Whittaker, Freddie. 2017. ATT chief executive broke rules over chair sacking, EFA investigation finds Schools Week, 24 March 2017

[13] Brighouse, Tim. Tes, 18 August 2017

inviting schools to set out their wish-list for spending before deciding what they can each have."[14]

E-ACT would be one of the first MATs to propose doing away with local governing boards altogether. Having trumpeted on its website in early 2016 that it "places a great deal of emphasis on the role of governors in driving forward educational attainment and achievement at all our academies and Free Schools"[15], it outlined the key duties of the local governing boards:

- Setting strategic direction, policies and objectives.
- Approving the school budget.
- Reviewing progress against the school's budget and objectives.
- Appointing, challenging and supporting the Principal.

E-Act's model required two elected parent governors, two elected staff governors, (amazingly) two local authority governors and eight appointed E-ACT governors.

However, this democratic bonanza was soon to end. In January 2016, the BBC News website reported:

"An academy chain is scrapping the current form of governing bodies for its schools in England.

The E-ACT academy group says it will replace them with "academy ambassadorial advisory bodies".

These new bodies will "play a central role in celebrating the academy's achievements", E-ACT has told its school governors in a letter.

But governing bodies, with parental representatives, will no longer hold their local schools to account.

The academy chain says it was about providing the "best possible education".

A school governor described it as "authoritarian" and "repugnant" …

…A letter sent to governors tells them that the academy chain has decided to change its form of governance.

Instead of local school governing bodies, there will be a centralised process for monitoring standards.

---

[14] Ibid

[15] https://www.e-act.org.uk/

There will be a single central governing body covering all schools in the group across the country, rather than governors at individual level.

Governors often include representatives of parents, school staff, local businesses and local politicians.

The letter to governors says the academy chain would contact governing bodies "to discuss an appropriate transition date" and the replacement bodies would provide a different type of function, such as an "interface with the community".

And it invites current governors to move over to the new bodies, but these would no longer be involved in areas such as hiring senior staff and monitoring budgets and standards.

A governor in one of E-ACT's schools in the Midlands said he was "shocked" at how governing bodies had been disbanded, which he described as "offensive and disrespectful to the people who freely volunteer their time to act as governors"[16].

What makes this perhaps even more controversial is that E-ACT itself has a troubled record.

In 2014, the academy chain lost control of ten of its schools after Ofsted inspectors raised serious concerns about their performance.

Until July 2015, the chain was operating under a financial notice to improve, imposed by the Education Funding Agency."[17]

E-ACT now proclaims a different model: "Another striking innovation of our governance model is the Ambassadorial Advisory Group or AAG as it is more commonly known."[18] The four roles now delegated to the AAGs are communication, community, celebration, concerns. But not control.

It may not be surprising that the parliamentary education select committee reported on academies, "it seems to us that parents, staff and students are in the dark over who is running their schools and that decisions are being taken behind closed doors"[19].

Centralisation of decision-making was a characteristic of the management of the pandemic in the UK and especially so in England, where the side-lining of

---

[16] Coughlan, Sean. 2016. Academy chain to scrap governing bodies, BBC News, 19 January 2016

[17] Ibid

[18] E-ACT website, April 2018

[19] BBC News 20 January 2018

metropolitan mayors and local councils became a source of real conflict. Some commentators saw the emergency powers the government accorded itself in early 2020 as an opportunity to accelerate the dismantling of the National Health Service: "In recent weeks, ministers have used special powers to bypass normal tendering and award a string of contracts to private companies and management consultants without open competition."[20] After the government instructed NHS Trusts not to purchase their own protective equipment and ventilators, but to leave procurement of sixteen such items to be handled centrally, the writers suggested that "Centralising of purchasing is likely to hand more responsibility to Deloitte …the shadow chancellor of the Duchy of Lancaster said, 'The government must not allow the current crisis to be used as cover to extend the creeping privatisation of the NHS'"[21].

The summer of 2020 saw the easing of the overall national lockdown and the imposition of local lockdowns in response to spikes identified by local data. But this data was initially not made available to local government, so the decisions were taken by central government, while local officials had all the responsibility for enforcing the regulations. As Jessica Studdert of the New Local Government Network tweeted, "At every turn of the Covid-19 crisis, the Govt has centralised decision-making into command and control with a preference for big blunt schemes over sophisticated local strategies & expertise – often with huge real life consequences for people not getting response they need."[22]

---

[20] Garside, Juliette and Neate, Rupert. 2020. Serco deal raises fears that NHS faces 'power grab' by private sector, The Guardian 5 May 2020

[21] Ibid

[22] Twitter @jesstud, 9 May 2020

Chapter 18
The Seven Deadly Sins of the
Academy System: No 5 Cronyism

It seems inevitable that venality, secrecy and centralisation of power will lead to cronyism. We have already seen how the decision of two senior ministers to appoint a political chum to the Office for Students, bypassing all the safeguards put in place specifically to avoid charges of cronyism, led to a very public dressing-down from the Commissioner for Public Appointments but no other apparent sanction or admonishment.

Michael Gove's spell as Secretary of State brought about the inclusion of powerful but unelected colleagues in his department. John Nash, a former venture capitalist and Conservative party donor, was created a peer in 2013 so he could become an education minister in the House of Lords. He had previously set up a small academy chain, Future Academies, which sponsors five schools in London. He served as Parliamentary Under Secretary of State for Schools from January 2013 to June 2017 and then as Parliamentary Under Secretary of State for the School System until September 2017. In May 2016 Nash and his wife were criticised for allowing his unqualified and unpaid daughter to teach history in the trust's secondary school, to advise on a new curriculum and to be involved in the appointment of staff, prompting concerns from parents and a teachers' union.

The Guardian reported:

"Lord Nash set up Future in 2006 and was a generous Conservative donor before being given a peerage in 2013 and made the minister in charge of academisation. He is the director of Future Academies, a governor and co-chair of Pimlico Academy, which is part of the chain, and a trustee of Future, the funding charity behind the chain. Lady Nash, a former stockbroker, is also a trustee of Future, co-chair of governors of Pimlico Academy, and chair of governors at two primary schools in the chain"[1].

For many of these people and their relatives, whether at the highest level of government, as school leaders or as humble unqualified teachers, the concept of being interviewed in a competitive situation is unheard of. So it was for the headteacher of Castle School in December 2014, appointed without the promised involvement of school governors and untroubled by the need to make a written application. And so indeed it was at the National Governors' Association in 2013, when a new and senior post could be settled on the lately retired chair by invitation of the chief officer, by whom she had herself been appointed four years earlier and subsequently line-managed.

While venture capitalist John Nash was getting his feet under the DfE table, Theodore Agnew, who founded the aforementioned Norfolk-based Inspiration Trust was also persona very grata at Sanctuary Buildings. Here is his official 'gov.uk' biography:

"Theodore Agnew was appointed Parliamentary Under Secretary of State for the School System on 28 September 2017 and lead non-executive board member at the Ministry of Justice in July 2015.

Lord Agnew previously served as a non-executive board member at the Department for Education, where he was chair of the department's Academies Board from 2013 to 2015.

Outside of the department, Lord Agnew founded Somerton Capital LLP in 2007 and co-founded the WNS Group (a US listed company) in 1990."[2]

With his background in insurance claims management (where he pioneered the outsourcing of jobs to India) and later running a global outsourcing company, Agnew was enormously influential in the setting up of multi-academy trusts in the early years of the coalition government, and was then translated to the House of Lords, where he replaced Nash as the government's academies minister. Agnew is described as "well connected in Westminster, having served on the boards of several key think-tanks. He was a trustee at Policy Exchange, a right-wing think-tank founded by Michael Gove"[3]. Agnew chaired the board that

---

[1] Syal, Rajeev. 2016. Unqualified daughter of minister teaches in his academy schools, The Guardian 12 May 2016

[2] https://www.gov.uk/government/people/theodore-agnew, August 2020

[3] Whittaker, Freddie. 2017. Academy boss and Tory donor is new DfE minister, 29 September 2017

oversaw the RSC for East Anglia, which itself oversees the schools of the Inspiration Trust.

Inspiration Trust has found what may be a new way of furthering its influence. Its late chief executive, Rachel de Souza, now Children's Commissioner for England, is a founder director of the exciting new organisation called Parents and Teachers for Excellence (PTE), launched in September 2017 (see p184). Another director is Jon Moynihan, venture capitalist and chair of the finance committee of Vote Leave. This leading Brexiteer, who has donated £70,000+ to the Conservative Party and £60,000 to Vote Leave, leads an organisation rather cheekily pledged to shift the education debate from the "elites in Whitehall". PTE is not a charity, and its campaign "has been orchestrated" by the director of communications at the DfE under Michael Gove, and Rachel Wolf, former director of the New Schools Network for supporting the foundation of free schools later led by Toby Young[4]. And so the circle completes.

Allen writes about the democratic deficit inherent in the governance arrangements for academies[5]:

"A growing number of academics and practitioners refer to the 'democratic deficit' within the governance arrangements of academies, because control is placed outside established public accountability systems. The Academies Enterprise Trust, the largest multi-academy trust in operation, is an interesting example. The trust in question operates scores of academies up and down the country and, until recently, had a board comprising of only four (unelected) trustees. Surprisingly, the DfE line on governance arrangements is that Trusts are best able to decide the format that suits their needs, even though such small groups of unelected individuals are potentially responsible for large sums of public money – upwards of £250m."[5]

Given the way the structure was set up, it is hardly surprising:

"A handbook published in 2014 by the Institute of Chartered Secretaries and Administrators, and endorsed by the then chair of the National Governors' Association, noted uncritically that 'Generally, the first port of call for academies looking for governors is the connections of those already on the board'."[6] The

[4] Dickens, John. 2017. Vote Leave campaigner and Tory donor behind Parents and Teachers for Excellence campaign, Schools Week, 22 September 2017

[5] Allen, Andrew 2017 The academy revolution is ousting governors, Democratic Audit, 26 January 2017

[6] Paxton-Doggett, Katie. 2014 How to Run an Academy School, London: ICSA p105

sin of cronyism and its very close relative, nepotism reached, hopefully, its nadir when it was revealed that Lord Harris of Peckham has so arranged the business of his forty-nine school Trust that, after his death, "its 'principal sponsor' – or controlling individual – will stay within the family …passing to his wife or, alternatively, to his two sons."[7] It is a remarkable moment when decisive control of nearly fifty state-funded schools can be passed from parent to child as a personal legacy.

The rapid mobilisation of the Oak National Academy online learning platform in April 2020 to deliver video lessons and other resources was much admired as a quick and effective response to the mass closure of schools. The government used little-known powers given to the DfE in the 2002 education Act and enabling it to support any project providing education or educational services in the UK. One of the leading figures is head of a Norwich secondary school which is a member of Agnew's Inspiration Trust. "The ONA project board includes Leora Cruddas, who champions the academies programme in her position as chief executive of the Confederation of School Trusts; Daisy Christodoulou, the traditionalist-leaning writer and thinker whose past employers include ARK Schools and Future Academies, the chain of the Tory peer and former minister Lord Nash; Jon Coles, who leads the United Learning Trust, England's largest academy chain …"[8]

Linked to cronyism, of course, there are the even shadier behaviours which often cross the boundary into criminality, with features redolent of the findings against Harvey Weinstein and his Miramax company – bullying, intimidation of staff and pupils and the use of non-disclosure agreements to cover up cheating, discrimination and assault.

But the ONA names remind us once again that the new education establishment is as close-knit a clique as Gove claimed the Blob had been ten years before. If anything, the new Blob embraces a much narrower view of what constitutes education. The old establishment usually encouraged and welcomed healthy debate about teaching methods and school structures. This Blob seems very homogenous. It is also well-embedded in the ownership of schools, unlike

---

[7] Mansell, Warwick. 2019. Education's new royal family: how control of England's second- largest chain of academies will pass to the family of its founder upon his death, Education Uncovered, 7 November 2019

[8] Mansell, Warwick. 2020. Department for Education used little-known legal power to fund Oak National Academy, Education Uncovered, 28 April 2020

the twentieth century establishment. It controls both the infrastructure *and* the delivery mechanisms of schooling, as well as much of the research base. And again, the constant reappearance of familiar names has become a wearyingly familiar aspect of the pandemic crisis. Gove, Cummings, the Warner Brothers, Agnew, Nash, O'Shaughnessy, Harris …the names go round and round, running our schools, owning shares in the technology companies that one minute are analysing voting data for an EU referendum, the next advising on the handling of a health crisis, while producing resources for the schools that they hold in trust for our children.

Chapter 19
The Seven Deadly Sins of the
Academy System: No 6 Isolationism

Is it possible, one might ask, to laud school autonomy, while developing a structure for schooling founded on the "ideological pursuit of competition and marketisation of the education system"[1]? Is one of the most dispiriting sights in the country nowadays the formerly unimaginable "boaster poster", strung along a school's railings, proclaiming its inspection triumphs?

Multi-academy trusts might seem to offer both economy of scale and a model of school federation which should provide a fertile breeding-ground for cooperation and collaboration. However, we have seen that many of the economies of scale have been outweighed by the replication of expensive central administration structures with rocketing costs. While small-scale geographically coherent trusts are likely to offer the benefits of collaboration, many of the larger and widespread trusts get in the way of local cooperation while providing no easily accessible alternative.

The most extensive and probably most successful example of school-to-school collaboration was the London Challenge, between 2003 and 2011. Both the government and Ofsted accepted that there was a substantial and sustained improvement in the performance of secondary and, later, primary schools in this period: "One of the distinctive features of London Challenge was a focus on partnership and shared purpose between schools, whilst avoiding stigmatising schools through the use of negative language"[2].

---

[1] Rosen, Michael 2018. @michaelrosenyes, Twitter, 11 March 2018

[2] Kidson, Marc and Norris, Emma. 2014. Implementing the London Challenge, York: The Joseph Rowntree Foundation
https://en.wikipedia.org/wiki/London_Challenge#:~:text=One%20of%20the%20distinctive%20features,require%20the%20most%20intensive%20intervention

The City Challenge model was based on collaboration and co-operation between schools, their leaders and their staff[3]. Despite its unquestioned success, the challenge model was not supported by the incoming coalition government in 2010. What happened instead, in the first tranche of new academisations, was that 'successful' schools were encouraged to convert as stand-alone academies, often to the dismay and the detriment of nearby schools, while 'failing' schools were required to academise under sponsors, often removing from them the likelihood of working closely with neighbourhood schools – the outstandingly successful strategy adopted by the city challenges. In addition, such schools had to cope with the stigma of negative language specifically condemned by challenge participants. As we have seen, the new Conservative regime at Somerset County Council in 2010 had the brass neck to proclaim first, its neglect of Castle School, and then its vulgar haste to shuffle the school off into academy status, as an adoption of the 'school-to-school support' model developed in London.

And while individual schools had to learn new ways of cooperating, as local authorities lost the capacity to support them, through clustering and federating, the larger trusts brought overt competition to schools in a way that had been shunned by the state sector in living memory:

"In January 2015, a press release from Ark Academies Trust printed its own GCSE results in 2013 and 2014, alongside the other nine largest academy networks, which happened to show that Ark was 'the only one of the top ten largest academy networks to see GCSE results improve in 2014'."[4]

In February of 2018, Ark came face-to-face with rival United Learning over the opening of a free school in north London. United Learning had taken over a local secondary in 2014, which still had 399 unfilled pupil places. Ark's proposals, supported by the DfE, were to open a secondary free school less than a mile away, while the local council rejected the plans over traffic concerns and

---

[3] Hutchings, M., Greenwood, C., Hollingworth, S., Mansaray, A., Rose, A., and Glass, K. 2012. Evaluation of the City Challenge programme (Research Report DFE-RR215), London: Department for Education, p. v; Armstrong, P. 2015. Effective school partnerships and collaboration for school improvement: a review of the evidence; Research report, October 2015, Department for Education

[4] Gann, Nigel. 2016. p177

"inappropriate development within the green belt." United Learning's CEO "blasted local and national officials over their handling of the case"[5].

Competitiveness and mud-slinging are unlikely to offer the advantages of close collaboration, and with large financial turnover at stake, this is unlikely to be the last such turf war between trusts. An Ipswich headteacher writes of her local cluster of two high schools and seven primaries, the two high schools having different national sponsors, and the primaries representing "four different academy arrangements – two national chains and two locally formed MATs" – with one remaining LA school. While urban schools have always had to have an element of competition over issues such as recruitment of staff and pupils, this has in the past happened within the restraining embrace of a local authority whose key responsibility was the welfare of the children. Academy chains have no such responsibility, resulting in the separate clustering of higher and lower achieving children: "We need an admissions process that does not pit schools against each other or favour children from families who can pay for bus fares or a rented address."[6]

Maija Salokangas and Mel Ainscow of Manchester University (Ainscow's work on the city challenge was very influential) studied a single academy over ten years, while linking its experience to wider research encompassing similar corporatised schools in the US, Australia and Sweden (New Zealand, it should be noted, is quietly shelving its experiment with charter schools, and returning all existing ones to the state system): "An emphasis on competition, high stakes testing and parental choice is further disadvantaging low income families, and, rather than introducing reforms that lead to improvements in educational approaches, they have mainly focussed on structural reforms that focus on organisation and management"[7].

While trusts and councils fight over the opening and closing of schools, three-quarters of primary schools throughout England work in collaboration with each other, waiting to see if, or more likely when, their LA support services will

---

[5] Allen-Kinross, Pippa. 2018. United Learning and Ark in north London turf war, Schools Week, 9 February 2018

[6] James, A H. Academisation makes it harder for local schools to work together, Schools Week, 5 October 2017

[7] Salokangas, Maija, and Ainscow, Mel. 2017. Inside the autonomous school: Making Sense of a Global Educational Trend, London: Routledge

disappear and leave them with little choice but to choose which chain of schools will swallow them up.

Such isolationism is a form of exceptionalism. Instead of recognising the strengths of other models, welcoming diversity and collaboration, it emphasises the values of going one's own way, appreciating and lauding only those achievements of one's own, and always celebrating one's own 'success', spurious or not, rather than the system as a whole. This was almost uniquely the UK's attitude in its handling of the pandemic in the first 6 months of 2020, proposing different solutions, 'world-beating' processes and 'moonshots', claiming better performance, against all the evidence presented by the available data, and suggesting that the publication of contrary views was inaccurate and unpatriotic[8].

---

[8] Helm, Toby. 2020 They rang and asked us . . . @tobyhelm, Twitter, 26 April 2020: "Downing Street trying to get us to say trust in government not declining and to rewrite this story with new headline. Request refused. We are not edited by Downing Street"

Chapter 20
The Seven Deadly Sins of the
Academy System: No 7 Precariousness

Maybe it didn't look like it at the time, but for most of the population of England, the provision of schools throughout the twentieth century was remarkably ordered and secure. While rail services were decimated, hospitals constantly being reorganised, whole industries subject to savage cuts, the provision of primary, secondary and special schools remained very recognisable from the passing of the 1944 act until the early twenty-first century. Small rural schools were always under threat, and many unviable ones closed, but thousands of others survived. One of the protecting factors has been that few county councillors would vote for their constituents to lose their beloved local school.

But no one votes for MATs, and no very identifiable person – especially if they live and work hundreds of miles away – is going to be held responsible when a MAT decides that your village school is just too expensive to make its preservation worthwhile.

Financial Instability

In this age of seemingly permanent commitment to austerity, with the costs of Coronavirus and Brexit yet to come, the outlook for small schools is bleak. Teachers' unions claimed before Christmas 2017 that nearly 18,000 schools were facing real-terms cuts in per pupil funding. That is something like nine out of ten schools in England and Wales. The following spring, the BBC reported that the Kreston accountancy network suggested that eight out of ten academies were in deficit. They went on to predict that "two more years like this and the entire sector could face insolvency"[1]. Since staffing costs account for almost three quarters of schools' budgets, it is likely that redundancies will grow.

Individual schools are vulnerable – such as the Somerset single primary school trust that is accused of failure to ensure robust governance arrangements, failure to ensure good financial management and effective internal controls, failure to ensure effective planning and oversight of capital project, and failure to ensure spending has been for the purpose intended and that there is probity in the use of public funds. The EFSA issued the school with a financial notice to improve following the school's urgent request for financial support[2]. This is a school with fewer than 300 children that now 'required improvement' since its inspection in 2017. It had been rated 'good' when first inspected as an academy in 2013. The school had just six governors/trustees/directors, three of whom were also the three members responsible for holding the governing board – i.e. largely themselves – to account. It served a not particularly affluent part of a country town and it appears that the governors were struggling to meet the stringent requirements of academy leadership. While these people were clearly well-intentioned, they allowed a good school under good leadership to come perilously close to either closure or, maybe more likely, being subsumed by a multi academy trust and losing their local community leadership. Whoever allowed this conversion to happen will probably not be the ones counting the cost. Whoever dreamed up the system that enabled this to happen almost certainly will not.

Multi academy trusts are also suffering. Even the venerable Ark Schools, who we saw proudly trumpeting their achievements compared to close rivals, recorded an operating loss of £4.1m up to August 2017, with seven of its academies in deficit. Nevertheless, the accounts say its financial outlook "remains extremely robust"[3] – which must be true as the managing director received a 2% salary increase. Other academies found more inventive ways of throwing taxpayers' money around, as we saw above. Most noticeably, a free school which lasted just three years, paid Bolton Wanderers FC just under £600,000 for rent and utilities for a school roll of fewer than 100 children. One

---

[1] Shoesmith, Nathan. 2018. Entire Academy Sector Could 'Face Insolvency', The Speaker. 17 March 2018 https://www.speakerpolitics.co.uk/headlines/230-entire-academy-sector-could-face-insolvency (Reported on BBC News 17 March 2018

[2] Reported in the TES, 9 February 2018

[3] Reported in the TES, 11 January 2018

governor received £3,287 for travel, subsistence and accommodation expenses in attending, at most, four meetings. At that time, the football club was, like the school a year earlier, struggling to avoid relegation[4].

The sight for parents of letters from their children's school begging for donations is becoming wearily familiar. Operators of dozens of academy schools rely on emergency handouts from the taxpayer, with large and small chains suffering alike. "More than half of the biggest multi-academy chains had issued warnings about funding, citing pay, staffing levels, building maintenance and mounting deficits. It has now emerged that some smaller trusts have had to ask for cash advances from the state to stay afloat."[5] Sir Andrew Carter, Executive Headteacher of South Farnham School Educational Trust in leafy Surrey, got his knighthood in 2014, a couple of years before suggesting that parents should stump up, say, £500 a year for attending one of his state-funded schools. Four years later he was at it again, suggesting at an Academies Show: "send a letter to your parents tonight and ask for £1 a week"[6]. It must be hard for these people to bear it, that their schools are so wonderful, and that those ungrateful children get to go to them *for nothing*.

The Guardian goes on to report that "The Department for Education says that school funding is rising from almost £41bn in 2017-18 to £43.5bn in 2019-20, and that every school will receive an increase in funding through the national funding formula this year"[7]. The Secretary of State later had to admit that this was not true. The bonanza promised to early-converting academies, which took so much away from local authorities managing the many schools to give to the few, had soon disappeared. It had become a rare school that had adequate funds to hang on to all its staff, let alone to do all that was expected of it.

The Trouble with Sponsors

We have to presume that, if Michael Gove and his team had any vision of how his policies would look after a few years, it was of a generally very stable

---

[4] Camden, Billy. 2017. Struggling school paid £600,000 to football club, Schools Week, 24 March 2017

[5] Savage, Michael and Mansell, Warwick. 2018. Dozens of academy schools need bailouts from taxpayers, The Guardian, 3 February 2018

[6] Allen-Kinross, Pippa. 2018. Struggling to afford CPD? Charge parents £1 a week, says leading head, Schools Week, 27 March 2018

[7] Savage & Mansell, ibid

collection of multi-academy chains and single academy schools. When, as happens in all sectors, things were not working out for a particular school, there could be a new leadership sent in or a swift transfer to another chain, with the minimum of disruption.

Nobody on that team seems to have asked themselves what might happen if no sponsors wanted that school. After all, just as in the health service, the routine stuff is what makes the money. Outliers and troublesome cases are expensive, and no one wants to take responsibility for them – that's why private health companies really don't want to engage with complex operations and lengthy treatment programmes. So, of course, with schools. Who would want to run a school with a large per pupil cost and uncertainty about the future roll? Who would want a school that finds it really difficult to recruit teachers and other staff due to its history or its geography? Why wouldn't United Learning refuse to take on any more PFI schools, when the costs are, on the one hand, irrevocably inflexible and, on the other, rising annually at well above the current rate, and the chain will have hardly any control over the buildings? Especially when the PFI provider goes bust, like construction giant Carillion did in early 2018, and no one has a clue what might happen next. And certainly, not many chains are likely to leap at the opportunity of taking over a school that is £1m or more in deficit.

Similarly with schools that don't measure up to Ofsted's and the DfE's standards. By the end of 2017, the remaining 'requiring improvement' schools, according to Ofsted's Director of Education, were the hardest to improve, due to "unstable leadership, the difficulty they find in recruiting and retaining teachers, and tough socio-economic circumstances"[8]. Who would have thought it? Meanwhile, the sixty schools branded 'inadequate' for more than a year were still waiting to find sponsors to take them over, as required now by law. In all of these schools, the very causes of their continuing 'failure' were the reasons for their performance failing to improve, and the current system offered few or no solutions.

Fortunately, schools can sometimes be passed from one sponsor to another if they are failing. This exercise was costing £17m in 2016, probably rising to around £20m in the following year. The then academies minister initially "agreed to publish the figures in April 2016, but asked civil servants to bury the

---

[8] Staufenberg, Jess. 2018. Remaining 'requires improvement' schools will be hard to fix, Schools Week, 15 December 2017

information in a larger report, in case it 'highlights high brokerage costs'"[9]. MATs like Bright Tribe can walk away from schools, while schools, it appears, cannot walk away from MATs, because a school that has joined a MAT has no legal separate existence – although a Cheshire primary school did try very hard to leave its MAT and prove the opposite. Studio schools and University Technical schools seem chiefly at risk.

Free Schools pose particularly intractable problems. As we saw earlier[10], the DfE has produced some rather questionable statistics on the opening of free schools. Warwick Mansell[11] did some forensic work on these figures, suggesting that the government's 2018 target of building (or opening?) 100 free schools per year was unlikely to be approached, especially if you allow for the closure rate running at over 10% per year (a closure rate like this among established schools might be regarded as scandalous). Meanwhile, the cost of opening such schools has been largely hidden. As it happens, some £2.6bn had by then been spent on the 321 free schools, including £93.2m on legal, property and technical advisers. How many children attend free schools? The New Schools Network, their main support structure, was remarkably coy about this figure, while claiming that 680 free schools were open (or approved to open) with a potential 400,000 school places ("once full")[12]. The current number of children attending free schools in 2020 seemed to be about 80,000 (out of 347 schools claimed by the Education Policy Institute), which suggests that free schools are very small compared to others, and also that they have comparatively low occupancy rates.

The coronavirus pandemic struck in the early spring of 2020. By that time, schools had experienced almost ten years of cutbacks to their finances, to the professional support available to them, to the academic research they rely on to continuously improve their practice, while most staff had lived through a time of static or deteriorating pay. The government, by and large, was not compensating schools for the hugely increased costs of cleaning raised by the pandemic. Even a scheme to provide laptops for deprived children to allow them to access online school support during pandemic lockdowns or self-isolation came a cropper. Schools discovered at the end of October – just before half-term – that their

---

[9] 'Schools week reporter'(sic). 2017 Costs of rebrokering academies to be published for first time, Schools Week, 23 August 2018

[10] Chapter 15

[11] Mansell, Warwick. 2017. Education Uncovered 20 October 2017

[12] New Schools Network: https://www.newschoolsnetwork.org/, 12 April, 2018

allocations would be slashed by up to 85%. This was despite the fact that the firm supplying the laptops happened to be a Tory donor.[13]

Meanwhile, incompetent, sometimes provably criminal, school sponsors come and go, and individual schools are hawked around from trust to trust because the deficit they carry with them would not be manageable. While MATs can walk away from schools without sanction, schools are stuck with trusts they can no longer – trust. Government policy switches from all-out academisation as soon as possible, to a waiting game, ensuring that school governing boards eventually and often against their better judgment give up the fight to remain with their underfunded and understaffed local authority, and accept the inevitable.

Why Is There Such Uncertainty Amongst Schools?

Rarely in the history of education in England can there have been such lack of clarity about government policy. The fact is that a brief account of non-LA state-funded schooling goes something like this:

- 1988 – 1997 City Technology Colleges and Grant Maintained Schools encouraged by Conservative governments with low level take-up.
- 1997 – 2001 GM schools become foundation schools under the Labour government.
- 2001 – 2010 Labour government decides a few of the lowest performing schools (in cities) will become sponsored academies.
- 2010 – 2011 As above, with academisation of low-performing schools accelerating, and a few 'outstanding' schools applying to be stand-alone academies.
- 2011 – 2014 Process accelerating, with all schools eligible, and more schools forced.
- 2015 Announcement that all schools will be required to academise by 2022, and if governors of forced academy converters disagree with the DfE's decision they'll be sacked because it's going to happen anyway.
- 2016 Or maybe not, we'll just have to see, maybe they all will anyway by 2022, actually we just don't know, but if we don't say anything, a lot

---

[13] Dickens, John. 2020 100k more laptops for schools – but access is slashed, Schools Week, 31 October 2020

of schools will decide to convert just in case in order to avoid being made to.

- 2020 The process of forced conversion continues, despite the pandemic.

What looks to have been a deliberate tactic to undermine the earlier certainties of state education seems to have been the driver that has pushed many of the more recent converter schools into the arms of corporate trusts.

Section V
Endgame

Chapter 21
Corporatisation and The Ethical Shift

Where we consider what the disruption brought about by academisation may have achieved.

"It ain't what you don't know that gets you into trouble. It's what you know for sure that ain't so that does." Mark Twain

"We live in an era of fraud in America. Not just in banking, but in government, in education, in food, baseball. I thought we were better than this, I did really."[1]

Addressing the Seven Deadly Sins: Corporatisation and The Ethical Shift

In April of 2020, the second month of UK lockdown, there was a brief debate on Twitter between Sam Freedman and Rupert Higham. Sam Freedman is a fully-signed-up member of the new educational establishment, being the Chief Executive of Ark's Education Partnerships Group. "EPG works in developing countries to help improve the quality of education, including through well designed public-private partnerships and effective systems of school accountability"[2]. Freedman joined EPG from Teach First, where he was Executive Director. "He has extensive experience in education, including a period as Senior Policy Adviser to the Secretary of State for Education"[3]. Freedman is not the most closed-minded member of the education

---

[1] Mark Baum in Lewis, Michael. 2010. The Fifth Risk, London: Penguin Random House

[2] arkonline.org

[3] ibid. epg.org.uk

establishment. Rupert Higham is a Lecturer in Educational Leadership at the UCL Institute of Education in London.

In the exchange of views, Freedman suggests that the government's handling of the pandemic has been incompetent, but that does not mean it 'actively' intended that people should die. Higham's response to this claim could just as easily apply to the academy debate. "Intent and motivation don't work in organisations like it does in people. When investigating institutional racism, we don't look for proof of the racism of individuals but for evidence of discriminatory impact of systems …if safeguards are ignored or overturned, then the 'motivation' of the organisation is discriminatory, regardless of individuals. With COVID-19, alerts, plans and contingencies were ignored. The 'motivation' was thus to put economic and political considerations above lives."[4]

My contention here is that the catalogue of sins committed in English academy schools was unlikely to have been endemic in a national provision dominated by a culture of non-profit-making public service. But the academy policy extended to all schools from 2010 was not merely *prone to* abuse, owing to the built-in capacity of the schools to provide opportunities for high salaries for professional educators and 'on-the-side' profit opportunities for a cohort of people who are not professional educationalists. On the contrary, the perverted *motivation* of the education service in these ways has been an integral element of the academy system and it is impossible to imagine the model *without* these inherent characteristics. Because what would such a model look like?

The Values We Have

Education is not value-free. Perhaps some might suggest that schooling could be. But the model of schooling that a nation chooses must reflect the values of the leaders who construct it.

For all its faults, the system of local authority administration and provision of statutory state education from 1902 to 1988 provided a profoundly ethical foundation for schooling. The structure was recognisable throughout England and Wales and staff could move from one end of either country to the other and be sure of the ways and means by which the structure worked – and be clear about its values. Some local authorities had strongly individual characteristics with key strengths (or weaknesses) while others might be more focused on

---

[4] Higham, Rupert and Freedman, Sam. 2020 Intent and Motivation, @rupert_higham, @Samfr, Twitter, 19 April.

efficient administration, but a teacher or an education officer knew how things worked and understood the range of ways in which senior officers and headteachers interpreted the mission. In all those local authorities, the ethic underlying the mission of school provision from top to bottom was one of public service, of intervening in the lives of children and adults in a way that would aim to enhance their lives and the lives of the communities around them, with no place for private gain beyond the agreed rates for the jobs done. At its best, children were provided with a schooling that was "emancipative and educative"[5]. A national system locally administered was the common description.

So the gradually accelerating introduction of models of state-funded independent schools from 1988 was a radical change. It was claimed by politicians to be a shift from a centralised, albeit on a local basis, model of local government-managed schools (a premise which was always arguable), towards a nationwide network of autonomous schools managed by headteachers supported by like-minded governors/trustees. Salokangas and Ainscow consider how "making schools autonomous has been seen as the remedy to help cure the ills of the education system"[6]. This may be more generous to the scheme's devisers than they merit, as it is unclear that this was ever analysed or evidenced before it was thrown together as a policy over the course of some twenty-two years. The intended outcomes, they suggest, were ambitious, offering educational and managerial innovation, improvements in student attainment and greater diversity of provision and, as a result, increased parental choice. But "whilst these are seen as the desired outcomes, it has to be remembered that remedies can also cause side effects … although a reform is introduced in order to address particular issues within an education system, once implemented, it may also produce outcomes in addition to, or perhaps opposed to those that are intended"[7].

"When Someone Shows You Who They Are, Believe Them the First Time." Maya Angelou

---

[5] Holmes, E 1911 What is and What Might Be: A Study of Education in General and Elementary Education in Particular, London: Constable p.vi

[6] Salokangas, Maija and Ainscow, Mel. 2018. Inside the Autonomous School: Making Sense of a Global Educational Trend, Abingdon: Routledge p10

[7] Ibid pp11-12

But this may be too kind to the policy-makers too. The absence of any advance consultation and of evidence-based policy construction, let alone the use of emergency powers in 2010-11 to push through legislation, suggest that the DfE under Michael Gove and Dominic Cummings saw it as a predominantly – perhaps even purely – ideological move drawn out of the innovative disruption cupboard knocked together by Oliver Letwin and John Redwood[8] to explain how to denationalise everything a Conservative government could lay its hands on[9].

Intended and other possible outcomes, the evidence now suggests, were never more than crude headlines about school autonomy, freedom from local government which might – horror of horrors – be quite left-wing, raising of standards (to be determined and overseen, somewhat paradoxically, nationally) and release from the notorious education blob, consisting of anyone who knew anything about it.

We have therefore seen how a policy, derived from an ideological mantra for smaller, lighter-touch government and a society based on the concept that private interests will produce a more efficient state, grew out of the education department run in tandem by two of its most extreme adherents – Michael Gove and Dominic Cummings – and came to infect the UK government in two of the nation's key moments of the 2010s – the EU referendum of 2016 and the 2020 coronavirus pandemic.

Certainly, the agenda included a notable absence of values, and relied on three key assertions:

- Local government was not up to administering an education system that would deliver the priorities identified by the governments, Labour, coalition and Conservative, to place England higher in the international rankings.
- People with business experience are better at providing services than the public sector.
- Politicians and business people know better than anyone else, including professional educationalists, practitioners or academics, what schooling should offer and how it should do it.

---

[8] Letwin, Oliver and Redwood, John 1988. Privatising the World: A Study of International Privatisation in Theory and Practice, London: Cassell, 1988

[9] See also Meek, James. 2014. Private Island: Why Britain Now Belongs to Someone Else, London: Verso

These assumptions in turn assume – though maybe less explicitly – that the outcomes of schooling are more important than the processes and, since certain outcomes are easier to measure than others, that content is more important than method.

The fundamental values that the world of public education espoused during the major part of the twentieth century held true even though they might have been put into practice in different ways, with different aspirations, in primary, special, secondary modern, grammar and comprehensive schools. They presumed that, for example, schooling is a means of positive social engineering, and is not purely transactional; children from disadvantaged backgrounds need positive discrimination to enable greater equality of outcome, so poverty cannot be ignored; children with exceptional learning needs require some sort of positive discrimination, too; decision-making in administration and management should usually be fair, therefore transparent; lay people should have some role in the governance of schools; and humanitarian values take priority over all others.

While many people in business espouse similar values (see, for example, the B Corp movement: 'bcorporation.uk', which is a body of businesses committed to prioritise societal and environmental needs alongside financial ones), the overriding priority of business is personal and/or shareholder profit.

Rotten leaders make rotten organisations. Some of the top people at the Department for Education between 2010 and 2014 became the top people at Vote Leave in 2016, and then became the top people in government in 2019. In the rush to Brexit, they made promises to the EU, to their followers and to the British public that they had no intention of keeping. In particular, they saw the 2019 Withdrawal Agreement, a contract signed with the EU in apparent good faith, as something they could dump in the autumn of 2020 without a backward glance. The commitments made about the Irish border were critical to the Agreement, and there was some surprise when Johnson agreed to terms almost identical to those that he and others had violently rejected when offered them under Theresa May's leadership. But all became clear:

" …Johnson and his most important confreres, Dominic Cummings and Michael Gove, never really saw this as anything other than a clever dodge, a tactical retreat. On his blog in March 2019, when May was in power, Cummings addressed 'dear Vote Leave activists': 'don't worry about the so-called 'permanent' commitments this historically abysmal cabinet are trying to make on our behalf. They are not 'permanent' and a serious government – one not cowed by officials and their bullshit 'legal advice' with which they have herded ministers like sheep – will dispense with these commitments.' In May this year, Steve Baker, former chair of the European Research Group, wrote in the Critic that Cummings 'said we should vote for the original withdrawal agreement without reading it, on the basis Michael Gove articulated: "we could change it later"' [10]

Spreading the Gospel

The corporatisation of schools has two strands. It enables people with corporate business backgrounds to engage in schools, and it encourages people engaged in schools to adopt business strategies and values.

Corporatisation, then, in recent years, has put each of these societal values in question, at both macro, governmental level and micro, school level. In a period of growing austerity, with fewer and poorer public services and rampant poverty, inequality continues to increase. Academies have less transparency, less accountability, and less capacity or taste for lay engagement with governance.

Effectiveness: What Has It All Been For?

So in this book I have laid out some of the broken eggs left for us after the most radical rearrangement of schools in England since the 1870s. The question now is, "Where's the omelette?"

Perhaps the most remarkable fact in this whole saga is that, after nearly ten years of creeping, then rushing, academisation, we have no independent evidence that schools are performing any better than they were.

Do Academies Produce Better Measurable Outcomes for Their Pupils?

There is still no definitive evidence to show that academies work. They do not seem to produce better results per se than LA schools: "Academies do not provide an automatic solution to school improvement ...there is significant

---

[10] O'Toole, Fintan. 2020. Johnson lied to Europe, but he lied to Britain too, The Guardian, 11 September 2020; Baker, Steve. 2020. Boris: take back control, The Critic. 24 May 2020

variation in performance at both different types of academies and Multi-Academy Trusts."[11]. An Education Policy Institute report of 2018 found that academies do not perform better than maintained schools[12]:

- *Overall, we find little difference in the performance of schools in academy chains and local authorities. The type of school – academy or local authority – is therefore less important than being in a high performing school group.*
- *Indeed, we find that both academy chains and local authorities feature at the very top of our performance tables, and at the very bottom ...*

This remained the case as time went on: "Maintained schools in England out-perform academies and free schools in national exams taken at the end of primary school, while pupils in multi-academy trusts also do worse than their peers elsewhere, according to official figures"[13]. Indeed, "the number of children leaving school without basic qualifications by the age of 18 has risen by nearly a quarter in the past three years" according to the former Children's Commissioner for England.[14]

Are Academies Promoting Equality?

The Education Policy Institute found the following shocking results based on DfE data in the late summer of 2020:

- The attainment gap between disadvantaged pupils and their peers has stopped closing for the first time in a decade. Policymakers have not succeeded in responding to earlier reports warning of a major loss of momentum in closing the gap. Disadvantaged pupils in England are 18.1

---

[11] Andrews, Jon and Perera, Natalie. 2017. School Performance in Academy Chains and Local Authorities – 2017 https://epi.org.uk/publications-and-research/performance-academy-local-authorities-2017/; Education Policy Institute, 2017; Adams, Richard (2019a) 'Off-rolling' hides true extent of disadvantage gap in schools, The Guardian, 5 December 2019

[12] Andrews, Jon. 2018. School Performance in Academy Chains and Local Authorities – 2017, Education Policy Institute, June 2018

[13] Adams, ibid

[14] Children's Commissioner for England, 2019

months of learning behind their peers by the time they finish their GCSEs – the same gap as five years ago.

- The gap at primary school increased for the first time since 2007 – which may signal that the gap is set to widen in the future.
- The stalling of the gap occurred even before the COVID-19 pandemic had impacted the education system.
- Researchers have identified the increasing proportion of disadvantaged children in persistent poverty as a contributory cause of the lack of progress with narrowing the disadvantage gap.[15]

Do Academy Trusts Turn 'Failing' Schools Around Better Than LAs?

"Councils are best when it comes to boosting the inspection grades of inadequate schools, analysis of official figures suggests"[16]. "'Inadequate schools' that had remained council maintained were more likely to be good or outstanding than those that had become sponsored academies". This outcome from research by Angel Solutions, responsible for the 'Watchsted' site which analyses inspection outcomes, strikes at the heart of the DfE's rationale for academisation.

Do Academies Increase Parental Choice?

There is no evidence available that parents are more likely to get the primary or secondary school of their choice, or that choice is greater where there are academies rather than maintained schools[17].

[15] Hitchinson J, Reader M, Akhal A. 2020. Education in England: Annual Report 2020, Education Policy Institute/Fair Education Alliance; https://epi.org.uk/publications-and-research/education-in-england-annual-report-2020/

[16] Burns, Judith. 2018. Councils beat academy trusts at boosting failing schools, BBC News, 5 July 2018.

[17] Weale, Sally. 2020. Thousands denied a place in first choice of primary school, The Guardian, 17 April 2020

Are Teachers in Academies Better Qualified?

"The worrying number of unqualified teachers in Birmingham schools": One in twenty teachers working in Wolverhampton schools does not have qualified status – the highest proportion since rules were relaxed in 2012[18].

Do Teachers Prefer Teaching in Academies?

"The majority of teachers in England are unsure of the benefits of working for a Multi-Academy Trust [MAT] and two thirds (sixty-eight per cent) would choose a role in a standalone school over a job working within a MAT, according to research from Affinity Workforce …nearly two thirds of teachers (63%) have no understanding of how working for a MAT differs from teaching in a normal school, and even teachers that are already working within a MAT are unsure of the advantages it brings (54 per cent)."[19] The Teacher Tapp website found in a survey of 4,743 teachers that, given a choice between working at a local authority school and one belonging to an academy chain, 65% would choose the LA school against 10% choosing the job in the academy chain[20].

Are Academies Better for Children, Now That More Than Half of Secondary Students Are Taught In Them?

"New analysis has found that UK teenagers have the lowest levels of life satisfaction across most of Europe, with researchers from The Children's Society warning that a particularly British fear of failure could partly be to blame. The charity's annual Good Childhood Report has examined international data and found a strong link between life satisfaction and fear of failure. Children aged 15 in the UK had the greatest fear of failure, and the lowest overall life satisfaction across the 24 European countries in the study. Over one in three UK 15 year olds (36%) scored low on life satisfaction.[21]

---

[18] Miller, Claire and Rodger, James. 2018. The worrying number of unqualified teachers in Birmingham schools, Birmingham Mail, 2 August 2018 https://www.birminghammail.co.uk/news/midlands-news/worrying-number-unqualified-teachers-birmingham-14978209

[19] Schools Improvement. 2018.Teachers unsure of benefits of working for a multi academy trust, 25 July 2018

[20] teachertapp.co.uk, 16 August 2019

[21] The Children's Society, 28 August 2020

Are Academies More Cost-Effective Than LAs?

As we have seen, there seems to be wastage on senior salaries and other expenses built into the academy system. Were academies more efficient than maintained schools, they should be weathering the real cuts in education funding better, but they are, like maintained schools, struggling, and seeking financial support from both the ESFA and parents.

A cost-cutting exercise conducted by Lord Agnew in 2018 came up with a number of suggestions following visits to schools. These gems included: replacing experienced teachers with new, young, cheap, teachers or support staff; using spare staff to manage three classes at a time; cutting the number of hours in a school week; disposing of elements of the curriculum; downsizing lunch portions; keeping back for the school half of the money raised by students for charity.[22]

One estimate of the worth of public assets transferred to the private sector so far is £66bn[23]. Even back in 2012, the DfE was unable to estimate the value of school grounds that had been transferred to academies[24]. Michael Gove's reply to my query back then read: "I note Mr Gann's concern that my Department does not keep a record of how much land is currently held by Academies. I am not convinced that collecting this information would add any additional protection for the land or provide any benefit for the school or its pupils." He did not, of course, mention any possible benefit to the wider public. In 2019, "The DfE has admitted it does not know how many academy trusts are operating under funding agreements that completely relinquish public control of state school land".[25]

The land and the buildings are not the only assets that state-funded schools possess. During the twentieth century, far-sighted chief education officers, directors of education and their LA committees enriched their schools with works of art. In Cambridgeshire, some of those works of art were the buildings themselves. At the behest of Chief Officer Henry Morris, Impington Village College was designed by Walter Gropius, opened in 1939, and "could not avoid, over the following months and years, commanding the attention of architects,

---

[22] Dickens, John. 2019. Agnew's army fires cost-cutting salvos, Schools Week, 28 March 2019

[23] The Torygraph, @TweetForTheMany, 29 June 2020

[24] Gann, Nigel. 2012. Playground Robbery, The Land v12 Summer 2012

[25] George, Martin. 2019. DfE does not know how much academy land it has lost control of, TES, 14 February 2019, https://www.tes.com/news/exclusive-dfe-does-not-know-how-much-academy-land-it-has-lost-control

educationists, artists and critics ...the building of Impington was conceived by an architect of international fame, who took delight in translating what he recognised as a great idea into a building suitably sited, designed and furnished."[26]. The building might have been even more spectacular had a sculpture proposed for the college grounds been affordable. Instead, Henry Moore's Family Group was installed in a school in Hertfordshire, where nearly seventy years on, its ownership by Hertfordshire County Council had to be enshrined in law when the school where it did finish up became an academy under the sponsorship of John Nash's Future Trust. Elsewhere in Hertfordshire, "it emerged that some of the county's new academies had claimed ownership of other works from the county council's art collection as their own"[27]. It is impossible to estimate how many valuable paintings bought by local authority education committees for their schools in counties such as Hertfordshire, Cambridgeshire and Leicestershire have passed into the ownership of academy sponsors.

The summary of the House of Commons Public Accounts Committee report of 2018 read as follows:

"In the rush to convert large numbers of schools to academies, the Department did not pay enough attention to ensuring that its scrutiny of applicants was sufficiently rigorous. It is now strengthening how it examines prospective academies' financial viability and sponsors' ability to improve the schools they are taking on, but these issues should have been addressed much earlier and the changes do not go far enough. It is particularly worrying that the Department still does not seem to be learning the lessons from high–profile academy failures that have been costly for taxpayers and damaging to children's education.

"The one-off costs to the Department for Education of converting schools to academies have been £745 million since 2010–11, but the full cost of conversion, including spending by schools and local authorities, is unclear. We are concerned, however, that the Department is failing to give a clear sense of direction for maintained schools, academies, local authorities, pupils and parents. Its policy for converting schools to academies is unclear, and there is substantial

---

[26] Rée, Harry. 1973. Educator Extraordinary: The Life and Achievement of Henry Morris, London: Longman 1973 p75

[27] Price, Deborah. 2019. Henry Moore sculpture worth millions to stay at Stevenage's Barclay Academy, The Comet, 14 February 2019

regional variation, not only in the extent to which schools have become academies but also in the quantity and quality of support available to struggling schools."[28]

It is difficult to imagine a more damning summing-up of a then eight-year-old policy from inside parliament itself. What we have ended up with is, arguably, not even a system. "Tony Blair said that the aim (of limited academisation) was to create 'a *system* of independent non-fee paying state schools' but it always appeared questionable whether that model was compatible with the notion of a 'system' …"[29]

So where, exactly, is the omelette?

Can It Be Mended?

One of the most damaging, and unexpected, political scandals that came to light in early 2018 – and there was some stiff competition – was the disclosure that British citizens and their children from the Caribbean who had migrated to the UK in the late 1940s and 1950s at the request of the then government were being denied benefits, losing their jobs and being deported to the West Indies, where many of them had never lived. This was happening as a result of the 2014 Immigration Act, designed to create a hostile environment for "illegal immigrants" and illustrated by then Home Secretary Theresa May's "Go home or face arrest" van advertisements that toured six London boroughs in the summer of 2013. When the suffering of numerous citizens came to light, it was presented as a policy side-effect – the result of over-zealous or misdirected civil servants wrongly interpreting their duties under the act.

When the application of a policy of a political party in power produces "unwanted" outcomes, it is often presented as a side-effect. But when the evidence climbs, and continues to climb to a significant extent, and things are not put right, it becomes clear that the so-called unwanted outcomes must be the result, not of bad luck or of poor implementation, but of either culpable lack of foresight, or deliberation.

---

[28] House of Commons. 2018. Fifty-second Report of Session 2017-19, Public Accounts Committee, 11 July 2018

[29] Glatter, Ron. 2018. The 'independent state school' and its aftermath: Which way now? Keynote paper for British Educational Leadership, Management and Administration Society (BELMAS) UK Review conference on England, Birmingham, 25-26 September 2018

So it was here, in the middle of April 2018, when it was shown that critical documents proving the arrival of the immigrants had been destroyed under instruction, six months after May had become Home Secretary in 2010. This tipping point caused Caroline Lucas MP to tweet: "Let us be very clear about what's happening. The Govt wants to create a hostile environment for migrants. This isn't a design flaw, it's central to their programme."[30]

The fee-paying "public school" system, which children typically enter at the ages of seven or eight years, has for years been held up as the ideal education for Britain's young, despite the evidence of the long-lasting impact of separation from parents, and the apparently endemic violence. But after the publication of a series of studies and personal reminiscences over some thirty years, Alex Renton concludes that "in the boarding schools cruelty and bullying, by children and adults, was a function of the system: not a disciplinary practice but an ingredient in the magic of that unique education."[31] In short, you cannot have the public school system without the so-called undesirable side-effects.

Is it possible that the academy system is so riddled with the accumulation of evils recorded here as a matter of poor luck or unfortunate coincidence? Could it be that the absence of foresight of the system's devisers was naivety? Can we put it down to just a remarkable collective bout of stupidity? Was it, perhaps, a compilation of costs of the system that would hopefully be outweighed by the benefits? The DfE has shown an interest in placing risk assessment at the heart of school inspection. No one at any time, as far as we can see, performed a risk assessment on this massive handover of control of our schools lock, stock and barrelful of money to the private sector at any stage in this now ten-year-old policy.

Or was it seen all along as a set of, in fact, desirable outcomes, that would reshape the education system, and eventually all public sector provision – would reconstruct the ethical basis on which state education and other services exist – and in time change the expectations and culture of the entire country?

Greed and deceit are not anomalies curable by ever more stringent regulation, when the advantages they may bring are built into the system as acceptable outcomes. When, as in the capture of Castle Primary School, the regulating authority itself – the DfE and the Secretary of State aided, wittingly or not, by

---

[30] Lucas, Caroline. @CarolineLucas, 16 April 2018

[31] Renton, Tim. 2017. Stiff Upper Lip: Secrets, Crimes and the Schooling of a Ruling Class, Weidenfeld and Nicolson 2017. pp. 7-8

local government officers and trust leaders – sponsors breaches of transparency, accountability and the rule of law, and turns a blind eye to the bullying of volunteer governors, what can we expect of the system itself, and of some of the people working within it? I contend that these processes are not incidental hazards of corporatisation, but key elements of it, and therefore should be seen as intended, or at the very least foreseeable, consequences.

And where, I ask again, is the omelette?

Chapter 22
What Might Be

What Now? A Caveat

What might happen now? The last few years in British, and particularly English politics have been more turbulent than at any time since the Second World War. So predictions may well be worthless – especially in the sphere of state education. In addition, the impact of Covid-19 is impossible to measure or foresee. Could this be a tipping point, where the realisation hits home that continuing austerity and growing poverty (turning to actual widespread destitution where the economy collapses) feed inequality in education? David Laws certainly appears to think so, and he was a significant player in the austerity regime[1]. From being a need identified in local, mainly urban, hotspots, where children were appearing in school unfed and often inadequately clothed, the poverty of schoolchildren became a national concern during the lockdown of spring 2020, and impossible to ignore. This led people in all sectors of education to ask fundamental questions about the nature of the work they were being told to perform[2].

In fact, the contention of this book goes further. In chapter 3, I wrote about competence as a requirement in a political administration, a bar that governments since 2010 have signally failed to clear. My assertion here is that, since 2010, the key players in the Department for Education have been *actively working against* the interests of children, parents and staff in English state-funded schools. It is now apparent that the government has been working *actively* against the interests

---

[1] Millar, Fiona. 2020. 'The human stuff matters': heads call for a kinder school system post Covid-19, The Guardian 5 May 2020

[2] Sweeney, Niamh. 2020. When the Covid-19 crisis finally ends, schools must never return to normal, The Guardian 7 April 2020

of the people of the United Kingdom through austerity, Brexit and its management of the pandemic.

The Fightback?

Resistance to all sorts of current government policy is being reported and is even occasionally successful. Teaching and other school staff unions (where the amalgamation of the NUT with the ATL is grounds for optimism) and parent groups are becoming more militant. The low hanging fruit of secondary schools and a few primaries has now been picked, but academisation by force and by governing board choice is reaching both urban and rural areas where conversion has not been regarded as inevitable. Throughout 2019-20, very active campaigns were being waged by combinations of parents and teachers against both large chains such as Ark, and smaller trusts.

Popular movements such as this, are fuelled by nationwide concerns about funding, not just of schools *per se*, but for children and families driven into poverty and destitution by the government's mishandling of the pandemic. The demand for proper consultations, unlike the one conducted by Somerset CC and Redstart Trust, is growing, supported by organisations such as the 'Anti Academies Alliance' and 'Rescue our Schools'.

Cronyist appointments such as Toby Young's to the Office for Students are being reversed in the face of political and professional resistance. Many of this government's policies are cause for shame, but occasionally the shame is thrown back on the decision-makers, and they have little option but to back down. The A Level results fiasco of 2020 led to a shameless bout of blame-laying between Ofqual and the Secretary of State over a systemic flaw for which both share responsibility. But this, at least, was public and, for once, not a disaster that they could lay on the teaching profession – or the old Blob. All the many faults in the system, many of which have been exposed during the pandemic, can only be laid at the door of the current ruling establishment.

New Structures

There appears to be little enthusiasm for a return to the old system of local authority management of delivery, which has reached such a stage of dismantling that it probably could not be revived. But there is much support for a return to some degree of localism. The demand for a new education act addressing five systemic structural issues is rising. These are: the growing crisis in teacher recruitment and retention, increasing professional and parental disenchantment with the curriculum and examination system, the over-centralisation of governance and accountability, school admissions based on a fiction of parental choice and the actuality of school choice, and the funding deficit[3].

I suggested the following model for a new system of schooling in earlier work:

"What might a more democratically accountable *and* educationally robust structure for the piecemeal system we have now look like?

At local level, we could seek a partial restoration of the local coordination of educational provision. The challenges faced by educational establishments should be addressed by the creation of **Local Education Boards** to cover all areas of England, coterminous with local authority boundaries. These would replace both existing local authorities' responsibility for schools and the regional schools commissioners with their headteacher boards.

The Boards would be partly directly elected by the public and partly elected by governors of existing educational establishments. Boards would be responsible for:

- The oversight of the efficiency and effectiveness of all educational provision from early years to further education (re-establishing local input to colleges of further education), *including* all independent and private providers.
- Ensuring universal access to high quality comprehensive provision and public accountability.
- Enabling cooperation between educational providers from all sectors.
- Ensuring fair admission arrangements and equality of access (including the provision of transport).
- Ensuring provision of appropriate education for children regardless of need.
- Disseminating best practice amongst all providers.
- Enabling innovation in educational practice.
- Providing information to the public and an appeals process in the event of unresolved complaints.

---

[3] Brighouse, Tim. 2018. Social mobility: Time for a new Butler act for the 21st century, The Guardian, 3 April 2018

Boards would be responsible directly to parliament for their performance, and subject to inspection against agreed criteria, including achievement levels across the locality.

Boards would also take responsibility for ensuring multi-agency approaches to children's social care, working with local authorities while current arrangements obtain.

The Boards would provide oversight and some level of standardisation, while enabling and encouraging innovation and experimentation within a controlled environment.

No extra costs need be caused by this structure, as they would replace many of the functions currently carried out by local authorities[4].

At school level, the status of all schools currently academies or free schools would be required to reflect their position as community-based charities – whether as stand-alone academies or as members of a chain or multi academy trust. They would be required to be membership charities, with membership including:

- Any parent or carer of any child enrolled in the school (or 16+s who are enrolled), would automatically take up membership.

Other individuals could apply for membership, for example:

- Any member of the community served by the school who would like to be a member.
- Any individual with a connection to the school who would like to be a member.
- Any person with a skill or quality that the school would find helpful, and would like to be a member.

Membership duties and responsibilities would include annual election of a third or a quarter of the board with local responsibility for the school (in chains and MATs, this would be a step in the election of the overall collective trust board). Members would receive an annual report from the board on the school's performance across a wide range of measures agreed by the membership, at an annual general meeting. In order to involve staff and to observe rules on

---

[4] Gann, N 2013 in House of Commons Education Committee: The Role of School Governing Bodies, Second Report of Session 2013–14, Volume III (House of Commons 2013)

employee engagement with charity governance, employee membership might offer a distinctive category of membership, either non-voting, or voting for a limited form of board membership.

All grouped academies would be limited geographically and to an optimum size around two dozen, and would have overall governance developed on these lines.

This membership, above all, would be empowered to hold the board to account on an agreed set of performance standards and, ultimately, under extreme circumstances (where the board's probity or effectiveness is seriously compromised) to remove it altogether. It allows any member of the community, and encourages parents, to become 'social shareholders' in the school. They will have already made a financial investment in the school through paying taxes and council charges. By investing their time and interest, care and responsibility in the school, their returns include a successful and energising school, a vibrant community and a generation of young people with the skills and qualities to lead that community into the future."[5]

This would not be a step backwards to an age when local government 'controlled' schools, in the government's rhetoric. The academy structure can continue to grow and thrive, not based on the increasingly discredited 'business' model, but on a model of cooperative and community organisations, transparent, accountable and in the shared ownership of the communities they serve.

Instead of direct performance accountability to parliament, I would now advocate the creation of a national education service which sets broad aims and objectives for schooling at a strategic level. Such a service would comprise education professionals from all levels of state-provided and independent education together with academics and cross-party politicians. The balance of such a multi-disciplinary body would need thorough consultation before construction.

---

[5] Gann, Nigel. 2016. Improving School Governance: How better governors make better schools. 2nd edn. London: Routledge. Pp193-4

A Vision Statement: Some Values Worth Fighting For

For a set of basic values for a national system, we should look to a culture that:

- Can stand up robustly and remain in good condition, having *Firmatis*, that is: Durability.
- Is useful and functions well for the people using it, having *Utilitas*, that is: Utility.
- Delights people and raises their spirits, having *Venustatis*, that is: Beauty[6].

The wide and deep engagement of local people in their schools should join these fundamental values of public education to underlie its structures at every level. Accountability to them must be enshrined in law.

Can we change the way we do education in the UK? Can we change the way we do government? It may prove impossible to do one without the other.

Schooling in The Community: What Might Be

Looking back to the curious conversion of Castle School at a distance of some six years, we might wonder what the fuss is about. The village seems to have a good school again. There are local people serving on a local governing board – with no actual powers, but if the governing trust fulfils its purpose, it will listen to them, and the head of the school will work in partnership with them and address any concerns they have.

But I think something has been lost. The school no longer 'belongs' to the local community. They no longer have rights concerning the school. Indeed, the school no longer exists as a legal entity. And the dismissiveness of the local authority's officers and the new management of the school, the steam-rollering of the community's wishes and, indeed, legal rights, the arrogance and underhandedness of DfE officials and local government officers may live long in the village's memory.

---

[6] These were the principles laid down by Vitruvius Pollio (died 15 BC) for the construction of buildings two thousand years ago. It is arguable whether schooling in England currently meets any one of these expectations. Vitruvius understood that any construction needs a culture underlying it, not merely practical and technical skill in its building.

So it should. What are schools for if they are not for us and our children? And what does it teach us about the world if the administration of our schools does not reflect the highest moral standards?

Where in the saga of Castle School – and the similar stories of so many similar schools – did anyone in 'authority' stand back and ask the school's community what they wanted, with a genuine respect and a sincere desire to know?

And where were normal human relationships, other than those based on officialdom and 'our leaders know best'?

Capturing a Castle is all very well. What should we do with it once it's captured? Take it apart stone by stone? Rebuild it better? Turn it into something entirely different?

And what to do with the people who lived in it, worked in it – the people to whom the castle really belonged?

One of our greatest writers and thinkers, Samuel Johnson, was not a softheaded liberal by any means. But he understood this fundamental principle: "Getting money is not all a man's business: To cultivate kindness is a valuable part of the business of life"[7].

The State We've Got Ourselves In

As you will have spotted, this book is actually about *fairness*. Fairness can be found at the root of every valued relationship, of every successful organisation and of every good society. Without fairness, other virtues serve little purpose.

A health service that favours some and disfavours others is not fair. A jobs' market, a benefits system, a police service, a housing provision, a justice system, that does not treat people as of equal worth, regardless of their wealth, birth, colour, class and gender is itself worthless. It leads to a society where, from birth, some people are, or feel, more entitled and more privileged than others.

If an education provision, a schooling system, is unfair, it strikes at the very roots of our society, because from day one, some children can see that other children are getting a better deal because of who they are and how much money they have. Perhaps that is inevitable in most areas of life. But our education system must minimise that inequality, neither exploit it nor add to it.

---

[7] Boswell, James. 1851. The Life of Samuel Johnson LL.D, Vol.3, London. Wordsworth Editions, 1999

A schooling that unfairly, almost arbitrarily, divides children into sheep and goats, or that by design provides some young people with fewer and worse facilities than others, or that allows the use of precious resources differentially between schools and groups of schools, is a virus as destructive and as potentially terminal as Covid-19. It blights and destroys rather than enhances life. It teaches us to accept, from the moment we enter it, that for some people who run our schools, the mission takes second place to the money; and that privileged gangs of people with self-advancement as their only motive can control the organisations funded by us that are supposed to enable our growth and wellbeing.

No organisation or service paid for by taxpayers can be seen to be fair, unless it is moderated by the people it serves. The participation of the public is critical in its leadership and accountability.

A schooling system that embeds inequality and enables greed, selfishness and competitiveness is unfair.

Our children deserve better.

Bibliography

Books

Affolter, T & Donnor, J 2016 *The Charter School Solution: Distinguishing Fact from Rhetoric,* Abingdon: Routledge

Ainscow, M. 2014 *Towards Self-Improving School Systems Lessons from a City Challenge*. London: Routledge.

Arendt, H 1951 *The Origins of Totalitarianism,* London: Penguin

Aynsley-Green, A 2019 *The British Betrayal of Childhood: Challenging Uncomfortable Truths and Bringing about Change,* Abingdon: Routledge

Baggs A, Bush, R & Tomlinson, M 1974 *A History of the County of Somerset, Volume 3,* London: Victoria County History

Ball, S & Junemann, C 2012 *Networks, New Governance and Education,* Bristol: Policy Press

Baxter, J 2016 *School Governance: Policy, Politics and Practices,* Bristol: Policy Press

Boswell, James. 1851. *The Life of Samuel Johnson LL.D, Vol.3,* London. Wordsworth Editions, 1999Brecht, Bertolt. 1947 *The Life of Galileo,* London: Methuen 1960Chitty, 1999 *The Education System Transformed,* Tisbury: Baseline Book Company

Connolly, C 1938 *Enemies of Promise,* London: Routledge and Kegan Paul

Costas, J & Grey, C, 2016 *Secrecy at Work: The Hidden Architecture of Organizational Life*, Stanford, Stanford University Press

Daube, Jonathan. 2017. *Educator Most Extraordinary: The life and achievements of Harry Rée, 1914-1991,* London: UCL Institute of Education

Davies, Nick. 2014 *Hack Attack: How the Truth Caught Up with Rupert Murdoch,* London: Chatto & Windus

Dewey, J 1916; this edition 2011 *Democracy and Education,* New York: Simon and Brown

Dewey, J 1938; this edition, 1997 *Experience and Education,* New York: Touchstone, Simon & Schuster

Duane, M 1991 *Work, Language & Education in the Industrial State*, London: Freedom Press

Edwards, T and Parsons C 2019 *How to Dismantle the English State Education System in 10 Easy Steps*, Winchester: Zero Books

Ellis,T. McWhirter, J. McColgan, D and Hadow, B. 1976. *William Tyndale: The Teachers' Story*, London: Writers and Readers Publishing Cooperative

Emerson, Ralph Waldo. 1841 *"Self-Reliance"*. In Eliot, Charles William (ed.). *Essays and English Traits.* Harvard Classics. Volume 5, with introduction and notes. (56th printing, 1965 ed.). New York: P.F.Collier & Son Corporation

Foot, M 1962 *Aneurin Bevan: A Biography: Volume 1: 1897-1945*, London: Faber & Faber

Francis, P 2001 *The Best Policy? Honesty in Education 1997-2001*, Much Wenlock: Liberty Books

Gann, N 1999 *Targets for Tomorrow's Schools: A Guide to Whole School Target-Setting for Governors and Headteachers*, London: Falmer Press

Gann, N 2016 *Improving School Governance: How better governors make better schools*, London: Routledge 2nd edition

Gaventa, J 1980 *Power and Powerlessness: Quiescence and Rebellion in an Appalachian Valley*, Chicago: University of Illinois

Gentleman, Amelia. 2019 *The Windrush Betrayal: Exposing the Hostile Environment*, London: Guardian Faber

Goodfellow, Maya. 2019 *Hostile Environment: How Immigrants Became Scapegoats*, London: Verso Books

Grant, T 2015 *Jeremy Hutchinson's Case Histories*, London: John Murray

Halberstam, David 1969 *The Best and the Brightest*, New York: Ballantine Holmes, E 1911 *What is and What Might Be: A Study of Education in General and Elementary Education in Particular*, London: Constable

Holmes, G 1952 *The Idiot Teacher: A Book about Prestolee School and its Headmaster E. F> O'Neill*, London: Faber and Faber

House, Richard. 2020. *Pushing Back to Ofsted: Safeguarding and the Legitimacy of Ofsted's Inspection Judgements – A Critical Case Study*, Stroud: InterActions

Keltner, D 2016 *The Power Paradox: How we gain and lose influence*, New York, Penguin Random House

Kogan, M., Johnson, D., and Packwood, T 1984 *School Governing Bodies*, London,Heinemann

Kulz, Christy. 2017. *Factories for Learning: Making race, class and inequality in the neoliberal academy*, Manchester: Manchester University Press

Laws, David and Marshall, Paul. 2004. *The Orange Book: Reclaiming Liberalism*, London: Profile Books

Letwin, O and Redwood, J 1988 *Privatising the World: A Study of International Privatisation in Theory and Practice*, London: Cassell, 1988

Lewis, Mark 2018 *The Fifth Risk*, London: Penguin

Lilienthal, David. 1944 *TVA Tennessee Valley Authority: Democracy on the March*. Harmondsworth: Penguin

Lukes, Steven 1974 *Power: A Radical View*, London: MacMillan

Martin, W 2004 *The Best Liberal Quotes Ever: Why the Left is Right*, Chicago: Sourcebooks

Mason, P 2016 *Postcapitalism: A Guide to Our Future*, London: Penguin Random House

Meek, J 2014 *Private Island: Why Britain Now Belongs to Someone Else*, London: Verso

Murray, N 1996 *A Life of Matthew Arnold*, London: Hodder & Stoughton

Newman, Janet 2001 *Modernising Governance: New Labour, Policy and Society*, London: Sage Publications

O'Connor, M., Hales, E., Davies, J. and Tomlinson, S. *1999 Hackney Downs: The School that dared to Fight*, London: Cassell

Origo, Iris. 1947. *War in Val D'Orcia*, Harmondsworth: Penguin

Orwell, G 1946 *Politics and the English Language,* in *Collected Essays, Journalism and Letters of George Orwell* 1968, London: Secker & Warburg, quotes from 1980 edition

Paxton-Doggett, K 2014 *How to Run an Academy School*, London: ICSA, 2014

Reay, D 2017, *Miseducation: Inequality, education and the working classes*, Bristol: Policy Press

Rée, Harry. 1973. *Educator Extraordinary: The Life and Achievement of Henry Morris 1889-1961*, London: Longman

Renton, Tim. 2017. *Stiff Upper Lip: Secrets, Crimes and the Schooling of a Ruling Class*, Weidenfeld and Nicolson 2017

Sallis, J 1988 *Schools, Parents and Governors: A New Approach to Accountability*, London: Routledge, p.133

Salokangas, M and Ainscow, M 2017 *Inside the autonomous school: making sense of a global trend*, London: Routledge

Schattschneider, E 1960 *The Semi-Sovereign People: A Realist's View of Democracy in America*, New York: Rinehart and Wilson

Seabrook, J 1988 *The Leisure Society*, London: Blackwell

Simon, B 1988 *Bending the Rules: The Baker 'Reform' of Education*, London: Lawrence and Wishart

Swire, S 2020 *Diary of an MP's wife*, London: Little Brown

Thomson, P 2020 *School Scandals: Blowing the Whistle on the Corruption of Our Education System*, Bristol: Policy Press

Trump, Mary. 2020. *Too Much and Never Enough: How my family created the world's most dangerous man*, London: Simon & Schuster, 2020

Watson Tom and Hickman, Martin. (2012) *Dial M for Murdoch: News Corporation and the Corruption of Britain*, London: Allen Lane

Watts, J 1980 *The Community College: Continuous Change*, in Fletcher, C & Thompson, N (1980), *Issues in Community Education*, Lewes: Falmer Press

Wilkins, A 2016 *Modernising School Governance: Corporate Planning and Expert Handling in State Education,* Abingdon: Routledge

Wilkins, A. and Olmedo, A 2018 *Conceptualising Education Governance: Framings, Perspectives and Theories* in A. Wilkins and A. Olmedo (eds) *Education governance and social theory: Interdisciplinary approaches to research*, London: Bloomsbury)

Willis, Paul. 1977. *Learning to Labour: How working class kids get working class jobs*, Farnborough: Saxon House

Winkley, D. 2002 *Handsworth Revolution: The Odyssey of a School*, London: De la Mare

Yeo, Colin. 2020 *Welcome to Britain: Fixing Our Broken Immigration System*, London: Biteback Publishing

Journals and Reports

Allen, A 2017 *The academy revolution is ousting governors*, Democratic Audit, 26.1.17

Allen, A & Gann, N 2018 *Embedding Democratic Engagement in School Leadership: comprehensive schooling structures in an academised system*, in Forum Vol 60 No 2, Didcot: Symposium Books Ltd

Andrews, J and Perera, N 2017: *School Performance in Academy Chains and Local Authorities – 2017* https://epi.org.uk/publications-and-research/performance-academy-local-authorities-2017/; Education Policy Institute, 2017

Armstrong, P 2015: *Effective school partnerships and collaboration for school improvement: a review of the evidence* Research report October 2015, DfE

Balarin, M, Brammer, S, James, C, McCormack, M 2008 *Governing our Schools: A research study commissioned by Business in the Community*, Bath: University of Bath

Department of Education and Science 1977 *A New Partnership for Our Schools (The Taylor Report)*, London: HMSO

Department of Education and Science 1984 *Parental Influence at School*, London: HMSO, May 1984

Department of Education and Science. 1986. *Education (No 2) Act 1986*, London: HMSO

Department for Education (DfE) 2010: *Academies Act 2010*, London: Department for Education

Department for Education 2014: *ARK Schools: In-depth sponsor profile*, April 2014

Department for Education 2015 *The constitution of governing bodies of maintained schools: Statutory guidance for governing bodies of maintained schools and local authorities in England*, The Stationery Office, August 2015

Department for Education 2015 *Being inspected as a maintained school or academy*, Website last updated: 3rd September, 2015 https://www.gov.uk/guidance/being-inspected-as-a-maintained-school-or-academy)

Department for Education 2015 *Effective school partnerships and collaboration for school improvement: a review of the evidence; Research report*, October 2015, Department for Education

Department for Education 2015 *The governance handbook: For trustees of academies and multi-academy trusts and governors of maintained schools*, November 2015

Department for Education (DfE) 2016: *Education and Adoption Act 2016*, London: Department for Education

Department for Education 2016 *'Educational Excellence Everywhere'* London: The Stationery Office

Department for Education 2016 *Next steps to spread educational excellence everywhere announced,* Press release, 6 May 2016

Department for Education (updated 11 May, 2016) *Convert to an academy: guide for schools*, https://www.gov.uk/guidance/convert-to-an-academy-information-for-schools/1-before-you-apply

Department for Education 2018 & 2019 *List of trusts receiving letters from ESFA about high executive salaries*, https://www.gov.uk/government/organisations/department-for-education 6th July 2018 & 24th May 2019

Gann, N 2011: *Academy Conversion: a view from the governing body*, in Forum Vol 53 No 3, Didcot: Symposium Books Ltd

Gann, N. 2012. *Playground Robbery*, The Land v12 Summer 2012

Gann, N 2013 in *House of Commons Education Committee: The Role of School Governing Bodies, Second Report of Session 2013–14, Volume III* (House of Commons 2013)

Gann, N 2014 *Educating Ethics: The Probity of School Governance*, in Forum Vol 56 No 3, Didcot: Symposium Books

Gann, N 2015 *The Business of Governing Schools*, in Forum Vol 57 No 3, Didcot: Symposium Books

Gann, N 2016 *Capturing the Castle: an exploration of changes in the democratic accountability of schools*, in Forum Vol 58 No 2, Didcot: Symposium Books

Gann, N 2020 *Recapturing the Castle: looking to the de-corporatisation of schools and a post-viral revival of educational values*, in Forum Vol 62 No 3, Didcot: Symposium Books

Glatter, R 2018 *The 'independent state school' and its aftermath: Which way now?*, Keynote paper for British Educational Leadership, Management and Administration Society (BELMAS) UK Review conference on England, Birmingham, 25-26 September 2018

Hitchinson J, Reader M, Akhal A. 2020. *Education in England: Annual Report 2020*, Education Policy Institute/Fair Education Alliance; https://epi.org.uk/publications-and-research/education-in-england-annual-report-2020/

House of Commons 2010 *Academies Act 2010*, London: The Stationery Office

House of Commons 2013 *The School Governance (Roles, Procedures and Allowances) (England) Regulations 2013, DfE 2013; Statutory Instrument 2013 No 1624*: The School Governance (Roles, Procedures and Allowances) (England) Regulations 2013, coming into force 1.9.13

House of Commons Education Committee 2016 *The role of Regional Schools Commissioners*: First Report of Session 2015-16, London: The Stationery Office, 20th January 2016

House of Commons. 2018. *Fifty-second Report of Session 2017-19*, Public Accounts Committee, 11 July 2018

Hutchings, M., Greenwood, C., Hollingworth, S., Mansaray, A., Rose, A., and Glass, K. 2012. *Evaluation of the City Challenge programme (Research Report DFE-RR215)*, London: Department for Education, p. v;

Johnson, M & Mansell, W 2014 *Education not for Sale: A TUC Research report*. London: TUC

Kidson, Marc; Norris, Emma 2014 *"Implementing the London Challenge"*(PDF). York: The Joseph Rowntree Foundation

Morse, Amyas. 2016 *Comptroller and Auditor General's Report on the Department for Education's financial statements 2014-15*, London: National Audit Office

NAHT, ATL, NUT, UNISON & NGA 2015 *The Education and Adoption Bill*, http://www.naht.org.uk/welcome/news-and-media/key-topics/organisational-structures/education-and-adoption-bill-briefing/ October 2015

National Governors' Association. February 2011 *Guidance for NGA Members on the Academies Act v10 180211*, Birmingham, NGA

Ofsted (Office for Standards in Education, Children's Services and Skills) 2010 *London Challenge*, London: Ofsted.

Ofsted (Office for Standards in Education, Children's Services and Skills) 2015 *School Inspection Handbook* (issued 28th August 2015), London: The Stationery Office

Office of the Schools Adjudicator 2015 Office of the Schools Adjudicator *Annual Report September 2014 to August 2015*, November 2015

Parenti, Michael. 1970. *Power and Pluralism: A View from the Bottom*, Journal of Politics, 32

Sandbrook, Dominic. 2016 *How Will History Treat David Cameron?* New Statesman, 29 August 2016

Smith, Beckie. 2020. *Cummings seeks "weirdos and misfits" to work in No.10*, Civil Service World, 3 January 2020

Wilkins, A. 2014 *Governing Schools: The Role of Community and Professional Volunteers*
https://www.academia.edu/8901867/Briefing_Paper_for_ESRC_SASE_proj ect__findings_and_recommendations

Newspaper articles

Adams, R 2019 *'Off-rolling' hides true extent of disadvantage gap in schools*, Guardian, 5th December 2019

Adams, R 2019 *Maintained primaries outperform academies and free schools*, Guardian, 14th December, 2019

Ahmed, Nafeez. 2020 *Sagegate: Vote Leave Ideology Trumped Science and Safety*, Byline Times, July 2020

Allen-Kinross, Pippa. 2018. *United Learning and Ark in north London turf war*, Schools Week, 9 February 2018

Allen-Kinross, Pippa. 2018. *Struggling to afford CPD? Charge parents £1 a week, says leading head*, Schools Week, 27 March 2018

Allen-Kinross, P 2018 *Doomed Schools Company Trust 'double-counted' GCSEs*, Schools Week, 4th July 2018

Allen-Kinross, Pippa. 2019. *Academy rapped over consultancy payments to chair of trustees*, 1 February 2019

Allen-Kinross, Pippa. 2019. *"I'll deal with this treacherous whistleblower"* Schools Week, 5 April 2019

Baker, Steve. 2020. *Boris: take back control*, The Critic. 24 May 2020

Boffey, D and Mansell, W 2016 *Are England's academies becoming a cash cow for business?* The Guardian, 12th June, 2016
http://www.theguardian.com/education/2016/jun/12/academy-schools-cash-cow-business

Boyd, Milo. 2019. *NET Academies claims to have no plans to sell Waltham Holy Cross' land when it takes over in July*, East London and West Essex Guardian, 21 January 2019

Brighouse, Tim. 2018. *Social mobility: Time for a new Butler act for the 21st century*, The Guardian, 3 April 2018

Camden, Billy. 2017. *Struggling school paid £600,000 to football club*, Schools Week, 24 March 2017

Carr, James. 2020. *Investigation: diversity of education leadership roles fails to improve despite DfE pledge*, Schools Week, 21 June 2020

Chakrabortty, Aditya. 2018 *How parents and teachers are frozen out of our schools*, The Guardian, 30 July 2018

Chakrabortty, Aditya. 2019. *'Accidental Activists': Essex parents fight academy trust's takeover of school*, The Guardian, 28 April 2019

Conn, David. 2020. *Firm linked to Gove and Cummings hired to work with Ofqual on A-Levels*, The Guardian, 20 August 2020

Cornwell, David. 2005. *"I do give a damn", Interview with Stuart Jeffries*, The Guardian, 6 October 2005

Cusick, James 2013. *'Dump f***ing everyone': the inside story of how Michael Gove's vicious attack dogs are terrorising the DfE*, The Independent, 15 February 2013

Dickens, John. 2017. *The Lilac Sky Scandal: Accounts reveal Astonishing Financial Impropriety*, Schools Week, 16 June 2017

Dickens, John. 2017. *Vote Leave campaigner and Tory donor behind Parents and Teachers for Excellence campaign*, Schools Week, 22 September 2017

Dickens, John. 2019. *Agnew's army fires cost-cutting salvos*, Schools Week, 28 March 2019

Dickens, John. 2020. *High Court judge slams pricey legal rows as RSC's academy conversion ruled unlawful*, Schools Week, 30 June 2020

Dickens, John. 2020. *'Supersized' trust investigated by government just 14 months after opening with 10 schools*, Schools Week, 6 July 2020

Evans, Richard. 2019. *Norman Stone obituary* The Guardian, 25 June 2019

Evans, R and Pegg, D 2020 *Vote Leave AI firm wins seven government contracts in 18 months*, Guardian 4th May 2020

Evans R and Pegg D. 2020. *Fourth firm with Tory links awarded government work without tendering*, The Guardian 5 September 2020

Evans, Rob, Shahid, Nimra, Conn, David. 2020. *Minister relinquishes control of shares in firm given UK government contract*, The Guardian, 3 September 2020

Garside, J and Neate, R 2020 *Serco deal raises fears that NHS faces 'power grab' by private sector*, Guardian 5th May 2020

George, Martin. 2018. *Secrecy over Agnew conflicts of interest*, Times Educational Supplement (TES), 30 May 2018

George, Martin. 2018. *Exclusive: 'It's hard to argue for school autonomy,' says academy chief*, TES, 17 August 2018

George, Martin. 2019. *DfE does not know how much academy land it has lost control of*, TES, 14 February 2019, https://www.tes.com/news/exclusive-dfe-does-not-know-how-much-academy-land-it-has-lost-control

Grierson, Jamie. 2020. *Home Office wrong to refer to 'activist lawyers', top officials admit*, The Guardian 28 August 2020

Hackett, Geraldine. 2020. *John Lewis salesman lied his way to 1m job running schools*, The Times, 21 February 2020

Harris, John. 2020. *How the Tories are working to create a cookie-cutter country*, The Guardian, 17 August 2020

Hazell, Will 2020 *Michael Gove criticised for dropping the Windrush generation from curriculum*, The i Newsletter, 30th June 2020

Helm, Toby 2013 *Michael Gove's officials act to clean up abusive Twitter feed*, The Observer 16 February 2013

James, A H. *Academisation makes it harder for local schools to work together*, Schools Week, 5 October 2017

Kentish, Benjamin. 2019. *David Cameron says Boris Johnson asked him if Michael Gove was 'a bit cracked'*, The Independent, 16 September 2019

McInerney, Laura. 2017. *These Boards are corrupt, self-serving and secretive*, Schools Week 5 May 2017

McIntyre, N and Weale, S. 2019. *More than 300 English primary schools forced to become academies*, The Guardian, 11 July 2019

Mansell, Warwick and Savage, Michael. *Silver Birch Academy Trust in spotlight again over spending*, The Guardian, 12 May 2018

Millar, F 2020 *'The human stuff matters': heads call for a kinder school system post Covid-19*, Guardian 5th May 2020

Miller, Claire and Rodger, James. 2018. *The worrying number of unqualified teachers in Birmingham schools*, Birmingham Mail, 2 August 2018 https://www.birminghammail.co.uk/news/midlands-news/worrying-number-unqualified-teachers-birmingham-14978209

Mulholland, Hélène. 2020. *DfE in 'serious data breach' after naming whistleblowers*, Schools Week, 14 February 2020

Neate, Rupert. 2020. *'This isn't really Somerset': how the rich took over Bruton*, The Guardian, 10 July 2020

O'Toole, Fintan. 2020. *Johnson lied to Europe, but he lied to Britain too*, The Guardian, 11 September 2020;

Paton, Graeme. 2013. *Gove's department 'run like episode of Upstairs Downstairs'*, Daily Telegraph, 16 January 2013

Pegg D, Evans R, Lewis P. 2020. *Revealed: Dominic Cummings firm paid Vote Leave's AI firm £260,000*, The Guardian, 12 July 2020

Perraudin, Frances. 2015. *Michael Gove ran office 'like something out of The Thick of It'* The Guardian, 7th April 2015

Price, Deborah. 2019. *Henry Moore sculpture worth millions to stay at Stevenage's Barclay Academy*, The Comet, 14 February 2019

Rawnsley, Andrew. 2020 *Even Tories increasingly fear they have inflicted the worst of all worlds on Britain*, The Observer, 15th June 2020

Roberts, John. 2018. *Don't buy booze, funding agency tells Mats*, TES, 8 June 2018

Robertson, Alix. 2017. *The Expandables: Academy Trusts are supersizing*, Schools Week, 15 September 2017

Robertson, Alix. 2018. *Academy Trust Boss defends £1.5m in Payments to Family Firm*, Schools Week 19 January 2018

Rusbridger, Alan. 2019. *The election in the media: against evasion and lies, good journalism is all we have*, The Guardian, 14 December 2019

Savage, M and Mansell, W (2018) *Dozens of academy schools need bailouts from taxpayers*, Guardian, 3rd February 2018

Schools Week reporter'(sic). 2017 *Costs of rebrokering academies to be published for first time*, Schools Week, 23 August 2018

Shahid, Nimra. Conn, David. Goodley, Simon. Cutler, Sam. 2020. *Cummings recruit was fired after BLM tweet* The Guardian 3 September 2020

Smith, Mikey. 2016. *Tory ministers branded 'plonkers' after arriving late to meet flood-hit locals on the wrong side of collapsed bridge*, Daily Mirror, 4 January 2016

Staufenberg, Jess. 2017. *Remaining 'requires improvement' schools will be hard to fix*, Schools Week, 15 December 2017

Staufenberg, J 2018 *Named: The 92 academy trusts with multiple staff on £100k+*, Schools Week, 30th April 2018

Staufenberg,J 2018 *Second Harris academy has SATs results annulled*, Schools Week, 21st September, 2018

Staufenberg Jess. 2019. *Features: Rachel Wolf*, Schools Week, 23 July 2019

Staufenberg, Jess. 2019. *This is oppression: Non-disclosure agreements used to muzzle teachers*, The Guardian, 6 August 2019

Stewart, H and Weale, S. 2020. *Civil servants 'fall guys for No 10', say critics as education chief removed*, The Guardian, 27 August 2020

Sweeney, N 2020 *When the Covid-19 crisis finally ends, schools must never return to normal*, Guardian 7th April 2020

Syal, Rajeev. 2016. *Unqualified daughter of minister teaches in his academy schools*, The Guardian 12 May 2016

Toye, Christopher. 2017. *The false freedoms of becoming an academy*, Schools Week, 15 May 2017

Turner, Camilla. 2018. *Private schools' corporate greed is driving out middle-class families, former St Pauls' headteacher says*, Daily Telegraph 14 May 2018. www.telegraph.co.uk/education/2018/04/14/private-schools-corporate-greed-pricing-middle-class-families/

Wainwright, Daniel. 2019. *Ofsted: 1,010 'outstanding' schools not inspected for a decade* BBC News, 2 October 2019

Weale, S 2018 *300 schools picked out in GCSE 'off-rolling' investigation*, Guardian 26th June 2018

Weale, Sally 2019. *Academisation rebellion: parents resist school takeovers*, The Guardian, 5 May 2019

Weale, Sally. 2019. *School cash boost 'leaves most worse off than in 2015'*, The Guardian, 1 October 2019

Weale, S 2020 *Thousands of pupils in England miss out on first-choice primary school*, Guardian, 16th April 2020

Whittaker, Freddie. *'Communication' but no consultation on conversion* Schools Week, 19 December 2015

Whittaker, Freddie. 2017. *ATT chief executive broke rules over chair sacking, EFA investigation finds* Schools Week, 24 March 2017

Whittaker, Freddie. 2017. *Academy boss and Tory donor is new DfE minister*, 29 September 2017

Whittaker, Freddie. 2017. *Bright Tribe to give up struggling Whitehaven Academy*, 30 November 2017

Whittaker, Freddie. 2020. *Coronavirus: Unions report academy trust to health and safety watchdog over 'unsafe' return of pupils*, Schools Week, 2 June 2020

Online and other

ARK 2018 https://arkonline.org/news/sam-freedman-appointed-new-chief-executive-arks-education-partnerships-group, April 2020

BBC News 2016 *Academy chain to scrap governing bodies*, 19th January 2016 http://www.bbc.co.uk/news/education-35347602,

BBC News 2014 http://www.bbc.co.uk/news/uk-30226781, 1 December 2014

Bennett, Matthew. 2016. *Ark Schools: An example of philanthrocapitalism* Local Schools Network https://www.localschoolsnetwork.org.uk/2016/06/ark-schools-an-example-of-philanthrocapitalism

Benn, T 2014 http://www.newstatesman.com/politics/2014/03/tony-benn-1925-2014-ten-his-greatest-quotes

Burns, Judith. 2013. *'Culture of extravagant expenses' at academy group*, BBC News, 17 May 2013

Burns, Judith. 2018. *Drop 'misleading' statistic, government told*, BBC News, 2 July 2018

Burns, Judith. 2018. *Councils beat academy trusts at boosting failing schools*, BBC News, 5 July 2018

Campaign for Freedom of Information 2015 *Stop FOI restrictions* https://www.cfoi.org.uk/campaigns/stop-foi-restrictions/

Coughlan, Sean. 2016. *Academy Chain to scrap governing bodies*, BBC News, 19 January 2016

Fowler, J 2016 *Viewpoint: Farewell Education and Adoption Bill, welcome the Act*, February 26, 2016 (http://www.lgiu.org/category/education/)

Gove, Michael et al. 2016. *Restoring public trust in immigration policy – a points-based non-discriminatory immigration system*, Statement by Michael Gove, Boris Johnson, Priti Patel, and Gisela Stuart, Vote Leave, 1 June 2016

Gove, Michael 2020 https://www.gov.uk/government/speeches/the-privilege-of-public-service-given-as-the-ditchley-annual-lecture 1 July 2020

Hacked Off 2020 *Unelected: The insidious influence of Rupert Murdoch at the heart of the government*, July 2020

Hardy, Lloyd 2020. *Why is Dominic Cummings So Important?,* Open Source Intelligence, lloydhardy.com/news, 31 May 2020

Helm, Toby 2020 *They rang and asked us ...* @tobyhelm, Twitter, 26th April, 2020

Hencke, David 2020 *Britain Heads to Elective Dictatorship*, Byline Times, July 2020

Higham, R and Freedman, S 2020 *Intent and Motivation*, Twitter, @rupert_higham; @Samfr 19th April, 2020

Honeycomb-Foster, Matt. 2018. *Top Tory Nicky Morgan says she would refuse to serve under Boris Johnson*, www.politicshome.com, 10 September, 2018

Ingram, N 2016 : *The conversation blog* https://theconversation.com/forced-academisation-by-proxy-when-schools-have-little-choice-but-to-convert-56389#comment_93425).

Ireland, Tim. 2015. *Tweet archive of @toryeducation, the abusive sock-puppet of Michael Gove and/or his SPADs*, Bloggerheads https://twitter.com/bloggerheads, 3 March 2015

Komarnyckyj, Steve. 2019. *Firtash: How the Trump Impeachment Scandal Leads back to British Brexiters*, Byline Times, 23 October 2019

Mansell, W 2018 https://www.educationuncovered.co.uk/

Mansell, Warwick. 2019. *How could a local authority primary school headteacher simultaneously be working as director of education for an academy trust?* Education Uncovered, 31 October 2019

Mansell, W 2019 *Businessmen in near-complete control of schools educating more than 100,000 pupils, new analysis by Education Uncovered shows*, educationuncovered.co.uk, 6th November, 2019

Mansell, Warwick. 2019. *Education's new royal family: how control of England's second- largest chain of academies will pass to the family of its founder upon his death*, Education Uncovered, 7 November 2019

Mansell, Warwick. 2019. *Governing body refuses to release minutes of meeting where it decided to start academisation process, deeming it 'confidential'*, Education Uncovered, 15 November 2019

Mansell, Warwick. 2020. *DfE sets out in detail its reasons for cloaking academy decision-making in secrecy. But legal tribunal rejects them*, Education Uncovered, 26 February 2020

Mansell, Warwick. 2020. *Government operating 'almost feudal', dysfunctional system of oversight and influence over academy trusts, says ex-trust CEO*, Education Uncovered, February 2020

Mansell, Warwick. 2020. *Department for Education used little-known legal power to fund Oak National Academy*, Education Uncovered, 28 April 2020

Mansell, Warwick. 2020. *Head arrives at under-pressure secondary academy seemingly without experience of working in state education*, Warwick Mansell, Education Uncovered, 27 July 2020

Schools Improvement 2018 *Britain's best school has its SATs results ruled null and void in cheating storm*, schoolsimprovement.net, 23rd July 2018

Schools Improvement. 2018.*Teachers unsure of benefits of working for a multi academy trust*, 25 July 2018

Shoesmith, Nathan. 2018. *Entire Academy Sector Could 'Face Insolvency'*, The Speaker. 17 March 2018 https://www.speakerpolitics.co.uk/headlines/230-entire-academy-sector-could-face-insolvency (Reported on BBC News 17 March 2018)

Transparify 2016 *How Transparent are Think Tanks about Who Funds Them 2016?* www.transparify.org

Trendall, Sam. 2020 *Lord Agnew to take on ministerial responsibility* PublicTechnology.net, 28 February 2020

Wolfe, D 2016 *A Can of Worms: blog*: www.acanofworms

Youle, E 2018/19 *Top Academy Chain Accused of 'Cheating' During Ofsted Inspection*, HuffPost, 19th September 2018, updated 12th July 2019